To
The Christian Book Store
Portsmouth
England
Oct: 1996

Vera's Adventures

With Best Wishes
Vera Dorothy Erwine.

with Him—on a regular schedule. No day would find her busying about as "Martha" until first—those first minutes or hours before the day begins—she as "Mary" sits at His feet to fellowship with Him. Herein is her secret of a happy and fruitful life to the benefit of others.

Vera, now in her eighties, still as a matter of habit enjoys her daily walks with the Lord—physically, for the benefit of the temple of His Holy Spirit for serving Him, and spiritually, to have the joy of the Lord upon her for whatever is in His good plan throughout the day (Neh. 8:10).

The third area of discipline is servanthood. It shows through in that this lady, Vera Ervine, accomplishes much in life to the glory of God because she has a servant's heart (1 Cor. 10:31). Her life shows, as her story unfolds, a continual outflowing of ministry to others. You will see the gentle lady venture into many new experiences as she finds fresh and exciting ways to meet people's needs. Vera counts it a joy to control her own fleshly appetites for nonessentials that greater results will be realized for the glory of her Lord and Master.

America has been greatly blessed by having welcomed Vera into citizenship, giving her freedom to share her life with thousands of people—men, women, children—who owe a great deal to this dear lady. I thank God often for having known her (Phil. 1:3).

My title for this book would have been *The Disciplined and Charitable Lady*. May you be rewarded as you read her story.

—Myrtle Campbell

Part I

My Life in England

1
My Childhood

I was born Vera Dorothy Steers, in Brentford, a suburban town of London, England, county of Middlesex. I entered the world on October 15, 1906.

Brentford got its name from the river Brent, which winds its way through this small town. An historic battle was fought here in early Saxon days precisely at the location called The Butts. One of my father's sisters lived in a three-story house on this very spot. As a child, I heard about a secret passage in the basement of this house in Brentford which led over to the home of the Duke of Northumberland in the next town of Isleworth. The river Thames flows on the eastern side of Brentford and I grew up not far from the famous Kew Botanical Gardens.

My parents were both twenty-three years old at the time of their marriage. My mother and father were both devout Christians, and, although poor, desired the best for each of their children.

Their firstborn was my little brother Cyril. He was fair, and they adored their Cyril. When Cyril was four years old, mother had rather a struggle delivering me into the world, their second-born child. Children were born in the home during those days, and nurse-help had been engaged to aid my mother at this time. Alas, a tragic thing happened one day. Four-year-old Cyril felt hungry and went to the pantry alone to cut himself a "knobble," as he called it—a crust of bread. He cut his hand severely and lost a lot of blood. The beautiful, though injured, little boy was placed on a cot next to his mother. He died within a few days of pneumonia—or so the doctor called it. Right before he died, mother asked Cyril what they should name the new baby. Cyril said, "Call her 'Dolly,' and put her back in the bed, Mummy." So I was named

Vera Dorothy. The meaning of these names may interest you. Vera means "true." Dorothy means "gift from God." At this time of the loss of Cyril, I guess I was truly a gift from God.

Our house was a small duplex on a railway siding surrounded by prettily kept flower and fruit gardens. As time went on, two other daughters were born into my family—Elsie May arrived two years after me and Queenie Blanche made her appearance ten months after Elsie. Thankfully, we three sisters were healthy children suffering only common childhood ailments during our primary school days.

We were educated at a parochial school for which I am grateful. I was considered nervous and high-strung as a child, but also of quite studious and industrious temperament. I recall learning to knit at the age of five years, and, at six, I learned to crochet. I even made a bonnet for my new baby sister Phyllis Mildred who had come along into the family much later.

Let me describe my dad to you. My father was what I would call a gentleman of the first order. He was a "home man." I respected him and loved him very much. He was employed by the local gas company and, as I remember, was in charge of the meter system. During wartime, he organized and instructed a group of women in the task of changing wheels in all meters. This procedure altered the price of the gas. As you may imagine, customers had to place coins in a slot to obtain their supplies of gas.

My father had heart problems. This ailment had first appeared in his youth, and so he was rejected for war duty. He was accepted into the volunteer corps. My father never complained but occupied himself making ample provision for our family. He rented a land allotment where he grew vegetables. We children used to accompany him to this plot sometimes. As "little helpers," we would pick up the potatoes as he carefully dug them out. I was so proud of Dad when he would win prizes for the things he grew each year at the Brentford vegetable and flower show.

My mother was an excellent cook and always took first prizes for the breads and other goodies that she baked. She was a truly adaptive, flexible cook. I am thinking of one occasion during the war years, when protein foods were very scarce. One day Dad brought home a cow's udder. Mother prepared some excellent meals for us out of this.

My parents always tried to treat us children to an annual holiday. A few of these holidays were spent at southern resorts in England. At such times, my mother and father diligently planned the spending of our limited income. I remember a "holiday lesson" from Dad once while sitting on the beach at Brighton. Dad wanted to teach us the value of money. He held up a sovereign or a half sovereign (one gold piece) and informed us how many of those gold pieces were required to bring us away on holiday to Brighton.

My father was also a musical man. On Sunday afternoons, he would play hymns on our cottage organ. During his early married life, he belonged to a minstrel troupe. Dad played the banjo and all the musicians in the troupe would blacken their faces for show performances.

My father taught a young men's Bible class at the St. George's Church where he was a member. All of us children were christened at this church as infants. However, mother sent us to a Congregational church on Sundays when we were old enough. We grew up as members of the Congregational denomination.

Dad had served the Anglican Church (St. George's) well as a lay preacher, Sunday school teacher, etc. Sometimes he preached at the mission in the next town. I used to accompany him.

As the years passed, Mother persuaded Dad to join the Congregational church, which he did. He became an elder and served for many years. My father was respected by everyone who knew him.

Church window after bombing

I fondly recall the time when my mother's half brother Thomas Batty returned to England and stayed in our home for a few weeks. Uncle Tom had immigrated to America to further his education as a theological student. All of us children were extremely excited about his coming. He came to our cottage home in Brentford, Middlesex, bearing gifts for each of us kids. Each girl received a Bible. This was the first Bible that I ever remember receiving. Mine was the largest, and, according to our respective ages, Elsie had a slightly smaller one, and Queenie, the youngest at that time, got a little red New Testament. Queenie felt keenly disappointed with her smaller Bible; she shared her feelings with me later.

On this occasion of Uncle Tom's visit, some relatives on my mother's side arranged for all of us to spend Christmas together. Uncle Arthur, Aunt Alice, and Cousin Gwendolyn (who lived a short bus ride from us at Ealing) made a special effort to celebrate at this time because of Uncle Tom's presence. We had a Christmas tree and myriad gifts were hung on the branches of that beautiful tree instead of being placed underneath. I had my eye on a toy sewing machine, and that was what I got that Christmas. It was such a happy, memorable event. I remember other Christmases when my Great-Uncle Arthur (my mother's uncle) had been serving away in the Navy. One other Christmas he brought us a genuine Japanese tea set crammed with chocolates. Once he brought pretty dolls with painted china heads and bodies stuffed with sawdust. In my mind's eye, I can still see the bright blue shade of the dress on my own doll.

The only real drawback to Uncle Tom Batty's visit was the unwelcome visitors that he brought into our home—acquired on the ship in which he had traveled to England. That is, our home was infested with bedbugs for a considerable time after Uncle Tom's departure.

Father kept up a lively correspondence with Uncle Tom after he left us and returned to the States. One day, a letter of Dad's was returned and Uncle Tom was heard of no more. My mother was interested in spiritualism at the time and a medium told her that her half brother had been killed in a forest by a falling tree. Uncle Tom had become involved in spiritualism himself. In the last letter that we ever received from him, he asked why we hadn't told him about the death of Grandma. He said that he had "met her in a garden of roses." My father wrote back in answer to this strange letter and told Uncle Tom that Grandma Salisbury was indeed very much alive. This was the letter that was returned to us, so, to this day, I really do not know what happened to poor Uncle Tom. We fear that perhaps a lack of discernment got him mixed up with a cult of some kind. We can only hope that he lived and died a natural death. As for

Grandma Salisbury, she lived to be ninety-six years of age.

Growing up, we children were blessed to lead a rather sheltered existence. Part of our yard was paved and made a great outdoors play area. Here we engaged in the usual games of hopscotch, tag, and so on. Indoors, we played with selected table games and we all loved to paint with watercolors.

I still remember my favorite toys. I had some second cousins who gave me their beautiful baby doll and perambulator. I adored wheeling the "pram" around and was greatly elated when passersby would inquire, "Is it a real baby she has there?"

My mother had strict rules of behavior for us but was generous in nature to us as well. Mother hired a dressmaker to make our clothes and we dressed alike quite often.

All of us sisters had assigned work duties. We learned early in life how to cook, garden, and manage our money. Each of us kids stretched her weekly penny a long, long way. How-to-spend decisions took much time as there were three candy shops to shop and choose from—each one offering a rich, varied array of goodies.

I do not remember my first day at school, but I do remember some incidents that happened at school. My parents chose St. Paul's Church School for us. This school was free as were the council schools. We used to walk over the road into the church on special occasions to celebrate certain feast days. Every morning we were taught to memorize the catechism and we listened to Bible stories. Grace was said before and after meals, also. Inspectors would come periodically to test us over certain material we were supposed to have learned.

I enjoyed my school days and loved my teachers. I had a keen sense of what was right and wrong and, while in the infants' classroom, I once caused quite an upheaval because I knew that I was being punished for something I did not do. I was carried up to the front of the classroom and had to stand there for a time.

My favorite subjects were painting and reading. We were taught advanced subjects like Pitmans' shorthand and domestic science in the upper classes of this elementary school. Some of us went to private classes for typing. I did not become proficient in this subject.

My parents sent us to a private teacher for piano lessons, but we had to practice on our organ at home until I was able to buy my own piano.

I made some lasting friends in early school days and can remember some of their names to this day, such as Belle Wesson, and Gladys and Grace Bacon, the twins. We had exercise classes and sports. I was on a netball team and played defense. Several times each year we were taken in groups to see some of the Shakespearean play productions.

A very sad experience happened at the end of my school days. My youngest sister Phyllis Mildred had just recovered from the chicken pox. She returned to school and caught diphtheria. Severely ill, she was taken to an isolation hospital where she died of heart failure at six years of age. I was fourteen years old at the time. Phyllis was born to Mother late in life and was much loved by her. This death caused deep grief in the family. We three remaining girls had to be kept away from school in isolation also. It was end of term, and we missed all the fun. I was unable to say goodbye to my teacher. This was a very sad time for us all. Mother was distraught, and she gave us our bank money to spend at Christmas.

I felt somehow that I was to blame for my sister's death, because I had been asked to call the doctor to come and visit her, and I had not told him that it was very urgent. The doctor was busy and did not call on our home until in the evening. Phyllis Mildred was taken away by ambulance right away that night. We never saw her again.

Let me give you a glimpse of some relatives on Mother's side. (You have already been introduced, dear reader, to Uncle Tom and Great-Uncle Arthur.) I am not intending to go way back into my ancestry, but just to touch upon a few of the people I remember or have heard much about in my own lifetime.

Great-Grandfather and Great-Grandmother Salisbury were a grand-looking couple, according to their photographs. I remember Grandma Salisbury more vividly than I do her husband. Grandpa Salisbury was the inventor of powdered milk. He had a small factory in a little township called Perivale, England. The Salisburys had a fairly large family, and I was familiar with two of their daughters, Aunt Emma and Aunt Lizzie, as well as two of their sons, Uncle Arthur and Uncle Bill Salisbury.

As I remember, Grandma Salisbury lived with her daughter Elizabeth. Elizabeth's husband was Ernest. Great-Grandpa became addicted to alcohol. While he was drunk one day, some people stole his formula for making the powdered milk. I was told that, shortly afterwards, a famous malted milk firm started up in business.

It seemed remarkable to me that these two old relatives did resemble the count and countess of Salisbury, who were also living in England at this time. Grandma wore a little lace cap on her head and she loved to rock in her rocking chair. Such chairs were scarce in England and generally used only by very elderly folk such as Grandma Salisbury. The Salisburys were also caretakers for a mission close to their home on

Four generations on mother's side of the family—Great Grandma Salisbury, Aunt Emma, Mother, and Vera (baby)

Whitestile Road. This mission was situated on Junction Road in Brentford, Middlesex, England.

Aunt Lizzie was my mother's aunt and we were very close. I was her favorite great-niece. In my youth, while Brentford was still my hometown, I would often find my way around to Aunt Lizzie's apartment. She concocted the tastiest little cakes and jam tarts. It was a joy to visit her. I cheerfully ran errands for her as she was crippled by tuberculosis. I used to watch, fascinated, as she curled her hair with glowing irons heated in an open fire.

During World War I, I would often go out and queue up in order to buy a quarter-pound of margarine or butter for her, whichever I could get that day. Aunt Lizzie attained nearly the same age as did her mother, about ninety-six. We corresponded with each other after I left England for the United States. Eventually, she went to live in a retirement ward for the elderly in the West Middlesex Hospital. She was a popular patient with the staff there. My sister in England faithfully visited Aunt Lizzie there throughout her latter days.

Our grandparents on Mother's side died early in life, so we did not know them. Fortunately, our second cousins took a special interest in us as children. Here I want to introduce these cousins to you, my reader.

Edith Norman, who was living as I first penned these notes, used to tell me about her Aunt Rose (my maternal grandmother), who physically resembled her own mother. My mother lived with them at Harrow-on-the-Hill in her childhood days. Because we did not have the opportunity of knowing our maternal grandparents, Cousins Edie and Phoebe became attached to us and treated us with special kindness. They themselves never married. Their brother was engaged to be married, but died too soon. I recall visiting his fiancée at Banbury Cross. Her brother was a baker, and we relished eating those famous Banbury-Cross Buns. Mother lived with relatives at Harrow-on-the-Hill until she went out to work.

Cousin Phoebe lived all of her life at Harrow-on-the-Hill. As a young girl, she was involved in a cycle accident which left her partially paralyzed and an invalid for many years. We loved to go and visit these cousins. I often had extended stays with this family—probably at such times as when my mother was delivering her babies.

Harrow was the home and school of the "Big Boys" and fed into one of the two big universities. If I remember correctly, these boys went on to Oxford University from Harrow. We would often go over and take walks up Harrow Hill. Sometimes, when we grew older, we would cycle over to see the relatives in Harrow. I stayed during the summer holiday season and made good friends there.

Cousin Edie worked in His Majesty's Stationery Office, but Phoebe, the accident victim, was bedfast. As youngsters, we called them "Aunt Edie"

"Aunt Phoebe," our second cousin, during her first stage of healing

and "Aunt Phoebe," even though they were actually our second cousins.

A wonderful thing happened to Phoebe on March 29, 1932. The vicar from her church, the Church of England, regularly visited Phoebe and gave her Communion. On this particular day at Easter, Phoebe experienced a partial healing. She had been confined to her bed for about twenty years, using her left arm and hand to help herself as much as she could. She had been praying that God would heal her since her mother was aging and finding it more and more difficult to care for Phoebe. Aunt Emma had been a superlative nurse to Phoebe and her patient had never had a single bed sore, although paralyzed along the whole of her right side. As the vicar was administering the sacrament of the Lord's Supper, Phoebe lifted up both of her hands and praised the Lord! She received great blessing in this because now she could do more to help herself and her mother. Within two years, she was completely healed and could be active out of bed. Phoebe became a church visitor for the sick and a member of St. Raphael's Guild of Healing in the Church of England. The healing was a most sacred event in my cousin's life. She had a vision which she says was nearly indescribable. She wrote the following poem about it.

"O Blest communion, Fellowship divine,
We feebly struggle, They in Glory shine.
Yet all are One in Thee, for all are Thine
Allelujah!"

The Radiant Glory of the Divine Presence

Oh, Radiant Morn, Light of my Life
Thy Glory I beheld.
I heard the Angels' Heavenly Song
And Radiance filled my room.

My soul was wrapped in silent prayer
And heavenly glory "Oh, so pure" Streamed O'er

I saw the countless heavenly saints
Arrayed in spotless white
With Crowns of Jewels "Oh, so rare"
Sparkling in heavenly Light
The Glory of the Lord was there
The Son of Righteousness arose
All Glorious to behold.

Humbly I bowed at the Throne of Grace
A Sinner unworthy to see such a place,
And the sweet gentle voice of my Saviour said
"Fear not," I will keep thee unto the end.

This beautiful vision passed from mine eyes
The heavenly song was hushed.
I awoke and wept with sacred Joy
That my Soul had seen my blessed Home.
Where there is never a pain or tear
Buy Joy is always there.
And as I looked at the Altar fair,
I prayed that I might guide some weary suffering souls to find
That Bright and Happy Home of Rest.

—Phoebe Norman

Holy, Holy, Holy, LORD GOD Almighty,
Heaven and Earth are full of Thy Glory
Glory be to Thee, Dear LORD, Most High.

I was the first person to whom Phoebe wrote, and I remember the thrill I got when I received a postcard from her saying, "Come over to see me soon. I have some wonderful news for you and want you to give thanks in my church." I could see that her handwriting was different. She had been a right-handed person, and this card was inscribed with the right hand in a beautiful script—so smooth compared to her usual left-handed scrawl. Dear Phoebe outlived her elderly mother. Some years later, sister Edie watched Phoebe being transported to the hospital where she died of pneumonia. At the time of this writing, Edie is an eighty-six-year-old patient in a nursing home located a few blocks away from the home where she lived all her life. Edie had faithfully served her mother and invalid sister. She always felt responsible for her home. Edie remained single although there was one male friend whom she would have liked to have married. That man married someone else.

I can remember when Edie was a clerk in a candy shop. She would recruit me to help churn the ice cream and, of course, I was rewarded with some of the finished product. In later years, Edie became an invalid. We all found her rather difficult to understand by then. She possessed a warped, introspective outlook on life, and her close friends could see that she was demanding some of the care and attention that had been showered upon her sister Phoebe for so many years. Edie has since passed on.

Now let me turn to my father's side of the family. The name of my paternal grandfather was Henry John Farmer Steer. The thing I remember most about him was his singing voice. He lived with his daughter Mildred for whom my youngest sister was named. I did not get to know Grandmother Steer since she died much earlier. Alcohol had caused a lot of grief in this family, but, at the time that I knew Grandpa Steer, he was living a normal life.

It was the custom of my father to take long walks on Sunday morning after church while Mother was preparing dinner. Being a very active child, I was the one who went along with him. We would walk along Boston Road and turn into Colonel's Drive and then on to Whitestile Road, where Grandpa Steer lived. I always enjoyed these walks, which sometimes took us through wheat fields. It is interesting that Mother's relatives lived on this same street. Inside my Grandpa Steer's house, we would always go down a long connecting passageway. This led into a small conservatory where Grandpa spent much time amongst the plants and flowers that he loved to grow. My father must have inherited his passion for plants from Grandpa Steer. He had named his first son John Henry Farmer Steers. Somehow that "s" got added to our name and, ever after that, our family has gone by the name of "Steers." Most of our ancestors were dairy farmers, as the name "Steers" suggests. My father, although a lover of the soil, did not follow in the steps of his ancestors.

Dad was a quiet, humble man, content to follow a career with a local gas company. As a child, I found him very knowledgeable about a great many topics. He was an avid reader, and had been privileged to obtain a fairly good education for those days. He came from a large family. They were poor, but my father received a scholarship to attend the Old Ragged School set up by a Rothschild Legacy. This school was superior in instruction to the state grade schools. I would often go to Dad when I wanted information. He was a deeply religious man as well as musical. He usually spent Sunday afternoons playing by ear on our cottage organ, filling our house with the melodies of old-time hymns from a worn Sankey hymnbook.

Mother and Father were married in St. George's Church of England and, as I have already stated, their five children were all christened there. We have no wedding picture of my parents, but we were told that they had a carriage with gray horses for the occasion. Mother wore a dove gray wedding dress. We had a picture of the church's font decorated with flowers in our family album. This church is now an organ museum.

I remember a bit more about the Lads' Bible Class that my father taught, together with another man named Sid Maskell, at St. George's

Church. I used to hear them discussing some of the matters they dealt with in that class. Mr. Maskell was deformed, having developed a kyphosis (humpback) from wheeling a fruit and vegetable barrow for numerous years. He was our greengrocer, and delivered produce to our home twice a week. He was a very cheery fellow with high cheekbones and a bright countenance.

While we were still tiny children, Mother desired good Christian education for us. We lived too far away from St. George's Church, so we went with a neighbor's older daughter to the Sunday school at the Congregational church. We attended there for many years. Mother was our first parent to become interested in this nonconformist type of church, and she would accompany us for the evening worship services. We were in church and Sunday school all day on Sundays. We were introduced to the League of Young Worshippers by a beautiful lady named Miss Taylor. We had a short session before morning worship service, in which we were taught to read the Bible and to pray every day. I remember this lady coming to our house for me to sign the promise card which we renewed every year. She was shocked because I did not want to sign this card, but I knew that I had missed often in the reading of the Scripture portion.

Sunday school lasted for one hour each Sunday at 3 P.M. in the afternoon. Evening service was at 6:30 P.M. It was during these years that we had regular classes during the week for Scripture studies with examinations given upon completion when some of us obtained certificates or merit awards. We studied hard, and I continued until I was teaching and sat for the teacher's examinations. After awhile, Dad became interested in our church, and Mother persuaded him to attend where we children were going. He soon took an active part and was chosen to become a deacon in the Congregational church. He served in this capacity for many years and was respected by other members. Occasionally arguments arose in the monthly council meetings and Dad was chosen to chair these to help stabilize the meetings.

As we grew older, we were allowed to go with Dad to the food allotment which provided an extra source of nutrition for us during the war years of 1914–1918. Every autumn an allotment show was held, and Dad was often a winner of first, second and third prizes. He grew wonderful potatoes, brussels sprouts, parsnips, artichokes, etc. I remember the year he received a prize for his cabbages. He was asked to submit three cabbages, and they were a picture—pencil-shaped and perfect. He raised cucumbers in his little greenhouse, and he was careful to leave the blooms on the ends, a proof of freshness, I suppose. My only living sister at this time of my writing, Queenie, seems to take after Dad in her love for growing things. She is retired now, living in England; she recently won first prize for her homegrown tomatoes entered in a local gardeners' show in southern England.

Our backyard, or "garden," as such is called in England, was always resplendent with flowers. We eagerly anticipated the first appearance of daffodils poking through the ground after the winter. In the spring, bluebells graced the front of our house. Flowers bloomed in season the whole year round. There were two big loganberry bushes in our backyard, several gooseberry bushes, and a good patch of rhubarb—these made delicious preserves and pies. Thus the Lord supplied so many of our needs and preserved our health during the stressful war years. Also, food from our own yard did not put any more strain on our meager family budget.

Dad had been the eldest in a large family growing up and he suffered with a rheumatic heart problem all of his life. This condition did not prevent him from working hard to provide for his own family, however. Dad did have a sense of humor which counterbalanced Mother's serious-mindedness. One day, he pulled a joke on me which I did not appreciate at the time. He called and asked me to go into his little greenhouse and fetch something for him. Obediently, I went in and ran into a huge spider's web, which covered my face. I can see him laughing to this day, but this was no laughing matter to me.

One Sunday afternoon, we were waiting for a visit from Aunt Daisy. She lived in Acton, a short train journey away, and was expected to arrive for tea. We all had on our Sunday dresses and were in the garden. I was being quite overactive, and, I realize now, that must have irritated Dad. He grabbed the clothes prop and chased me around the garden with it. I dashed around until, finally, I got into a hole in the fence and snagged my good dress on a rusty nail. Mother came along and ripped the entire bottom of my dress off and I was made to wear it like that. You can imagine my shame and embarrassment when Aunt Daisy did arrive and saw my state. I recall Aunt Daisy as a very "dressy," formal person.

Mother was quite a versatile woman. She had worked as a professional cook before marriage and that talent of hers kept our larder full of home-made breads, pies, and preserves. We girls wore pinafores with crocheted tops that my mother made. Mother also embroidered black satin cushion covers, which were quite fashionable at that time, and these found a ready market. But I best remember Mother's activity in the "scullery."

Just outside our back door, there was a long, neat, asphalt area which led to the end of the back kitchen, or scullery, as we called it. Mother spent hours working in this area and she kept an eye on us children through its wide double window. The scullery contained a sink underneath a water tank. There were two faucets, one from this water storage tank and the other from the main. In another corner, there was an old copper complete with a fireplace. Monday was wash day, and our dirty clothes were boiled in this copper every Monday. Then the clothes were threaded through an old-fashioned mangle. All these clothes were then hung to dry on a lengthy line extending all the way to the far end of our lot. Being the oldest child, it fell my lot to fold laundry and pass it through the mangle. A few garments were ironed with our old flat iron heated on the gas stove. An efficient feature of our kitchen was the fact that a plate rack had been hung over the gas stove. This arrangement enabled stove heat to warm the crockery that would be used to serve our meals. This would be a good thing to adopt in this country.

Another feature of the scullery, installed by Dad, was a porcelain-lined bath tub which had an outlet directly into the outside drain. The outlet was covered when not in use by a specially fitted lid which Dad made. Our only refrigerator was a box-like container that we called the "safe." The safe had three sides of perforated copper and a door, placed in the coolest place near the back door. Milk, butter, meats, and other perishables were kept in the safe. Vegetables were kept in a recess under the mangle. Pots and pans were stored on shelves on another wall. We also had a pantry which had been built under the stairway next to our combination living-dining room. There was a nice open fireplace in this room with a small oven that Mother used as a warming oven and to cook puddings. We boiled water over open fire. The space was furnished with a sofa, dining table and chairs, an open Dutch dresser for crockery, and an old grandfather clock.

As you must have already gathered, dear reader, our family's life was closely connected with church life. I remember many other church activities. We were involved in church programs staged for our parents to view. When I was older, the young people of the church occasionally presented the whole Sunday evening service. I gave a sermonette during one such service. Sometimes, our Congregational church joined with other churches of protestant denomination. One such united service occurred on Whit-Sunday when we joined with the Wesleyan Methodist congregation, the largest church in our town. Each member church assembled at its own location, and then we all walked over to gather at the Methodist church. We truly looked forward to such occasions. All who had white dresses wore them to these services.

I have very fond memories of church Christmas parties. Long trestle tables were brought out of the storeroom and loaded with assorted goodies to eat. A special program would be presented for us children as we sat and gazed at a huge Christmas tree covered with gifts. I found it exciting to look and wonder what I might receive. I recall being very disappointed one year to receive a package tied with pretty ribbon containing only three handkerchiefs inside. Queenie got a baby doll. My disappointment was a child's very human reaction.

When I was a teenager, I was asked to help with our church newspaper. I really enjoyed this activity and the experience enhanced my self-confidence. After I joined the church, I became a member of the young people's Bible class and later was asked to teach a primary class. I have since preferred teaching this age group, and have taught them whenever I have been available.

My church selected several of us to go to Cambridge and take a Sunday school teachers' training course. In Cambridge, there was not room to house all of us in the college itself. My friend and I lodged outside in the city where several of the famous Cambridge boat crew members lived while studying at Cambridge. The crewmen were away from campus for Easter vacation, and I enjoyed seeing their winning oars hanging crossed on the wall of our room. This short course at Cambridge was extremely helpful, and we were able to apply some of the principles we learned quite handily in our teaching.

The annual Sunday school outing was a great event for the children. My favorite place was Hampton Court. Usually two tram cars full of children carried us to this festivity, and we sang all the well-known songs together along the way. Mother used to join us on these occasions. We carried a picnic lunch and a special tea was catered for all of us, either in Bushey Park under a marquee or in a tea-house in the city. There were organized races with much scrambling for wrapped candies as well as a multitude of other activities. We visited the beautiful palace gardens there, the maze, and the palace of Henry VIII. I loved to see the famous grapevine which grew inside a glass house. I heard that the roots of this vine reached down to the river Thames. Directly across from the palace was Bushey Park with its avenue of old horse chestnut trees. These were magnificent to behold at all seasons of the year. Tame deer roamed through Bushey Park. We also visited Eastcote over toward Harrow. We took a train ride over there and ended up in a large field where sports and donkey rides had been organized for us. This was the one and only time I ever rode upon the back of a donkey. I was terrified and did not enjoy

Sunday school class in Brentford, Middlesex, England, 1925

it. Yes, I always thoroughly enjoyed these Sunday school games.

As far as creative games at home, we girls would always play upstairs in our bedroom after being sent to bed around 8 P.M. Some of the games we devised were making tents of bedsheets by holding them up with our feet, pretending to hang ourselves on the bedposts by our nightgowns, or pretending to be legs of mutton in a butcher's shop. Sometimes we tried creeping downstairs without being caught. On one of these occasions, I remember listening to the conversation of our parents downstairs who were watching the first zeppelin brought down in flames during World War I. We kids were granted a special concession one evening when some neighbor children came over and asked if we could join them for a May Day celebration. We danced around their homemade pole.

Grace was said before and after all meals in our house, just as we were taught to pray before and after lunchtime at St. Paul's, the parochial school of the Church of England where we attended. When we were quite young, we had evening prayers at our bedside. We would say the prayers we had learned until we were mature enough to make extemporaneous prayers. Reverend Cook was the name of our vicar.

I remember another instance of my high activity level as a child. My mother told me that when I was quite a small girl, she had laid the table for tea when I got into mischief. A high tea usually consisted of a salad, cold cuts, and dessert or cakes. On this particular afternoon, when Mother's company arrived to take tea and sat down for their meal, it was discovered that all the tomatoes had been "tasted" by Vera. There were tooth marks in every tomato although none had been eaten. I don't remember being spanked for this, so I don't know what punishment, if any, was meted out for my behavior.

I do not remember a great deal about the youth of my sisters except that Elsie May (whose birthday was August 8) turned out to be the brightest of us sisters. Elsie was also a self-taught artist capable of extreme detail in her work. We girls would sit around the kitchen table together at home and enjoyed copying pretty scenes from postcards obtained from the local post office. We also did watercolor paintings of branches and flowers in our art classes in the grade school. All these years, I have kept my first attempt at outline and perspective drawn when I attended the Twickenham Polytechnic School in England. I studied under a royal academist in 1932 when I was twenty-five years old.

My mother was not too proud to do housework to help out during the war. I remember how nicely she kept us girls dressed, and she overprotected us in some ways. Family photos depict our long, fair hair, which was kept in ringlets over the shoulders. We were dressed almost alike. Mother found a dressmaker who made little navy blue suits for us; another time, we were outfitted in white serge wool dresses. Each of us was assigned Saturday chores, thus teaching us self-reliance. My job was to clean our bedroom each week as well as the staircase down to the front door. I thought this was a difficult assignment at the time because there were two beds crowded into a small room. My daily chore was the cleaning of the front doorstep with hearthstone and the stove with blacking. In the winter, I would relay the fireplace.

I was eight years old when the First World War began. There were hardships and scarcity of food. I can remember queuing up for a quarter-pound of butter or margarine. Sometimes it would be sugar or bacon. One half-pint of milk would be left on our doorstep for the whole family. I have known the time when I would have to go home from the grocer empty-handed after standing in line for a long, long time.

I learned some of the intimate facts of life from Belle Wesson, a long-time, close friend of mine in grade school. Her parents were broad-minded and took care that she got a business education. Belle and I always remembered the other's birthday and we stayed in touch for many years after school days.

One of the true delights of our childhood days was frequent bus trips to Kew Gardens. The entrance fee was one penny. We would take a picnic lunch and stay several hours. The scenes in the gardens changed as the seasons changed. I loved spring when crocuses grew underneath the trees in various bright colors. Hot houses in the gardens educated us about plants and trees from all over the world. Here are a couple of poems I wrote in 1936 while at Kew Gardens—the only poems I ever put on paper.

An Ode to Springtime

Spring is here, God's bounteous gift to man,
Wake up, fair earth, and let the world thy beauty see.
The time for sleep has passed, and now 'tis time
For Praise and Thanksgiving.
Oh! Wondrous Love, Who wrought this miracle,
Open the dreary hearts of men
To behold this glorious gift of Thine.

Crocus-Time at Kew

Down among the tender grasses
Blooms the crocus fair;
Gold, mauve, and white.
Caring naught for wind and rain,
Fulfilling her mission upon earth.
The joyous bee with song of mirth and gladness,
His work in God's earth begins
And into the heart of these flowers sweet
His song of praise doth sing.

Growing up, I experienced "growing pains" as most adolescents do. At about twelve years of age, I often found myself in argumentative moods. One evening I informed my mother that I would not be home for lunch the next day. Sure enough I stayed at school the following day during lunch and even kept my youngest sister with me plus another girl. We went to the recreation area adjoining the school, shared our friends' lunch and played on the swings and giant strides. My father habitually went home for his midday meal. When it was almost time for our afternoon school session to begin, I looked up and saw father at the gateway beckoning my sister and me to come along. I will always remember how ashamed I was to be heading home when it was time for afternoon classes to resume. The second school bell was ringing loud and clear as we were made to sit down at home and eat our noon meal. I remember that it was fried herrings, a delicious food. But, at this time, I was disgusted and ungrateful.

Growing up, I had a slight inferiority complex. There was good reason. First, I was myopic (near-sighted) and reticent to tell my parents. When I was twelve, I finally told Mother that I could not see things on the blackboard and was finding it very difficult to catch on to instruction in school. I was taken to the Richmond Hospital where the doctor pronounced me "blind as a bat." After getting my own glasses, I seemed to be living in a new world.

Another problem I had was a bad overbite which deformed my mouth. My upper jaw protruded and my lower jaw receded to such a degree that children at school poked fun at me. I inherited this malformation of the mouth from my family. I remember that one of my cousins on Dad's side suffered from a similar condition. Proper chewing and eating were difficult for me and I grew up lean and lanky. I was a very slow eater and probably did not assimilate my food properly. I actually pushed out my top front teeth and eventually had all my teeth extracted while in my early twenties. I bit through the first false set and had to have a steel top plate made. This was not satisfactory either, and I had another set made which proved to fit better. The problem was really not completely rectified until I came to the United States, however. Years later, Dr. Tatum operated on my mouth in Tallahassee, Florida, after my marriage to Bill Ervine. Since that surgery, I have had no trouble.

World War I came closest to us when a bomber strayed off course, flew over our town of Brentford, Middlesex, and lightened its load upon us. This was a frightening experience at night in our suburb of West London. The next day's light revealed the damage to us. A bomb had dropped in Whitestile Road and three houses had been demolished, killing one whole family. Mr. Curley, a soldier, came home at this time on leave to discover his wife and several children plus an elderly woman (who may have been his mother) had been killed. The whole town turned out for that extremely sad funeral. Later, two of those homes were rebuilt. The Curley home which had stood in the middle of the three was not reconstructed. Some relatives of mine lived on both sides of the deceased family. My father's eldest sister, Aunt Louise, had come here with her family to escape the London bombing and found herself very close to Brentford's bomb disaster. Two other bombs fell that fateful night in our town—one on the water works property and another near Kew Bridge.

Following World War I, England experienced a happy, carefree period of prosperity. I myself enjoyed those school years. I was encouraged to read Dickens (one of my favorites), some poetry, and the classics. I also discovered a magazine called *Psychology* or *The Psychologist*. It was reasonably priced, with brief, pertinent articles. I am sure that this magazine helped me along in life. Also, a Christian psychologist came to our church one day. I do not remember his message, but he gave us a motto to follow: "Doing does it." This has remained my motto throughout life since that time.

Now a bit more about my sister Elsie May. Elsie's first job after leaving school at fourteen was as an office clerk. She worked with our cousin Doris (Dad's side). After a year or two of this office work, she took up a domestic position. She was with a prominent family in our town named Stallabrass who were very good to her and she was very happy. She became quite ill with a lingering ailment and left her job, being in and out of work for a time. She was wrongly diagnosed by her doctor and was treated for indigestion. Finally, Elsie was admitted to a London hospital where her condition was properly diagnosed as ulcerative colitis. She made rapid progress with the right medication and diet. Believing that a change of scenery would speed her recuperation, she went to stay with Cousin Doris, now married to Don Collis and living in the beautiful seaside town of Bournemouth. She was involved in a car accident there and hurled out of a car. This incident aggravated and stirred her latent illness, and my dear sister found herself in the hospital again. This time, it was the local hospital. Surgery was performed, but she did not recover, dying at the age of twenty-eight years. This was a crushingly sad time for our family. I was living away from home at this time, studying in a nursing program. Three members of my family died during my nurse's training, all in this same hospital. A certain young man related to the Stallabrass family was deeply grieved at the loss of Elsie. I heard later that he had been in love with her.

My sister Queenie was a beautiful girl, three years my junior. Being the youngest girl (after the death of Phyllis Mildred), she tells me that she often felt slighted. While Elsie was alive, we were all allowed to join the Girl Guide movement. We enjoyed this diversion. I was old enough to become an officer and I also enlisted as a Tawney Owl with the Brownies. This group was connected with the Brentford Congregational Church. Personally, I was not too happy about joining the Brownies. I recall that the habit of saluting other officers made me quite nervous. I think this was because I had not grown up in this organization. It was new, and I was pushed into it. As far as I can remember, it did not last long for me.

Queenie was the only one left at home with Mother and Father after the death of Elsie. Queenie was apprenticed for dressmaking with Madam Bailey when she first left school. Queenie became disillusioned with this job when she found that all she was allowed to do was to make up the fireplace, keep it fed with coal, and pick up pins. She left this employment without telling Mother and went with a neighbor girl to Acton Teddy Bear Factory. There she was hired and given the job of stuffing toys. She stuffed the big Donald Duck for the Wembley Exhibition, and she was proud to bring home money that she had earned. This was not a healthy job for her. She later found employment nearer home with another family as a mother's help. She learned to cook and, to her joy, she was assigned the care of the family's big shepherd dog. This animal became her friend. Then Queenie was called home for a time since Mother became ill and needed her.

I was living away from home at this time. Four years after the death of our sister Elsie, we lost Mother to kidney problems. Mother was admitted to the Cottage Hospital, developed kidney poisoning, and died July 9, 1940.

Queenie found employment with a family in Ealing, a nearby town. It was wartime now and people were desperate to get help. To get Queenie to work for them, the family allowed my father to come and live in their home, too. Thus, his needs were also taken care of. The lady of the family for whom my sister worked was kind and helpful. She found out that Queenie wanted to take up cooking as a career. This lady had noticed real potential in her and Queenie was sent to the Polytechnic School for advanced cookery classes. While there, she was honored by the opportunity to prepare a meal for a titled lady, who heartily congratulated her on her good cooking. It must have been during the Battle of Britain that the home of the helpful family was bombed. All escaped without injury, but the family went to live elsewhere. Queenie and Father went back home. Most homes were provided with bomb shelters during these war years, and there was one in the garden near our house.

Before long, Queenie was conscripted for war work. Since she was caring for my father, a semi-invalid, in her home, she was given the option of working in a factory near our home. She went to work for Sperry's, makers of gyroscopes and other aviation instruments. She became most adept at this kind of work. In time, she was made a forelady for her section. Her job was to test the finished articles and give final inspection. It was tedious work, but she remained with the firm for many years and received a gold watch for her services when she finally left.

My sister Queenie and her husband Victor were married in the Congregational church—a simple wedding—her first marriage and Victor's second. I recall that a good friend of ours from childhood was married in this church, and Queenie and I were honored to be chosen as her bridesmaids. The dresses we had made were of a delicate lavender shade. Elsie was ill at this time and so missed being one of the bridesmaids.

2
Life Beyond School

The First World War was behind us when I left school at fourteen years. My cousin Doris recommended me to her boss for a position at Griffith Brothers, a men's clothiers situated in High Street which was walking distance from my home. My work entailed pricing all the goods that came into the store with a cost code and selling price. Brentford was the main place of business and there were seven other branches in outlying areas in the south of England. All of the wares were sent out from this main office or store. I had to ticket them and put them into stockrooms. These old buildings have long since been torn down and modernized. I worked for that firm for about two years.

One of my duties there was to prepare the manager's tea. I would get fresh butter and rolls and serve them with tea. We had to be careful not to leave food around, since that locale was infested with rats. I would often glimpse one of those when the building was quiet. Congenial people worked here and we were a happy bunch of employees. After my sister Elsie left school, she worked in this office also. I had left by then. My wages were ten shillings per week; after two years, I felt due for a raise in salary. The boss insisted that he could not pay more for the job I was doing. Therefore, I looked around for different employment. As far as I remember, the hours were very long there. I had time off to get my dinner at home and I had one-half hour for tea and always dashed over to Aunt Nellie's home on the corner of The Butts for tea.

Incidentally, my reader, I returned to my hometown of Brentford in 1983 for a visit. I found a completely changed town. My own home in Layton Road was no longer there and many new high-rises had replaced the cottages where we had lived. I was glad that our home church had been restored after being bombed and is now classified as an historic building.

My impression of my early adult life is that I was fairly self-reliant, and I do acknowledge God's protecting hand guiding and leading me. Along about this time, I was anxious to better myself and to earn more money. I heard about another job vacancy at a business house along the High Street and I went to inquire. I landed that job. This time I was a saleslady and had to canvass the area carrying a small suitcase packed with pretty ladies' undies. These were samples made by girls who did sewing in the shop. Another garment that we sold was the famous Jean Corset. I was amazed at the number of women who wore these corsets. My company was exclusive agent for this garment and I was required to go into homes and take measurements of the ladies desiring to purchase them. As I look back, I am surprised that a young girl like myself was entrusted to do this kind of work. However, it was all an experience in life.

I did this job for only a short time, as in the course of my canvassing, I encountered a lady customer who took an interest in my welfare.

"You should have a better job than this; I will speak to my husband who may be able to get you a job in the office where he works," she said. Sure enough, he did, and I soon found myself at Cadby Hall, the headquarters of Lyon's Tea Shops. I was given a simple math test and employed as a clerk in the stock department.

I commuted back and forth to Hammersmith of West London daily and found my job interesting and rewarding. Lyon's employed a big staff and supplied facilities for social life as well as educational classes. Some of the sports grounds were in the country, and many of us would enjoy these on the weekends. At the end of each quarter, some of us were sent to take inventory of the special tea shops. These were the Maison Lyon's Tea Shops in London. I made a good friend this way and looked forward to these occasions. We worked together and also visited in each other's homes. At mealtimes on these special jobs, we were privileged to sign the bills. I was in my late teens when I worked for Lyon's. They had employed more staff to train them for the World Exhibition at Wembley. Lyon's did all the catering, so when the exhibition opened I was transferred to their offices in that area. This was another experience for me. I commuted back and forth on the district railway. We had a free pass into the exhibition and so, at lunchtime, we would be found watching the many interesting things in these grounds. My cousin Edie lived in Harrow, not too far from Wembley. Once Edie and some of her friends took part in an old world show of some kind. She had to go to the stadium two and three times a week dressed as a Victorian lady. I had an opportunity to take part in this show one time. A friend of hers could not attend and so I dressed up in her crinoline dress and wig complete with black beauty spots. I paraded in the stadium. By the way, this has always been used to present great football events. At the close of the exhibition, Lyon's staff was absorbed into the main office, so I continued to work at Cadby Hall. I remained with this firm for about four years.

Along about this time, I had health problems. For one thing, I was not eating right. I used to try and save money by cutting down on nourishing foods. I remember having a cough all that winter. Also, there were people in my office who had tuberculosis. My very dear friend who lived in East London came down with this disease and died at an early age. One of the men had been taken off a bakers' delivery route because he had tuberculosis and was in this office spreading his germs. I was doing my best to keep well, but it was good that I decided to make another change and was able to overcome the disease which had infected one of my lungs already. I did not know I had been infected at this time. It was not until I had X-rays in preparation for my emigration to the U.S.A. that I was told I had a scar on my left lung. However, I was not ill enough to be laid up, and I grew stronger, able to throw off any ill effects.

Lyon's catering firm was proceeding with business methods, and it was at this time they decided to use computers in their offices. I was not impressed by the changes occurring, so I decided to leave Lyon's when an occupation new to me opened. Here is how I found my new employment: Billy Pierce, a close friend in my church, was working in the home of an artist, a Mr. Altson. Billy was doing some specialized decorating for the artist. Mr. Altson's daughter Ruth was mentally ill and a companion was needed for her. I was exactly Ruth's age, twenty-three years. I thought I could do this job; Mr. Altson interviewed me and I got the position. My association with the Altsons lasted over a period of five years.

Let me tell you a little about this dear girl and the family. Mr. Altson was Jewish, an artist and widower, who worked exclusively for the Maharajah of Nuwanegar in India. Ruth was left alone quite often as her mother had died a year or two before this time. Her brother Ralph lived at home with his sister, but each went his or her separate way. Being a family of artists, they were continuing their studies at the Polytechnic School nearby. Mr. Altson traveled with the maharajah and was his guest in his Indian palace for six months of each year. Mr. Altson was a well-known cricket player in England for the other half of each year. I often wondered why Mr. Altson painted religious pictures with Hindu themes. I did not know in the beginning that he was Jewish either. While her father was away, a sad thing happened to daughter Ruth. Upon his return, he found Ruth in a most distraught condition, weeping continually for weeks at a time. A private nurse took care of her at first. Then, in the next stage of her illness, she began to laugh, shutting herself away in her room. She received the finest medical help available and the diagnosis was schizophrenia. She had been molested, but she would never divulge what had happened to her. In her delirium, sometimes she would say, "I've told you about the baby, haven't I?" This was the beginning of my life's work as a nurse. I was Ruth's companion for two years. I kept her occupied with things in the house, taking her on occasional out-of-doors shopping trips, picnics, and to other places of interest. She was placed in a private hospital at Salisbury for one year. I remained in the Altson household as a paid servant with special responsibility to care for Ruth's needs. I visited her once a month, wrote to her, and carried or mailed things to her. During this year, Ralph had taken a bride, and the two of them lived in the next town along Bedford Park where they had an apartment with studio, as they were both artists.

I was given one section of the Altson house as my own living quarters; another part of the house was rented to a single lady, and the rest was closed until Mr. Altson should return from India. I was given daily help for the cleaning. Ruth returned home from the hospital and I took care of her for another two years. Then, as there was no improvement in her condition, she went back to the hospital.

Ralph and his wife announced one day that they were going to emigrate to California and wanted Mr. Altson to go with them. This was a very difficult decision for him to make, having Ruth in the hospital. They did decide to go together and they departed for the U.S.A. I visited dear Ruth in the hospital from time to time, but she steadily deteriorated. Another change for me was imminent. Ruth had one close, wonderfully faithful friend. She also became my friend and, about this time, we decided to go on a hiking holiday, an account of which follows.

My First Hiking Holiday in England

We set out Friday morning, July 7, 1939. My friend Eileen James and myself left Waterloo, London, on our way to Godalming in Surrey. From there, we intended to use an itinerary planned for us by the Rambling Association.

The weather was not very promising, being dull and cloudy as we set out. However, we were in high spirits and intended to make the best of our holidays.

We lost our map outside the station, but on inquiring found that someone had kindly taken it into the station. We found ourselves in the pretty village of Eashing about 1 P.M. Eashing has a quaint old bridge and an inn where we lunched on steak pies and cider, which got to my head. The inn proprietor and a yokel were playing Shove-halfpenny.

We continued on to Pepperharrow Park and then across Oakley and Thursley Commons—very extensive and lovely in parts with heathland and dense woods. Coming out onto the Portsmouth Road later, we got directions to Highcombe Bottom. We came through lanes and more heathland leading us right round the Punch-bowl. We longed for tea, climbed higher and higher, and passed several tumbledown houses . . . still, no sign of tea. Suddenly we found ourselves right on the main road, walked round the rim of the Punch-bowl and finally got our tea in the town. We hurried on to our destination which was "Wagonners Wells." A delightful spot, but a lousy hostel. The women's dormitory door wouldn't close properly and the "North London Belles" thought it a grand place. We got only snatches of sleep; pillows were hard and the blankets smelled stuffy. A crowd of Danes stayed for the night—a cycling club. The old warden was a jolly old chap, and gave us good directions for our next day's walk. We got up late and left Wagonners Wells about 10 A.M. We came through Liphook to Hollycombe and Redford. We took shelter in a phone box from a heavy rain shower.

We met a friendly clergyman who approved of our plans for the day and gave us even more explicit directions, wishing he could accompany us. We passed on to Woolbeeding. Tea was still hard to find, so we had ices instead. We continued through Cowdry Park about two miles, and fed the deer in this park. The road through here was very pretty, around hillsides and woodlands and later through pastureland to Ambersham. We passed along some picturesque lanes lined with hedges covered with honeysuckle and wild roses. We passed through a railway arch right onto Ambersham Commons. Here we ate some sandwiches. Halfway across this heathland, we found a road and signpost leading us left to Graffham. We had no difficulty in finding the hostel, beautifully situated, clean and friendly. We met some extremely nice young people and had a sing-song evening. The meals were served nicely, too. We slept in bunk beds for the first time away.

Sunday morning was very promising, gloriously sunny early and continued so all day. We spent the whole day traversing the Downs. We lost ourselves and arrived at Coldharbour Farm in a delightful valley. We had to come back over the Downs for Slinden. Everywhere was covered with thyme and wild flowers, also lots of wild strawberries could be found in this area. We found a clearly marked track to follow right into Slinden. A delightful little hut called "The Hikers' Home" was awaiting us at the bottom of the garden at the Newborough Arms. After tea, we went for a walk and explored the village. I was sad at the thought of Eileen leaving me the next day. Poor kid, her feet were paining her so. We had a very good night and breakfast. I ate most of Eileen's, also. We got lost in Rewel Woods when we started off again, but were soon on the right track again after meeting a rider on horseback with whom we had a chat. We were soon on the road to Arundel. Here we made a few purchases. We bought chocolate, etc., to eat later in the day. We shopped for a suitable sweater in a very nice shop as well as making a parcel of a few other things not needed right away. Eileen was able to take these items with her. She seemed anxious to be getting home, so we hurriedly passed by the castle and I put Eileen on the London train at the station. The booking clerk there put me onto a pretty road for Burpham. The cows in the fields were terribly restless as I strode by. I got a good cup of tea before crossing the Downs near Burpham. The village postmistress helped me with a few directions for my journey and I found a direct path leading to Kithurst Hill. There was a splendid view from here and the deep peacefulness of the place made me feel quite happy.

A signpost (not usually seen on the Downs) pointed me across the hills for Storrington. I encountered another lone hiker who had come up from Amberly. Also, I met another walker who had just killed an adder. He beckoned to me and showed me the creature hanging on his walking stick. The other hiker asked if he might accompany me and offered to share a flask of tea. We trod very gingerly now and avoided long grass. I found my new companion very interesting and a great nature lover. The time slipped by too quickly. Noticing the lateness of the hour, we parted with a friendly handshake and each went in a different direction. I went a long way off and had to return. After a very long walk, I found the village of Washington which was on the main road. I chased a bus for a few hundred yards and eventually caught it. Steyning was a sixpenny bus ride along. I met some experienced hikers who were staying at Graffham. They offered their company for our walk the next day. This proved to be a successful day. Our walk was rather shorter, but scenery was delightful.

We trekked through the picturesque village of Bramber; then through pastureland with a winding stream. The Castle of Bramber nestled amongst the trees, enhancing the beauty of this spot. Heading straight for the Downs, we reached the north side after passing through corn and hay fields as well as heathland. From the Devil's Dyke, we got a fine view of the county of Sussex. We were glad to find a refreshment chalet and rested here for a considerable time. We ventured down into the Dyke and through the small village of Saddlescombe which consisted of one farm and two or three cottages. Here we got delicious ice-cones and also watched the swifts in flight over a small pond. At the end of this ridge of hills, we came down right opposite to the hostel at the other side of some playing fields. We found a main road and some of the young folk had arrived early to spend an evening in Brighton.

I followed my itinerary next day to a certain point and then struck off alone. I traversed an uphill road for a good distance. Gazing back and down, I noticed a variety of colored rooftops dotting the new estate built on a large triangular plot of ground. Upon reaching the summit of this hill, I came to a road leading to Stamner Park and Brighton and Lewes

The Legend of the Devil's Dyke.

According to the ancient legend, Old Nick, beholding the great beauty of the Sussex Weald, and seeing many Church spires thereon, threatened to flood the weald in a single night—but—his evil designs were frustrated by the goodly Saint Cuthman, patron saint of Steyning.

'Twas evening in the realms below,
The Eternal Fire a great red glow ;
When Satan, caught with Wanderlust,
Resolved to take a stroll, just
To demoralise the world without,
The World he'd heard so much about.

A Flash of Flame...a loud report,
And "Nick" on the world, prepared for sport,
He chuckled at the scene revealed,
Then above his head did his pitchfork wield
With angry mien, for nestling in the vale below
Were myriad Churches—some high—some low

Fired with a murderous lust to kill,
He resolved to cut away a hill ;
This was his awe-inspiring notion—
That thru the Gap would flow the ocean,
But his self-set task—by no means light—
Must be accomplished in a single night.

He at once began, ere Dawn should come.
When Nick would have to cut and run ;
And a terrible noise he made that night
Exerting all his sinful might,
'Til an old woman in a cottage near
Awoke—filled with a nameless fear.

She heard weird noises in the outer night
And tremblingly did the candle light ;
She placed it on the window level,
Unknowingly shining its rays on the Devil,
Nick quickly saw the great, bright beam,
Which to him the morning sun did seem.

With an awful oath Nick hurriedly fled ;
What seemed Success was failure instead,
He firmly resolved to make no more raids,
But in future would stay in peaceful Hades
There never was a gruesome tale like
The true legend of THE DEVIL'S DYKE.

Legend of the Devil's Dyke

Road farther on. I slept on the hillside after having lunch in Rottingdean. A big military camp was located at Falmer. After trudging over the Downs, I got very thirsty and enjoyed a refreshing glass of cider. The art shop at Rottingdean had enticed me to make a few purchases, also.

Uncle Sam's donkeys were causing some amusement with their fair riders at Black Rock. I boarded a bus at Poole Valley; it was just starting for Lewes and arrived at the hostel in good time. I renewed some acquaintances with hikers as well as meeting more new people: some Danes, and a Chinese student from Paris who was touring England by himself. This hostel was clean and I decided to stay another night.

Thursday, my seventh day, was another sunny day. It was quite windy up on the Downs though. Today's walk took me over Offham Hill, Mount Harry, and Black Cap to Ditchling Beacon. It was quiet and peaceful, hardly a soul to be seen all day. The way was easy to find, and upon reaching Black Cap, I stayed for about an hour in that perfect paradise of a spot and then walked on to the next hill which was Ditchling Beacon, the highest point in Sussex. After a short rest, I decided to take the road under the hills for a change. The road was winding and pretty, bordered by masses of wild thyme, and yellow rock flowers grew in beautiful profusion. After walking another two miles, I came to the village of Plumpton and at the local inn was able to get a pot of tea. I went on down the road, sat in a hay field and wrote up some of this holiday's experiences. I enjoyed this respite and was reluctant to leave this scene of numerous wild flowers. I saw canterbury bells growing wild here. Later, I remember seeing a handsome white calf lying on a bed of hay in a barn I walked by.

Not being familiar with these roads, I made a circular return tour and arrived at the hostel fifteen minutes late for supper. I spent that evening with two Danish girls. We chatted and played Lexicon. Two other Danish people had had an accident with their cycles. They went on to Paris the next day. The two girls I spent my evening with returned to London with severe sunburns. I had been troubled with a toothache, so I went the next day to the dentist and had an extraction. I walked into Brighton this day, not caring to face the winds on the hills. The weather was a tad dreary, looking like rain. I ate sandwiches in a park along the road and walked on again, finally reaching Brighton at 2:30 P.M. I spent the afternoon on Palace Pier in a deck chair. We were entertained by the Sussex regiment military band. I weighed in at 129 pounds. After having tea, I decided to come home. I caught the 6:25 P.M. train, arriving at Victoria punctually at 7:25 P.M. I was soon home, relating my holiday experiences to my friends, feeling very fit and "full of beans," so to speak.

Phoebe restored to health

Mother and Father

Sister Elsie (right)

My First Love Affair

I have not forgotten my first "love affair": My uncle Victor knew a nice young man about my age and it was he who introduced me to Harold who lived in North London and who was unemployed. He came to Brentford, my hometown, each Saturday and took me to some place of interest in the vicinity. He was serious about getting settled with a partner in life, was a clean-cut young man and had no bad habits that I knew about. However, somehow I didn't care to continue the friendship. He was also faithful in writing me every week and took me to his home one day where I met his mother, who was a widow.

I didn't know how to break up the friendship, which lasted a few months. He found employment eventually and it was at this time that I decided to write and tell him not to meet me again. He was heartbroken and I felt cruel and was sorry for him, but I knew it was the best thing to do as I did not love him. We were both twenty-three years of age at the time. Later I saw him with another girl and so I was happy for him and trust that her friendship was more compatible than mine.

I did not come in close contact with members of the opposite sex for serious friendship until later in life. I found myself extremely busy with studies and getting my living. This is why I never married early in life. It was in God's plan for me, no doubt. I have had no children of my own, but when I learned from a friend about sponsorship of orphans, I was led to do this and have had much pleasure in keeping in touch and sponsoring several children over the years, one of whom I took care of for sixteen years. Yoon Mee is a Korean girl and is now out in the world on her own. A missionary interpreted her letters for me for a short period of time.

3

My Nursing Years

Life at Bethlem Royal Hospital During World War II

While I was wondering what my next job in life could be, some relatives of Ralph's wife tried to decide this for me. In fact, they had it all planned that I should go along with them with a plan they had in mind to open up a small restaurant in Holland Park. They wanted me to be the cook. This was a Belgian family and they were willing to teach me what I did not know about cooking. They wanted to make this restaurant an exclusive eating place and a special project and interest for their other daughter. I was not really interested, but went along with the idea for the time being. I remember learning how to make real mayonnaise. The cooking was simple as they served mostly roast meats and lunches only.

I was not long in this job and I cannot remember if this was a successful project for them or not. I was reading the local newspaper in my own hometown when I saw an advertisement for educated young ladies to train as mental nurses at Bethlem Royal Hospital. This immediately drew my attention as I was quite anxious to find out if I had done all possible in the care of Ruth Altson. I answered the advertisement and was interviewed by the head nurse whom we called "Matron." A medical examination was required before being accepted, and I remember my doctor was reluctant about passing me. He said, "You have to be a very strong person to be a nurse." I begged him to pass me and he did. So, I launched out with determination and entered for training in the year 1936.

I was nearly thirty years of age when I began training and somewhat older than most of the others in my school. However, I fitted in all right, was accepted, and moved into the nurses' home at Eden Park, Kent. This was a beautiful hospital and training school for psychiatric nursing and was in several acres of park land. It was actually the original Old Bethlem Royal Hospital known previously as the Old Bedlam, the first hospital of its kind, which was moved from London to this lovely area.

This was a private hospital and I enjoyed my training here very much. I had to work very hard, for in those days, nurses had quite a lot of domestic duties to perform, and the training stretched out over a period of four years. We were paid a small salary plus board and lodging. We received very little more when qualified. This hospital was one of the first to give shock treatments. At that time some patients were undergoing electric shock and others were undergoing insulin shock therapy. Occupational therapy was, of course, practiced also among all the patients. Our studies for the first two years were the same as in a general hospital and so we were glad when we were working on the medical wards so as to put into practice what we were learning. We had to go to London for state board exams and when we passed the first examination were given a black stripe for our caps.

We met with many interesting people in the hospital and had a number of exciting experiences as well. Let me relate what happened on two occasions: I was working on the convalescent ward and was entrusted with a group of patients who were going for an afternoon walk in the woods. I was given strict instructions to keep a certain patient next to me and watch her, as she was a runaway and suicidal. Needless to say I was careful but she was wary, and when we were a good distance out she decided to run away. I left the others and made a long, fast chase after her. I was almost exhausted when I outran her and she just turned around and laughed at me. Another time I had a scare in the refectory ward. As you may know, all doors are kept locked after passing from one place to another. At this time I was what was known as kitchen nurse. After each meal the cutlery had to be accounted for, and that was one of my duties. Suddenly I looked up and saw the gaunt figure of "Christine," we will call her. She had come through the living room and here she was in the kitchen. Someone had left the door unlocked. Christine watched me and went straight to the cutlery box and got out a knife. I watched carefully what she would do. She went to the refrigerator and cut herself a piece of cheese. It was some months later that I saw her again and on a different ward. She looked so different—a charming young lady with all of her faculties and behaving normally. I could just recognize her. She also knew me and I asked her if she remembered the above incident. She said she did and laughed with me about it.

I was working at this hospital at the beginning of World War II and would go home every other weekend. Sometimes it would be during air raids that I would travel back and forth on the district railway. On one such occasion, I was home when we had an air raid on my hometown. We still lived at the duplex home of 38 Layton Road, Brentford, Middlesex, where I was born. A German bomber plane released all of his bombs onto our town. This was a "stick of bombs," I remember they called it. We were living next to the railway and there were five or six bombs dropped quite near to our home—one on each side of the railway, one on the waterworks, one on Kew Bridge and another on a factory on the Great West Road. We had an air-raid shelter but there was no time to use it. We ducked under the table and I jabbed a knitting pin into my arm. After it was over, we looked around to find what damage was done and discovered the scullery ceiling was down and there were a few panes of broken glass.

The Battle of Britain was a very trying time period as we were bombed night and day every day. We nurses had to take our patients into the basement every night for a long period. We were rigged up with mattresses and air-conditioning, which was very loud and made it hard to sleep. Our sleep was fitful and I used to have nightmares. However, the patients were very cooperative. I did a lot of night duty at this hospital and we worked a ten-hour shift. We tried to keep healthy and the hospital authorities took care of us physically. We had free dental care and other amenities. The night nurses also enjoyed a health and beauty course. It was set to music, and we wore white blouses and black shorts. It was extremely helpful to our well-being. There were a lot of good memories at this place. I used to help arrange flowers, of which there was an abundance, for the wards. They were grown on the grounds.

When our patients were ready for home one of us would travel to London with them. This was a privilege we enjoyed. At Christmastime we worked with the patients to make decorations. We would choose a theme and work with it. Everything was kept secret and no one was allowed to pass through to the other wards until we had finished and were ready for awards to be given. I remember the ward on which I worked at one time made Dutch scenes. It seemed like weeks beforehand we were making tulips, windmills and Dutch figures. I have kept pictures of the completed scenes. We did not get first prize. Another floor had made extensive scenes, quite different, but ours were prettier.

One weekend during the Battle of Britain, the enemy decided to pay us a visit. I was sleeping in one of the hospital wards (a senior nurse was always on call on each floor) and I awoke to find an air raid in progress. Incendiary bombs were being dropped all over the hospital grounds. I dressed for an emergency; however, I was not called upon to do anything. Presently, as I watched from the window, I saw what I thought was a direct hit. A bright light showed a mountain of rubble flying in the air nearby. I was told my help was still not needed so I went back to bed. In the morning I found out the extent of the damage incurred. The people on duty for fire duty had done a good job by putting out all the small fires made by the incendiary bombs. The direct hit was made on the corner of the nurses' home. The damage was minimal. It appeared quite drastic at nighttime.

Work and studies were pursued during these trying times and when it was time for state board examinations, we went to our assigned places for these. One such time I remember I was given an entry ticket number thirteen. Well, many people thought this was an unlucky number, but it turned out otherwise for me. I was taking an oral examination when an air-raid siren came over the air. The examiner watched me and then went on with his duties. There was a written examination also at this time. Out of nine students, I was the only one who passed. There was a trick question which the others failed to notice. I record this because I am particularly thankful to God for His graciousness in helping me in various circumstances of life. I want to thank Him for the many times He has seen me through difficult times.

Sometimes we come up against people we find difficult to work with. All of us, I am sure, have experienced this in life. This was so in the hospital. The head nurse here was jealous of me getting my state certificate. She told me I was very fortunate to have gotten the honor of receiving the hospital Medal of Achievement, which was presented to me at a hospital board meeting. She herself did not train in the hospital so did not receive one of these medals.

Well, I stayed on as a staff nurse for awhile and did a good deal of night duty. When the charge nurse was off duty I did relief duties, which entailed walking from one ward to another picking up reports from the nurses in charge of the various units. I would have to condense these for a single report to give to the matron in the morning.

It was while working in this hospital that I received a message to go home. A second death had occurred in my family while at this hospital. My mother had been ill for some time. She was taken into the local cottage hospital and after a very short time died. Mother was sixty-two years of age, a loving and hardworking parent whom I have come to appreciate more as the years have passed. Her body was interred in Ealing Cemetery. My father especially missed my mother, and, as he was a heart case, had taken an early retirement. My sister Queenie lived at home to help take care of him.

I stayed on at Bethlem Royal Hospital for awhile and later decided to leave and further my nurse's training. The war was still on, so I decided to apply at West Middlesex Hospital at Isleworth, which was the nearest hospital to my home. I was accepted as a third-year nurse for general training. They had a nurses' home so I moved into it. There was a shortage of nurses and we had to work very hard there.

As we were living in the greater London area we were plagued by bombs dropping around us. One day we had a direct hit on the nurses' home. Fortunately for us, no one was killed as all were on duty at the time.

I remember the shortage of food too. We were all rationed for most commodities and it seemed like we did not even get our rations. Dinner consisted of a plate of gravy with a few flakes of meat. One redeeming feature was that we had a work break in the middle of the morning and we hungry nurses were glad to eat hunks of bread and drippings. Speaking of food, people used to adapt themselves to all kinds of substitutes. My father used to make bee wine and mother used to make homemade chocolate.

Everyone had to do air-raid duty about once a week. When it was our turn we would be stationed on top of the hospital, and, when there was a raid, we would have to watch for fire bombs and report them. There was a number of foreign nurses on the staff and I remember a German nurse whom we thought was a spy. She would be seen listening to news over the wireless (radio) when no one else was around.

After the nurses' home was bombed we were moved into Syon House next door. It was the home of the Duke of Northumberland, K.G. It was a beautiful place on the river Thames and this made us a temporary refuge. Later, because of the shortage of space, some of us were allowed, or were asked, to live out. As I lived nearby I took advantage of doing so. I cycled back and forth. We were given a monetary allowance for this.

I may have told you before that nurses in training were allowed a small salary, so it pleased me to be able to stay in my home until graduation. I found the training interesting. We were given many opportunities to work with the doctors and watch operations being performed. As senior nurses, we were given a lot of responsibility, also. We chose the diets for each patient.

Nurses at Bethlem Royal Hospital

It was while in this hospital that I became acquainted with the Nurses Christian Fellowship. I am also ashamed to say it was here that I became inebriated, my one and only time. All the nurses on my ward were invited to celebrate with a patient whom we had nursed back to health. Some of the nurses thought it would be fun to get me to drink two or three different drinks. I was not used to drinking any kind of alcohol so, of course, it really went to my head. I am thankful I made a decision not to drink again.

I made a number of friends in this hospital as I did at the last one. Some of these I kept for many years. After graduation we all separated and went our different ways. Some chose to stay and become ward sisters. One girl with whom I was friendly nicknamed me "Horsey." She got a job as a health visiting nurse. She caught tuberculosis and died early in life. Another went abroad and married. She lived in the Isle of Cyprus. Elizabeth Ekrum corresponded with me for many years. She was head nurse in the hospital where she lived for a number of years. Her husband died and she came back to live in England and bought a beautiful home in Eastbourne, a seaside resort. She worked at the local health clinic and raised her only child, who in turn became a nurse also. After I came out to America, I was able to visit Elizabeth in her lovely home when I went on vacation.

Nurse Training at West Middlesex Hospital

It was while I was in nurses' training at the West Middlesex Hospital that I became acquainted with my second cousin Gwen. She was my mother's first cousin and was married to a Mr. Driver. They had settled and lived at Weybridge Surrey. Their beautiful home was quite near the station. In fact, the deep railway cutting was at the end of their lot. Gwen invited me to stay with her and I spent a very delightful holiday there with this couple and Aunt Alice, who was living there with them.

It must have been fine weather because we used to have tea on the terrace overlooking a lovely garden. They had a canopied garden seat in which one could enjoy swinging. We used to take the Airedale dog out for a run on the common across the road where there was a lovely stretch of brush land with patches of yellow gauze, a prickly ground cover. My cousin later moved not far away into a nursing home. She was very incapacitated with arthritis. She wrote to me every Christmas until her death.

While training for general nursing I heard about the Queen's Nurses who worked in the district and in the homes of the people. This appealed to me so I wrote to headquarters for this specialized training. It was a six-month course after general was completed. I was accepted and my training home was in Holland Park, London. We had some narrow escapes in this area which was in the west side of London.

The first "V" bomb from Germany landed in the street behind us. I remember the night it came over. It was brightly lit and shone into my room like daylight. I don't know why we did not hear it after it roared over our roof tops. A whole side of a street was razed to the ground. The next morning it was my duty to visit a patient on the other side of the street. The police had cordoned off the area and I had to step over rubble to reach my patient.

London was noted for its fogs in those days, although it is different now. We had no lighting in the streets either, so it was most difficult to get anywhere at nighttime. We nurses had to find our way somehow to the homes of people in the area. I remember on one such occasion I was completely lost. I had to rely on the tramways and a little light from inside to get me home again. We used a very heavy type bicycle and carried our equipment in a basket in front and in suitcases on the back. We were taught how to sterilize dressings and utensils in the homes of the people or back in the nurses' home. In spite of the difficulties and problems arising during these years, I found the training interesting and satisfying.

At the end of this course I checked into the London Ear, Nose and Throat Hospital for a small operation. While there a bomb dropped in Tottenham Court Road. I was under anesthesia at the time and was told I jumped up while on the operating table. Also, the impact of this took a plate of food through a glass door while a nurse was carrying it.

In spite of the difficulties and problems, we tried to carry on in our usual routine. Because of the possibility of poison gas being used, we all carried a gas mask with us on our shoulders.

The home in which we trained was situated in a long row of typical London houses. We took up two of these. They were about four stories high with basements and glass doors leading out onto small balconies with wrought-iron enclosures.

There were about six nurses in training at one time. We used to make rounds in the mornings and evenings. A senior nurse would show us the technique and once in awhile an inspector came with us. It was important to carry out what we were taught. We were considered an elite group of nurses. We had our uniforms tailored and made to order by a London firm. Our dresses were a fine mid-blue stripe with short sleeves. Coats were of navy blue velour cloth worn with peaked caps for day wear and navy felt hats for dress wear. The medallion worn by Queen's Nurses was two shades of blue and, hung on a long, thick cord around the neck under a stiff white collar. We handed them in if we left the organization.

Because of my health problem, this nursing association chose to send me to the Margate District Nursing Association for my first job with them, and my earliest full-time job after training. I was very happy there and worked there for about four years.

I will endeavor to tell you some of my experiences in this southeast English resort town.

District Nursing in Margate, England
Queen's Nurse, July 1944–July 1948

I was happy to be settled in a full-time job at last, at least for awhile. The private nursing association here supplied us with a place to live and a maid to clean and prepare our meals.

I shared a two-bedroom house, a small villa, with Sister Urquart, a Scotch girl who had a little black Scotch terrier. These are one-man dogs and Scotty was no exception; he would have nothing to do with me.

I found out that we only did emergency work on Sundays, and I was, therefore, able to make use of my Sunday school training. I joined the Congregational church and made many good friends. These I kept for years.

We nurses also met with other Queen's Nurses who lived in nearby places like Ramsgate and Broadstairs, which only had one nurse to each district. We would get together sometimes and see each other at nurses' meetings.

Ellen, from Ramsgate, was particularly interested in hiking and cycling and I was able to take three holidays with her. I have kept notes on these and will include them later in my narrative.

Some of the church friends were very kind to me and I was always welcome to drop in for morning coffee anytime I was in the area. Miss Winifred Drew was a dear and the two Corby girls, all maiden ladies, were special to me. They have since died.

The Corby family was interested in the Girls' Brigade. They had organized a company in the Congregational church; it is similar to scouts, but they have religious training included. I helped by teaching a first aid course. In this way the girls earned their badges.

I was able to organize a graded school for the primary department. The teachers were required to come to the training class in the week, otherwise they were not allowed to teach on Sunday. I remember how bright and cheery we made our schoolroom. We painted it in pale blue and yellow and hung new pictures. The post-graduate training course I had taken at Cambridge helped me to organize the primary department.

On Saturday evenings we nurses used to go to a dance. It was old-time dancing, graceful and healthy exercise. We didn't seem to have any men folk in our group so we danced with each other. I remember the very pretty dresses I wore. One was cherry red voile with black velvet spots on it and the other a pale green satin which was given to me by Ruth Altson some years previous.

The Nursing Association had monthly meetings which we were required to attend. The chairlady, Mrs. Vernon, was very well-known in the city and put a lot of confidence in us. She really gave me a boost in life in general. At one of our meetings I brought to the notice of the committee the fact that it was very hard work for us to ride cycles in this windy and hilly district in which we were living and working. A discussion ensued and it was decided to provide us with small cars. The assistant nurse, who lived out, and I were given small black cars. I named mine "Blackbird" and Miss Urquart was given a larger blue car. I forget the makes of these cars. However, this made our work so much easier. We were rationed with gas, but I remember the amount was adequate and we were allowed to use our cars when off duty also. We kept a record of mileage for this purpose. I was able to get to my home occasionally by car. Very few people were driving at this time as it was wartime and we were given priority. The association paid for us to have driving lessons, and I remember the first time I was left to myself to drive alone. It was soon after this that Mrs. Vernon said, "Sister Steers, you will drive us to the nurses' meeting in Canterbury on such and such a day." I told her I had never driven in the dark and it would be dark when we returned. She said I would be all right and this was one way she encouraged us. I did carry us all to the meeting, and we got back safely.

Not being very experienced as yet, I did get the car banged up one evening. I was somewhat scared to have to report this accident, but, again, this lady passed it off quickly so as not to discourage me.

I had a few unpleasant things happen to me in Margate. I met a man on the train from London one day. He began talking to me and seemed pleasant enough. He told me he was an organist and he spent his lunch period playing a church organ in London and commuted back and forth to London daily. He was a divorcé and I knew no better than to have anything to do with him. I began to meet him on weekends and found out he was interested in spiritualism. He took me to one of the séances and the medium warned him about certain things in his life. I wondered what it was all about. After several weeks I also was warned by a person whom he had known for a number of years. This lady sent the message to me through a friend of mine. She turned out to be a wonderful Christian woman whom I came to know quite well afterwards. I was indeed glad to be told about him as he had tried to mess up this girl's life. I started to break up the friendship and then he tried to blackmail me. I became scared and went to Mrs. Vernon, who again put me completely at my ease. She knew this man and it seems that he was well-known as a troublemaker. The only way I got rid of him was by writing a letter to him giving some good reason for relinquishing our friendship. I heard no more, but was sorry for the other girl he had hooked.

On another occasion I became infatuated by a lay preacher who was temporarily serving in my church. He was married so nothing came of it. At another time we had a pastor whose wife became very ill with leukemia, and, like every other person I've known with this disease, got very tired of the constant blood transfusions. I did some private duty nursing on occasion and this lady was one whom I nursed. I think she wanted me to befriend her husband; she did not want to die and leave him. It was a sad time when she decided herself the day she would die. She called her three grown sons, who were in their late teens, and a younger one in school. They spent the last day and night with her and she died the next day. They left the neighborhood soon after this.

I felt that this may have been a chance for me to marry as quite a friendship had grown between us, but this was not to be. I am thankful it was not so, because my Christian beliefs are different than what I was taught at this time. God knows best about all things and He will point the way and provide for us in His time.

Going back to my church life, I remember that we supported the London Missionary Society. At a dinner, I gave the following talk about India:

> If we are not interested or have lost interest in missionary work it is our duty to stimulate our interest in that direction, and I think a good way to do this is to learn about the religious ideas of others in far-off countries, many of whom know nothing about Christianity, as we know very little about their religions. It was agreed at the last Jerusalem Conference by all present that the success of Christianity did not lie in belittling other religions and that wherever a greater study of these religions had been made sympathetically, it became all the more clear that Christianity was the only religion that would fulfill the world's needs.
>
> As I am a speaker for the Indian table, I want to stress the great need for Christianity in India. More than ever does she need to know Jesus Christ as Savior and Lord, as at this time she is entering into a self-governing stage of her history.
>
> Most of the population are Hindus, and a very religious people. It is encouraging to know that Christianity is particularly suited to the Hindu mind. They embrace a faith that once held lofty and beautiful ideas. Some of their hymns and poems express lovely thoughts about God. It is thought by some philosophers that certain passages correspond very much to verses contained in our Bible. They may have borrowed from our religion. If that is so, it is encouraging and proves the Hindu mind is capable of aspiring to it. They believe the universe is God. It is also interesting to note that their Godhead takes the form of a trinity: Brahma (the creator), Vishnu (the preserver), and Siva (the destroyer). Each is worshiped by different sections of the community as being the supreme power, and each one is reverenced by all. They think that nothing apart from God really exists, only appears to exist; and their ultimate aim in life is for final emancipation instead of eternal life as the Christian believes.
>
> The low caste people are especially to be pitied because they have very little in life to live for. One of the main theories of Hinduism is that whatever caste a man is born into, it is his duty to accept and only

> through constancy to duty in this life will there ever be a chance for a better life through incarnation in the next life. If they are good, that includes strict observance to ceremonies attached to the religion, they may be lucky enough to be born into a higher caste family next time; otherwise, they may be born into the shape of an animal, insect or fish.
>
> You may wonder how various gods came into the religion. It arose in the belief in incarnation. In a certain period of history, the priests had freedom to do anything they wished to stress their particular beliefs, and sometimes a character from a fable or some great philosopher or teacher would, years afterwards, be introduced as an incarnation of one of the triad and worshiped as a separate god. This gives us an idea of what Hinduism is about and the need in the lives of these people for the true and living God and Savior Jesus Christ.

Coming back to the times in which we were living, these were perilous times. The English people had many difficulties to cope with. Traveling was made difficult as name signs were removed in case of invasion. Also, various roadblocks were used to impede an impending enemy. A blackout regime was carried out till the end of the war, also.

There were all kinds of ideas put forth as to where the enemy might land in case of defeat. It was discovered after the war that it was a place quite near to Margate on the southeast coast. Thank God it never happened, and thanks to our American allies who helped to save the situation.

I remember the Normandy evacuation of our troops. Squadrons of planes were going over to France; there was a constant drove overhead to bring out as many of our soldiers as possible, and as they went, a prayer for their safe return.

Also, every available little boat was crossing the channel to lift a few of our men—a fight to the end. We thanked God for calm seas. Finally, the victory was ours, but at a great cost. We were rationed with food for several years after the war. Gradually things became normal. It took years to rebuild our cities and to plant flowers and shrubs instead of vegetables in every inch of spare ground as throughout the war years. So, England has survived and learned many lessons. I know that people became closer to one another and more helpful and understanding toward each other.

I would not like to close this episode of my life without praising our leader, Sir Winston Churchill; a great man who was influenced behind the scenes by two great women—his mother and his wife.

It was while living in Margate that I was able to go for some very nice vacations.

Walking Tour in the Wye Valley
April 26–May 3, 1945

It is with pleasure that I am recording some of the adventures and experiences of our week's tour in the Wye Valley. We were a party of four girls and my friend, Miss Ellen Meen, had invited me to join them some weeks previous. We were thrilled at the prospect of a rambling tour and were not disappointed. This tour took us eight days and covered approximately one hundred miles.

It was decided to do one of Stanley Barron's tours and Miss Reed, our chief guide, after many difficulties, arranged everything for us. We had each experienced this type of holiday before so were well equipped and prepared to thoroughly enjoy ourselves.

We were all up very early the first day of our holiday. Everything was in readiness, and Ellen and I were on an early London train with rucksacks on our backs. We had met at Margate and were traveling to meet the others in London. We were quite excited by the time we had met Misses Batstone and Reed, and I am sure that many who saw us thought we were a very happy party.

The time slipped by very quickly and we just had time for coffee before our long journey to Ross-on-Wye. This was uneventful but quite comfortable. We arrived at our destination at about 3 P.M., after four and a half hours of travel. We were quite glad to find it was not early closing day in Ross so we looked around for somewhere to have tea. We were soon refreshed and ready to commence our tour.

We were quite impressed by this country town. We made our way through the main street and out onto an open road. My first impression was how very much like Godalming in Surrey the place was. As we left the town behind we could see how the place was built, fairly high on sandstone cliffs coming down to the riverside.

It seemed that we came into the country immediately after we left the town. Although our walk was chiefly on the main road, we passed through some glorious country. A slight mist obscured some of the distant scenery, but we were almost intoxicated by the sheer beauty of everything we saw. The air was laden by the scent of the hawthorne. Everything in nature appeared at its best. The trees and grass and wild flowers were so fresh and green and the bird life so joyous. The meadows and banks were beautiful; some were full of buttercups, and the quietly flowing river Wye wound through the hills. The earth was a rich red color and was only cultivated in a few places. As we were told, it contained many boulders.

After walking four miles along this main road we reached Goodrich, where we turned into a secondary road for the youth hostel at Welsh Bickner. On our way we decided to view Kerne Bridge, a beautiful stone structure over the river and a very picturesque spot. We saw some swans on a small island in the river, also some day-old lambs frisking around in a nearby field. Some of the hills were covered with primroses reaching the footpaths. There were many other wild flowers to be found also, including herb robert, campions, cow parsley, forget-me-nots, and violets.

The hostel was in a very secluded spot, beautifully situated and overlooking the river, much to our delight. We were made very welcome here and served a hot meal on our arrival at 7 P.M. We were glad to retire early as we had a long walk planned for next day. The hostel was an old rectory and there was something grand about the place.

For awhile we enjoyed watching the scenery and activities going on from the dormitory window. A copper birch and cedar grew on either side of the garden and the tiny church was nestled among the trees below. I was able to look down onto the river from my bed.

Next day we were called early and after a sumptuous breakfast started out at 9 A.M.

We mounted Coppet Hill after leaving this delightful haven and from here we saw some more entrancing scenery. The winding river below and the wooded hills were very beautiful. We were able to traverse this hill by small footpaths; primroses grew in profusion at our feet. We were pleasantly surprised to find the river still coursing its way in the valleys on the other side and were not long in finding Huntsham Bridge, which we reached by footpath and road in one-half hour. We paused again to admire this lovely spot with picturesque bridge. We were delighted to see the various colors of the trees in their delicate spring shades. It was perhaps grander than the other side of the hills. Large patches of yellow broom and copper beeches added beauty to the vista.

Some workmen confirmed our directions for Symonds' Yat. We had to climb up on a gradual road round the hillside, and on reaching the summit we explored the top and found the huge rock which crowns the highest part. From here we could view three counties (Monmouthshire, Herefordshire, and Gloucestershire). The view was extensive; the river Wye appeared to almost encircle the hillside. We settled down in a sheltered spot for lunch. Afterward we found a cottage cafe where we were able to get a refreshing pot of tea.

We came down to the old ferry, another noted beauty spot, and crossed by the ferryboat which was manipulated by the boatman pulling hand over hand along a stout rope that was stretched across the river's width.

We continued our ramble along a delightful footpath in close proximity to the river and passed many caves in the rocky hillside on our right. At the mouth of one we discovered wild columbine growing, and water was gushing out of the rocks forming a little stream which ran into the main river. We passed on through a wooded area where wild flowers grew in profusion; there were patches of bluebells, pink campions and stitchwort among them. We came to open pasture areas and beautiful meadows where cattle grazed. For the whole day, for several miles, we were able to follow an easy footpath and were in a lovely valley. We came across a big old manor house when nearing Monmouth and learned it was being used as a military hospital. We thought how suitable it would be for shock patients.

We left the river and made a precipitous climb onto the main road into Monmouth. We had much fun scaling slippery slopes as there were no footpaths here to help us. We spent an interesting time choosing and purchasing view cards and especially good photographs of the places we were visiting. We did a little shopping and had a meal but did not find the town too interesting, except for the bridge which had a tollgate (no longer in use). The river Monnow flowed through the town thus giving it its name. We were quite glad to leave here and make our way to the hills again. The hills have an unexplained fascination for us, and we sometimes likened ourselves to Christian in *Pilgrim's Progress* while climbing difficult hills.

Over Church Hill we passed a tiny hamlet known as Penalt and we found there was yet another hill to pass over. It was worthwhile climbing for, over yonder, after passing through woodlands and making a very long and steep descent on an extremely rough pathway, we came to the prettiest village so far, lying nestled among the hills. It was very small and we found the hostel almost immediately. It was a whitewashed cottage, very primitive in every way.

Whitebrook possessed a well inhabited by a trout, we were told. Here we got our drinking water. A fast rushing stream passed through the garden. We used this for domestic purposes. The cookhouse stood apart from the house and everything got very sooty because oil stoves were used for cooking.

Saturday was a bright and sunny day and we took our leave quite early once again. We were exalted by the beauty of this village as we passed through with its glorious surroundings. The varying contours and heights of the grass-covered and wooded hills made it appear as a moving panorama of beauty.

We were now once again along the riverside and walked several miles on a good road to Tintern Abbey, passing on our way Bigswier and Brockwier Bridges. Before reaching the abbey we passed the particularly beautiful village of Llandogo, built partly on the hill slopes and in the Wye Valley.

We came into Tintern Parva where we had some delicious coffee and cakes, after which we made our way to the abbey. It is a picturesque ruin and famous as a monument to early English Norman architecture. The east window is of special interest. Sheep grazed within the abbey ruins. We continued along the road by the riverside and looking back we got a much better view of the abbey. We were able to look down upon it and thus we got a finer aspect of this old ruin. It was really majestic in its wonderful, natural setting.

The weather set in showery, but we were glad to have seen the abbey in sunshine. Trudging along in the rain, we were discussing where we might get a bus to help us along our journey (two of the party were

Tintern Abbey

pushing on to Usk that night instead of staying at Chepstow), when a lorry (truck) stopped behind us and the driver offered us a lift. This was unexpected but we gladly accepted. This part of our journey was on the main road and uphill for about two miles. He dropped us at the foot of "Wyndcliffe," a hill we intended to climb. On reaching the summit we got a good view of the Severn Estuary and Bristol Channel. It was windy and difficult to find a sheltered spot to eat our sandwiches. We at last sat down under a tree but hastily moved as one of our party saw a snake uncoil itself and enter its nest in the roots of the tree right behind us. We found a more open place in which to eat our lunch after this incident.

The next part of our journey was not so interesting. We made our way along the main road to Chepstow, passing a POW camp on our way. On reaching this town our first thoughts were for tea. This we got at an attractive tea shop known as the "Bunnery," and were supplied with delicious homemade scones (biscuits in America) and cakes. Ellen met an old friend here and both were excited at this unexpected encounter.

After tea, Misses Reed and Batstone caught a bus to help them along part of their journey, and we two spent an enjoyable evening by the river in a sheltered spot. Sitting on an old log we discussed our many adventures.

After an excellent breakfast the next day, we started off once again at 9:30 A.M. We passed through the village of Pwyll Meyric and then turned into a winding lane to the right. The hedgerows were very pretty along here. Cow parsley was growing in abundance. We also found wild purple orchid growing. We steadily mounted upwards passing through a wooded area known as Mounton and on through Shire Newton. The scenery became more interesting. We were walking northwest and still held a view of the Severn and Bristol Channel.

The village of Llanvair was tucked away in the hills and appeared quite isolated. We managed to get some tea at a cottage. The person living here knew the nurse-midwife whom we had met in Chepstow the day before. As we left this village behind we saw the ruin of Llanvair Castle, a small, crude structure not in the least imposing but of historical interest.

We came over a hill and looked down on a natural reservoir. Later, we came to some dense pine woods and open heathland, which was known as Wentwood. We were getting some showers but sunny intervals. We had climbed steadily most of the way since starting out, and suddenly we were surprised to find ourselves on the crest of a hill that looked down on a lovely landscape. Many of the fields had been freshly tilled and the sun and shade on the red earth and green fields gave a pleasing variation in the scenery.

We passed through Llandtrisent and Llancowel where we were able to walk by the river Usk. The weather remained cold and showery and we took shelter under a hawthorne tree, where a seat was provided on the river bank. Later, we reached the small town of Usk. We soon found the cafe where we were to stay for the night and recounted our day's experience to the others who had spent a restful day here after their adventures in the rain the previous evening. Our hostess soon had a hot meal ready for us and we felt better after this and the warmth of a fire. We found we had time to go to church so went along to the Methodist church and stayed after service for a special hymn practice. The Welsh singing was good to hear.

On Monday morning we started off again in good spirits, with a packed lunch for our journey. Crossing the river Usk we made our way under the hillside and saw much beautiful scenery. There were a few scattered hamlets, including Llanbadock and Glascoed. A kindly woman made us a pot of tea here. She was very proud of her sons serving in the forces, and it seemed strange she should be living in this lonely spot after traveling to Australia and back. A little later we found a sheltered hillside for lunch where we watched some folks planting potatoes.

We passed over Panpedi Hill from where we got a wonderful view of the countryside. The farmsteads around here made a pleasing sight. We then descended into Llan-St. Mary and up to Llanvaircross. From time to time we saw the mountains loom before us; the Sugarloaf was much in prominence, and traces of snow could be seen on the summit of a few distant ones. We also occasionally met the winding Usk. Many herds of Herefordshire cattle grazed in the fields.

We passed through the hamlets of Llanfoyst and Llanellen and so reached Abergavenny where we spent a short while. We completed the day's tour by taking a bus four and one-half miles out to Llangvihangel Crucarney. The weather had been getting cold and we were glad when we reached our destination.

We had arranged to stay at the Skirrid Mountain Inn which was situated on the main Abergavenny and Hereford Road. It was a very nice solid structure built in A.D. 1100. It is thought to be the second oldest inn still in use in England. It was very interesting inside. The lovely old antiques were well preserved and we were made very comfortable here.

The Skirrid Mountain or Holy Mountain is of interest as it is said that at the time of the crucifixion there was a great landslide causing a huge gap which can be seen for miles away. The next day was to be an exciting one for us as we had planned to climb the Sugarloaf Mountain, the height of which is 1,955 feet, and then we were to make a push into the Black Mountains.

We had been on the road a short while when a good-natured lorry driver pulled up and offered us a lift to the foot of the mountain. This was gladly accepted as it was an uphill road. It helped us considerably and we enjoyed this novel way of travel. We were rather impressed by the amount of vegetation growing on the mountainside, but it became more sparse as we climbed higher. The turf on the paths was soft and springy and, as the paths disappeared higher up, we made our way through heather and new bilberry plants. A few frightened sheep were grazing on the slopes and suddenly some large birds, which we were unable to identify, flew out of the heather. They made a loud, screeching noise and did not approve of being disturbed by us. At the top of the mountain we found a small plateau covered with turf and an obelisk marking the highest point. The inscription told us the name of the mountain belonging to the National Trust. As we looked around we could see nothing but hills, range upon range in varying shades of blue.

We settled on the slopes for awhile and ate our sandwiches. It was exciting clambering down the Sugarloaf and we experienced a feeling of satisfaction on our accomplishment in having reached the top. The village of Fforest is situated at the foot of this mountain and the village postmistress kindly made us tea, after which we were most refreshed and warmed. The temperature was low at this altitude.

We continued down into the vale of Llantony Abbey. This walk in the valley between the two ridges of the Black Mountains impressed us greatly. The grandeur of the mountains and the beauty of the valley as we passed along on this good winding road filled us with ecstasy. The narrow river Honddu and occasional mountain streams added beauty to the scenery. As we passed along, the mountains ahead changed in contour and coloring, many of which were still bearing signs of the recent snowstorm.

Many wild flowers and ferns grew in the hedgerows, including cuckoo pints and milkmaids. Marsh marigolds grew in the marshes.

Several bridges spanned the river at intervals, and ridges of larch added beauty to the landscape. Many of the hedgerows were formed by hazel nut trees. The young nuts were plentiful. Wild strawberry plants were growing here in abundance, too. When we reached Llantony Abbey we were able to have tea at the Abbey Hotel which was built into the old ruins and, as we sat in this very old dining room with many old pieces of furniture and chased silver and brass pieces, we were able to view the stately ruins of the old priory. High up in the crannies golden wild flowers grew, and pasture land grew between the ruined piles. The mountains behind added splendor to this sunlit scene. Many anglers come to this spot which is noted for its trout fishing.

We had four miles to walk before reaching Capel-Y-Finn, away up in the mountains. The winding road continued through the valley. Only a few fields are cultivated although the earth is very rich. There are very few inhabitants in this lonely place. Just a few scattered farms can be seen. The fields are chiefly used for grazing sheep. Many types of these are to be seen with their young lambs. At one place we passed a herd of cattle and one had a young calf. The parent bellowed at us along the way.

We, at last, reached our destination, a hostel nestled on a mountainside. David, our host, belonged to a monastic order of non-denominational creed and proved a unique character. We were made very welcome and after a hearty meal, were entertained by ghost stories as we sat around the fireside. We then retired early for bed. We were aroused in the night by the cry of a lost lamb and shortly after heard the shepherd and his dog going in search of the animal. Silence then reigned until dawn.

We were able to explore our immediate surroundings before breakfast and took Tiny the dog along with us. We found a very pretty waterfall in the monastery grounds. It was falling over boulders and formed a crystal stream which we could cross by stepping stones. The willow trees and pretty foliage here made a lovely spot which we wished more people could see. It is interesting to note the name of this place means "Chapel-on-the-Border."

We were later than usual starting out again on our tour. The weather appeared to be brighter and we were quite happy to retrace our steps to Llantony, a distance of four miles. It was a delight to walk in this beautiful valley. We did so enjoy the young lambs skipping and playing in the fields with the parent sheep.

We caught a bus at Llantony which took us back to the Skirrid Mountain. An ill omen met our eyes; a horse lying down. We proved this was a sign of rain which surely came before long. We were fortunate to get a hot lunch and shelter from the rain, which abated after an hour. The sun shone for us again.

We then took a road over Campston Hill and saw a few yellow hammers along here. We had made a hurried farewell on the bus to Miss Batstone as she was returning home and was catching her train from Abergavenny. We missed her company very much. The lane we now traversed had pretty hedgerows. Gypsy crackers were growing in large patches together with other wild flowers.

We had left the mountains behind us again and approached smaller hills on a more open road on our way to Grosmont. We rested in a field where sheep were grazing. The Sugarloaf loomed up behind this sloping field. A warm sun was now shining and clouds of varying types could be seen sailing over the hills.

As we journeyed on we viewed a perfect nimbus over the Herefordshire Hills, and as we continued along we saw fields of cowslips before entering the village of Grosmont. We made a gradual descent and this village proved to be one of the prettiest yet. The hedgerows were pretty. The Herefordshire cattle were grazing in lush meadows; we were simply charmed with this delightful spot where we were to stay for one night. As we went through the one street we were thrilled at the sight of the cottages with their washed walls and pretty, well-kept gardens. We passed the town hall, a unique building built of a special colored stone quarried from the rocks in these parts. The Angel Inn was very picturesque and deserved recognition, but I think we were all more charmed by the old Greyhound Inn, which was blue washed with flower gardens under the windows and actually growing on the cobbled pavement (or sidewalk as we say here). Forget-me-nots were growing between the curbstones. This lovely old place is where we had arranged to stay.

Our hostess proved to be a kindly woman and made us most welcome. Tea was soon made ready and served in the large parlor, where a fire burned. This comfort kept us indoors for awhile as a chilly shower had started since our arrival. We became interested in some travel books our landlady had given us to read. One proved especially interesting as the writer was describing some walks in the West Country that we had been doing.

Between tea and supper we went along to discover things of interest in the village. The church was especially interesting. Its roof sloped down very low and with the spire was covered with reddish-colored slates aged with moss. The main structure was of the same stone as the town hall. It was exceptionally large for the size of the village. This was due to Grosmont once being a borough. The castle ruins were on the other side of the street. It was sitting among hills with moat around it. The river Monnow was nearby.

We arrived back at the inn for supper after which we retired. We were very comfortable here; the rooms were spacious and very homey.

We started off about 8:30 A.M. the next morning and made our way up the main Herefordshire road, a walk of one and three-quarter miles. We took a bus into Hereford City. We spent a few hours here as neither of us had been here before. We were greatly impressed by everything we saw—not only its cathedral, but its churches. All Saints and St. Peters were beautiful structures and a credit to the community. The museum and art gallery were interesting, also.

The old house of Jacobean style we found of particular interest. This contained furniture of the seventeenth century, including children's cradles and walking cages and many old carved chests and chairs.

We were able to get a hot meal in Hereford, after which we made our way to the station and were soon on our way to London feeling happy to have had such a wonderful holiday.

Hiking Vacation in the Lake District England–1947

It would be rather remiss on my part if I did not include a short account of my vacation in the Lake District. I have found a few notes which I have kept over the years and will endeavor to unravel them.

There were four of us girls who went on this glorious hike. Some had been hiking before; however, I think this was my second holiday of this kind. Two of the girls were from London and two from the South Coast; three were nurses and one girl was an office clerk.

The sunshine greeted us on our arrival in the Lake District at 3 P.M. Here there were hills in various shades of blue as we left the railway station. I have omitted to record where we started from, but never mind, let's enjoy this trip at a leisurely pace.

Carver Memorial Congregational Church was beautifully situated. Further down the road we caught our first glimpse of Lake Windermere. Many visitors were enjoying the beauty by the lakeside with lovely blue hills surrounding it. Here there were a number of small boats. We particularly noted the beauty of dandelions growing along the pavement. We came to the ferry and passed over to the other side of the lake. We stopped for tea at a copse by the lake. Far Sawry and Near Sawry were two small villages along here. There were many beautiful trees in various shades of green and wild flowers in profusion. We found violets, forget-me-nots, king cups, primroses, yellow poppies, stitchwort, celandines, cowslips, bluebells and strawberries growing here.

We came to a small lake called Esthwater. This was very beautiful with a wooded island. Wild fowl were seen here. The reflections were exquisite. We found the lodge here where we were to stay overnight. We had a good supper, and, afterwards, walked through meadows to the lakeside. We saw milkmaids and birds in flight.

We started off the next morning, Sunday, at 9:30 A.M. We passed through Hawkeshead Village and saw Ann Tyson's cottage and Wordsworth's footpath and proceeded to a mountain pass to the right at the end of the village and later came to Coniston Village. We were climbing up and up to Old Man Coniston around the mountain. We found a sheltered spot and had lunch. It was very rugged here. We descended into Duddon Valley by a long rough footpath. We had tea overlooking the valley. We saw many sheep of various types grazing in the meadows; some had black faces and legs. It was interesting to watch them skipping and jumping around.

We had to come back to a small bridge where Miss Reid, one of our party, had to leave us to do a different walk. We took the road across Birken Moor. It was very lonely and we lost ourselves. At last we saw a sheep dog, the only sign of habitation, and soon saw the shepherd lad who directed us. We were very grateful as the place was very marshy. We came to a newly planted forest and at last a more defined path through this forest. We hurried along on a rough path down into Eskdale Valley and met our friend Reid again as we arrived at the hostel. It was 7:15 P.M. when we arrived here. It was a modern place and we had good meals. The warden here was a kind lady.

We started out at 9:30 A.M. next morning. We passed by footpath and mounted a precipitous height behind Woolpack Inn. We passed Great Barrow on the right and Granite Hill by EEI Tarn, a pool in the hills. It was very rough and a vast stretch of moorland with very little vegetation at eighteen hundred feet up and a terrific wind at the summit. Not much sign of life here and marshy in places. There were only a few patches of heather to be seen.

We saw a gamekeeper's cottage and a few cows lying down to catch the warmth of the sun. Harta Fell was now on our right. There were white crosses on boulders which helped us to find our way. We came down to Wastwater. The mountains ahead were very grand and colorful. The whole scene reminded me of the Lake of Tiberius. The mountains met the lakeside. We rested and ate our lunch in the shelter of an old shepherd's hut. After this, we continued down by lakeside to Mossdale Valley. It appeared to be very isolated; it had one hotel, a tiny church and a closed hostel. There were lots of yellow gauze in bloom and very few trees. Through the dale we followed the course of Gathnestone Beck by Blacksail Pass. A very majestic and rough pathway. We descended to one thousand feet. The river Liza ran below which fed Ennerdale Water.

We made another climb over mountains ahead which caused us some perplexity. It was still very desolate. We met two hikers who gave us some directions. It was steep and dangerous over these mountains. We came up to a moorland. There were no sheep and not much sign of life anywhere. Just a few marshes and mosses grew in this high place. When we descended, we came to the hostel called Old Barracks. We arrived an hour late for supper but grateful for having found the place at last. It was the only place around and was situated at the beginning of Honister Pass. Great Gable and many other mountains surrounded us. Two of our party hiked over Great Gable—Misses Reid and Batstone.

After a good night's rest, we set off with packed lunches for our next destination. We went down into a beautiful valley known as Barrowdale. The exquisite scenery changed as we went around the winding path. We passed through Seatoller and saw cottages dating back to 1628. Then we went into Rosthwaite which was very beautifully situated. We decided to go into Keswick as the hostel was only a few miles on. We took a bus the east side of Derwentwater and arrived about 11:30 A.M. We had coffee at Friars Cafe and ate our sandwiches in the park.

We looked up a road on our map back to Grange, first walking out to the villages of Braithswaite, Portinscale, Stair, and Swinside. At this last place we took a footpath along the mountainside overlooking Derwentwater. It was beautiful with wooded areas in places. The mountains were seen in exquisite colorings—blue, purple, etc. Hollows Farm, where we were staying, was about half a mile from the village of Grange, which was under a mountain. We enjoyed the meals here. The others had arrived before us. The next day we all visited Keswick. We had an easy day and walked into the town by the same mountain road on the west side of the lake. We had a quick look around, made a few purchases, sent a parcel home, and made our way to Friars Cragg. It was a delightful spot for lunch. We sunbathed all the afternoon. We saw Skidaw in the distance. We had tea in the only tea shop that was open as it was early closing day here. We arrived at the hostel early. We left our rucksack and went out for a walk again. We took a road back of the station to Spooney Lane leading to a footpath over Latrigg Hill. We found it gave a good view of the lake. We went back for supper and went to bed early.

We met some girls we had seen at Ethwaite Lodge. My friends had a desire to scale the mountains, but we decided to spend another day around Keswick. We booked another night at the hostel and set out along the main road to Penrith. It was particularly beautiful scenery with pretty hedgerows. We found primroses, celandines and violets. After walking for a few miles we came to the village of Treald. We had delicious coffee and chocolate biscuits.

We overtook some lorry drivers who were sitting on the roadside having their lunch. They offered us a lift into Penrith which we accepted. This was a market town with many banks and hotels. We had lunch here and returned by the 2:50 bus. Troutbeck was originally our destination. This was a very small place with railway halt. We enjoyed the bus ride back to Keswick. We had tea at Friars Cafe and after a walk around the lake, we did some sunbathing until suppertime. We chatted in the common room until dusk and then went to bed.

Friday, we started out before 9 A.M. It was gloriously sunny. We took the road to Grassmere, passing Castlerigg, Bleabury Fells, and Armboth Fellson on our right. Helvelyn was on our left and the beautiful Lake of Thurlmere (this is Manchester's Waterworks). There were pine trees in abundance here. Thurlsport Inn made us a pot of tea. A little later we got a good view of the lake and a scent of the pines. We came to a pony track. There were pines on each side of the slopes of Helvelyn. There were numerous becks rushing down the mountainsides. There were also sheep grazing here. We dipped our feet in the water. There were young bracken growing in places and patches of celandines. Just outside Grassmere we got refreshing lemonade and on into the village where we got tea.

The lake here was smaller and not so accessible but this walk had been very enjoyable. We found the bird life here active. We found our hostel nestled among the mountains. They gave us a huge supper here and were very generous with the food.

Reid and Batstone joined us again here and we started off together next morning. It was our last day. We went down into the valley of Grassmere. We had coffee in Tea Gardens and left the others who were staying another night. We then visited Dove Cottage, the home of Wordsworth and De Quincy. On the road to Ambleside we passed Rydal Water, a very pretty lake and winding roads under rugged hills. Most of the houses were built of rough-colored stones quarried from the hills here. There were many king cups growing in the marshes around the lake. Also reeds growing a long way out into the water. We passed through the town of Ambleside and caught a bus around midday for Windermere. From there we went down to Bowness Bay, a delightful spot with grassy banks by the lake. We ate our lunch here, then took a launch trip onto the lake.

It was picturesque and a warm, sunny day. We found islands on the lake and a castle. We had tea at the Chestnut Tree Cafe and found another good spot to rest. We made our way leisurely to the station in good time to catch the 8:30 P.M. train, to travel all night.

This ended a delightful holiday with lasting memories for later years.

Midwifery Training Part I
September 1948

It was my friend Ellen Meen who encouraged me to take further nurses' training for midwifery, so that I would be qualified to take over a district by myself. Although I did not practice midwifery after training, it was one of the most interesting studies I have ever taken.

I wrote to the Mother's Hospital in Tottenham Court Road in the east end of London and was accepted for Part I Midwifery training. It was mandatory to do this in a hospital, whereas the second part is done in the district.

This training was done in September of 1948 and graduation was in February of 1949. There were twelve nurses in this school, and the girls were very Spirit-filled. They organized Bible study groups and had services in the wards for the mothers. Although I was a Christian at this time, I was not entirely consecrated. However, during this time, I learned what it meant to become a full-fledged Christian.

The hospital was run by the Salvation Army, and the students were encouraged to witness to the patients. Most of the girls who were in this class were preparing themselves for foreign missionary service. There was much prayer for any whom they thought were not Christians. All the nurses in our school became Christians before leaving. I used to write to one of them who went to Chile as a missionary nurse.

The work there was hard but very thorough. We had to attend a certain number of deliveries and were often called out at nighttime to bring babies into the world. There were lectures to attend and case histories to write up, and, of course, there were examinations at the end of training. I remember we had a very strict lady doctor, tall and severe. We would stand around a bedside with young student doctors and she would thrust questions at us, expecting right answers for the benefit of the doctors.

I enjoyed this training very much, especially the study of anatomy and physiology in depth. I felt like I was living in a new world.

Each new baby that we delivered we would quickly bathe and return to the mother. We would place it in her arms and say a prayer of thanksgiving for the mother's safe delivery and for the baby. This was a thrilling experience for both mother and nurse.

I used to go home on days off, which were few, but there was not much time and I hardly knew what was going on at home. My father, who was very dear to me, was very good at writing to me and I appreciated this very much. He gave no indication that he was not well, so it came as a shock when I received an urgent call from my sister, who was looking after him, telling me he was very ill. He had hemorrhaged and had other complications. It was near the beginning of my training that I had to go home. My dear sister Queenie wanted my advice about hospitalizing our father. Three of our family had died at the Brentford Cottage Hospital and we didn't want him to go into this hospital. The doctor tried to get him into West Middlesex and Hammersmith Hospitals without success, as there were no beds available. Reluctantly, and with sad hearts, we had to let him go into the local hospital.

My father died on September 3, 1948. It was a very sad time for me and my sister. This was not the only death in the family at the time. We lost three aunts and an uncle, but it was the third death in our immediate family. I was allowed time off from my nurse's training to bury my father but had to make up the time at the end after all the other girls had left.

My sister and I are the only ones left in the family, and at this time we still have each other, although we live oceans apart.

I still had Part II of Midwifery to complete. This I was able to do with the Queen's Nurses. After applying, they arranged for me to do this at a training home in Slough, Buckinghamshire. After examinations, I moved into this home.

Nurses' Home, Slough, Buckinghamshire

Midwifery Training Part II
March–August 1949

Moving again! I was almost a hobo, but it was all an experience in life. It was also what I wanted to do. When I came to Slough, this very modern industrialized city, I had no idea where and what I would be doing next. God had it all planned for me. I have found it best in life not to worry about the future, just leave it to Him. So, I set to work in this new environment to do midwifery and found myself in a typical English cottage home where a few pupil midwives were housed with me.

To show you, my readers, how well thought of we nurses were, I'll endeavor to remember a few facts about our living arrangements. The cottage was nicely situated. Each nurse had a room to herself. A calling maid came at a certain hour with a cup of tea to awaken us. We may have been out in the night on a delivery; however, we were expected to show up for breakfast.

There was a gardener employed and a pretty garden in which we could relax. We chose our own place of worship. I had a friend living in Slough who had done her first part of midwifery with me and she recommended that I go to a Church of England church, which I found was evangelistic and fundamental. On days off I was able to visit with her also.

During this second part of training we were allowed to deliver the babies ourselves; we gave the mothers anesthesia (gas and air) in the third stage of labor and the fathers came to the center and carried the apparatus back to the home. The mother's room was previously made as clean as possible and had to be uncluttered. Everything was prepared beforehand. A sterile delivery pack was available for the immediate delivery. These mothers had to attend prenatal clinics. We attended these clinics which were held at the health care center at Birlington Road. This was an important part of our training.

Vera (standing) as pupil/midwife

What healthy babies these mothers had! I used to love to see them come to the postnatal clinic. There was quite a parade of perambulators (baby buggies) and they were kept so neat and clean. The babies were weighed and inspected each time and the mothers checked.

Mothers showing any signs of toxemia were referred to their doctor, and, if necessary, would have their baby delivered in the hospital. At the time of my training most mothers had their babies at home. First pregnancies had a choice of home or hospital, but they usually chose to have them at home. We carried small weighing machines to weigh the babies at birth. As I remember, the smallest one I delivered in the district was around six pounds and the largest was over ten pounds. The folks back in the office would not believe me about the largest one, and someone else went out and checked. I might add, it was a much easier delivery than the small baby.

While I was away from home my sister had been working at Sperry's, the manufacturer of instruments for airplanes. Her job was to test these parts and she became quite adept at this work. She had been conscripted for this work during the war years and remained with the firm. She was working quite near to her home and was able to look after my father, even going home at lunch periods. Now that Dad was not with us, it was very lonely for her at home. Dad's sister, our Aunt Milly, had been ill a long time with cancer and her husband, Uncle Victor, used to go to a London hospital to visit her. Queenie used to help out and go visit the aunt, thus she was thrown in the path of our uncle and an affection grew between them.

Victor was a rather helpless individual with regard to housekeeping and cooking, so my sister used to help him considerably after my aunt died; another relative in the family passed on. The next thing I knew, my sister was engaged to be married to Victor. This was a great shock to our family. Queenie was in her late thirties and it was her first love affair, I believe. No one in the family approved but she was determined to marry her uncle. He was no blood relation to her. She had a quiet wedding at the little church in which we worshiped. He was a Belgian and spoke French. She proved a faithful wife to him and nursed him through some very severe illnesses. It was strange for me to have Uncle Victor as my brother-in-law; however, we remained friendly in spite of our disapproval. This all happened while I was in Slough.

Aunt Hilda, Dad's youngest sister, was living in the States near Pittsburgh and had been there a number of years. She had married Alfred King who had settled in the States after the First World War. He came back and married Hilda and took his bride back with him where they lived the rest of their lives in the small steel town of Alliquippa, Pennsylvania. Aunt Hilda was fond of her brother and they corresponded over the years. She heard about Queenie through the cousins and did not approve of this marriage either, so she immediately wrote to me and asked me to go out and live with her and Uncle Alf. She had often hinted in letters for one of us to go out and join her. She said she didn't have any of her side of the family out there with her and she thought there was no reason why I could not come. She said she and my uncle would sponsor me out there.

It was a blessing all around as our home was now dissolved. Queenie was now going to live in Victor's little cottage and she was giving up the rented house in which we were raised and that had been home to us for many years. In any case, I had to make another start in life and so had to make a quick decision. My sister and Victor had offered me a home with them, but I did not think it wise to do so.

I wrote and told my relatives that I would come and thanked them. There was much to do and very little time in which to do it. It was one of the busiest times in my life. Moving around I had made many friends and so I found myself having to write many letters to some and visiting others, especially relatives, to say goodbye. There was a constant communication with the immigration offices in London and booking my transportation to the States.

During this time I had to take examinations for my midwifery courses, and it was not until just before leaving England that I found out I had qualified.

Part II

Life in America

4
Exit England—Enter U.S.A.

A few friends and relatives saw me off at Southampton as I embarked onto the *Queen Mary*. I left my native shore on October 19, 1949, and arrived in the United States five days later. This was a new beginning for me. I was single and forty-three years of age. The ship was indeed palatial; I traveled second class, however. A friend of my Aunt Hilda had a son who was an officer on board ship and I had previously arranged to meet him. This we did and during the voyage he took me all over this beautiful boat. It was a privilege and most enjoyable. The first thing we noticed when we boarded the ship was the abundance of food. The menus were full of good things to eat; it was unbelievable. However, we were glad to indulge after such stringent rations. There was still rationing going on in England although the war was now over. It was while on this trip, which took five days to cross the Atlantic, that we were involved in a race with the *Normandy*, a French ship. We waved to each other as we passed mid Atlantic. The *Normandy* won the blue ribbon.

The days on the ship were very enjoyable. I taught a group of people to play Lexicon, which was all the rage in England at the time. There was much enthusiasm over this game. The ship's officers also entertained us with thought-provoking games. Each morning there was something new to work with. After our leisurely days aboard the *Queen Mary* there came the excitement of reaching our destination. Only those who come into New York harbor for the first time and see the Statue of Liberty can really know the thrill one gets and it is something you do not easily forget. As I remember, we left the boat as our names were called and as the luggage was hauled. I remember, too, that they had all my stuff out on the deck and I had to pay an import duty on some wool that my aunt had asked me to bring. By this time Aunt Hilda and Uncle Alf had joined me. How glad I was to see them again! They were faithful in coming to meet me.

After some hurried refreshments there was the long ride back to Pittsburgh by train and then by bus to Alliquippa, where we arrived quite late. Then I had to meet all the cousins who had waited up for us. I was so tired I wanted to go to bed but they didn't seem in any hurry and we just sat around talking. Eventually, after retiring for the night, I peeked out of my bedroom window and was astounded to see so many lights. Austerity was still prevalent in England.

I soon had to think about getting a job. I went to the local hospital but they were unable to help me. I saw a notice in the local paper about a Red Cross course advertised, so I made my way there to take in these classes. The next day they had captured my photo which was on the front page of the newspaper. These people were able to help me and suggested that I go to see the officer at the Nurses' Planning Association in Pittsburgh, to find work. I used the buses and found this office. A very pleasant lady welcomed me. I remember what she first said to me: "Isn't it a pretty day?" This is typically American and I had not heard it before. She had a few jobs vacant. I learned here that I could work as a qualified nurse for a year and then would have to sit for the state board examinations. When she learned that I had just finished training as a midwife she said she had just the job for me. A certain home for unmarried mothers needed a nurse to take care of them, and get them to the hospital for their delivery. Well, I was scared, as everything was so new to me and I did not know their routine yet. It turned out that someone else got this job and so she sent me to the Allegheny General Hospital, where they needed a night nurse for the newborn babies. I was employed here and worked with the babies for nearly two years. They had a nurses' home so I moved in and went home to my aunt's place when I had a weekend off. Another nurse from Scotland worked one end of this big floor. We both worked single-handed and did not stop or contact each other during the eight-hour shift. I cannot realize now how hard we had to work here. We both took care of thirty babies each with no helpers. This included prematures in isolettes which had to be fed every two hours. I became quite friendly with Jean Taylor, the Scotch girl who worked on the top floor of this hospital with me at night. We arranged to have a vacation together and went to Washington, D.C., in July 1951. She left before I did and went back to Scotland where she took another postgraduate course for home nursing and was much happier doing that. I kept in touch with Jean and met her

Vera Davis (left) and friend Jean Taylor in Washington, D.C.

in Edinborough when I went back to the homeland after three years.

While I was living in Pittsburgh I found a Baptist church on the north side which was fairly near the hospital. I attended and became a member and was baptized. Pastor Boyko had a radio program to which I listened and at times would help him with his mailing list. I was wondering what to do and where to go for my vacation one time, when Mrs. Boyko came up with the idea of going to a Bible conference. I agreed to go and found myself attending Lake Erie Bible Conference, which was a distance of one hundred miles away. I went alone but made some longtime friends while there. They had a musical couple who had offered a prize to the person who had come the longest distance for the conference. Who should it be but me! I received a voice record of their songs, and what was so important about this gift was the fact that it had their favorite verses inscribed around the record. These became my favorite verses after this also. These were the verses: "Trust in the Lord with all thine heart and lean not unto thine own understanding. In all thy ways acknowledge Him and He shall direct thy paths" (Prov. 3:5–6).

Just before coming to this conference I had been very ill with the flu. I remember the large fever sores I had with this illness, and I was quite run down. I did not feel capable to go back to a hard job again. It seemed to me that God spoke very clearly to me through these verses, and I made up my mind then and there to go back and turn in my resignation and trust God to give me another job. I had great peace regarding this decision and so I enjoyed the rest of my stay and went back with my mind fully made up. It was by working a short time on day duty that I had met some people with whom I became friendly—they had arranged a special picnic in a park for my benefit, the first of its kind I had ever been to. This was a lot of fun, I remember. When I got back from my vacation I found out I had another day off, and so I contacted this friend by telephone and told her I

My first home in the U.S.A.

Aunt Hilda and Uncle Alf

was leaving Allegheny General Hospital and was going to hunt another job. I must tell you here how wonderful God is to us if we trust Him fully. He had just the job ready for me. My friend said that her husband had told her that they needed a private duty nurse for the lady for whom he chauffeured. She called the house and I was told to get in touch with the doctor, with whom I went to interview, and was engaged right away. I was asked if I would take two shifts for which I would be paid. Mrs. Laughlin was an elderly lady who needed very little nursing care. She was a millionaire who was able to have the best of care. I was asked not to wear a uniform even. I moved in and was given a room to myself at the top of this beautiful house—English-style with sunken gardens which was situated in Sewickley, a suburb of Pittsburgh and close to my aunt's home.

We had two maids living there besides a gardener and chauffeur. My job there chiefly was to be a companion to this lady. I was with her from 3 P.M. to 7 A.M. The seven-to-three nurse did most of the nursing care necessary.

I remember how much I enjoyed my little radio. I was a new Christian and used to listen to all the good Christian programs that I could. I used to go out for drives with my lady in the afternoons and enjoy her lovely garden. This certainly was a great contrast to my previous job. I was pleasantly occupied and able to save money for a return trip home to England. This job lasted ten months. I had promised to go to England with two girls who were missionaries and whom I had met in my church. It turned out they did not go after all, and I went alone to visit Queenie and my friends and relatives. I had been planning on getting my job back when I came back from vacation, but they did not want to make so many changes and so engaged another nurse to take my place. I had to take my things to my aunt's place and leave from there.

I also had to settle with the income tax officer before leaving the country because I was not yet a citizen. I had by this time filed my intention of becoming a citizen at Beaver County, where my aunt and a dear friend of hers, Mrs. Elizabeth Whitelaw, sponsored me. There I received my first papers towards citizenship.

My First Trip Home

I was truly thankful to God for taking care of all of my needs. My health had not been too robust. Since I had come to the States I had suffered with boils. I was not without one on some part of my body the whole time I had been here. After seeing several doctors without a cure I decided I would make a visit to my doctor in England. I remember when I was working in the hospital a young intern had lanced one on the back of my hand without anesthesia and I fainted.

My friends who were to have accompanied me felt badly about letting me down as they had urged me in the first place to go with them, so they arranged to meet me in New York on my return journey and take me to their mission headquarters in Morristown, New Jersey. They invited me to stay with them for a couple of weeks. I traveled cabin class on the *Queen Elizabeth* going back—another beautiful ship, but not quite so palatial as the *Queen Mary*.

It was very exciting for me to be back in my homeland and I spent the time visiting friends and relatives, and the highlight of this first trip home was that I visited Scotland and stayed in Edinborough. While in the States several people had asked me about Scotland and I had to tell them I had never been. I made up my mind if possible that I would visit Scotland when I went back. I arranged to do this before leaving and Cousin Edie, my mother's cousin, promised to go with me. My dear friend Winnie Drew gave us an address of a Christian hostel where we stayed for two weeks. It was most enjoyable but I remember we had very rainy weather. It was not possible to choose sunny days for trips into the mountains as we had to book up days ahead; however, the sun peeked out for a short time so we could take some photos. I was able to meet my Scotch friend whom I had met in Allegheny General Hospital. She was happily settled in a new job doing socialized health care. There were the lovely shops to visit in Princes Street, the Castle, and beautiful gardens, and other places of interest.

One of the first things I did on returning was to visit my local doctor about the boils. After hearing how long I had had them, he referred me to the West Middlesex Hospital where I did my nurse training. I was the last patient to be seen that day. I remember the doctor was washing up and ready to leave, and when I spoke to him he wanted to know if I was a Canadian. I had evidently acquired an accent. He did not examine me but gave me some good advice. This was the cure: I was to take brewer's yeast every day and expose my body to sunlight. Before I had finished the first can of yeast I was cured, and with this simple treatment I had no more boils.

When it was nearly time to go back to the States, I wrote to my aunt to let her know when to expect me and gave her my friend's address to reply. She never got my letter. Uncle had neglected to answer, as he was busy taking care of aunt, who was ill with a heart attack and was in the hospital herself.

My friends in the H.O.P.E. Bible Mission met me in New York as promised and took me to Morristown, New Jersey, where I enjoyed my visit with them. I learned firsthand what it was like to run a mission station. These three girls worked very hard. They were up very early and worked before breakfast. They had acquired a beautiful piece of property on which were two natural springs, and these girls were making a swimming pool by digging out the earth. This is where I got in on the act and was able to carry out my doctor's orders. I donned a swimsuit and helped them make the pool, and caught some sunshine at the same time. Gradually they added buildings over the years and they now have a lovely campground where they bring some of the New York kids in the summer for a special treat.

I was thinking it was time for me to make my way back to Pittsburgh and the girls knew I had no job to go to, so they urged me to find work in this area. I was not anxious to go back to a hospital, and there was a nursing home nearby which had advertised for a nurse, so I applied. I remember they showed me around and I was impressed with how nice everything was, so I said, "You have shown me everything except the living quarters." "Oh," they said, "we do not have a nurses' home." That was not suitable for me. When I went back to my friends, they said, "We want you to get a job in our *new* hospital." I reluctantly let them phone the hospital for me. The outcome was I was asked to go and interview with the director of nurses immediately. She was a charming person and offered me any job I wanted, as they were restaffing the whole hospital. I chose the three-to-eleven shift and was to take charge of the newborn nursery. I worked for two weeks in the old hospital until they made the final move.

It so happened they had built a new type nurses' home—the first of its kind in the States. Two nurses shared an apartment. We had a kitchen and bathroom in the center and our furnished bed/sitting rooms at each end. I shared one of these with a Jewish nurse, Minna Miller, with whom I worked for several years. She was a splendid nurse who did the day shift. I still hear from her at Christmastime.

While working at Morristown Memorial Hospital my friends helped me to choose a church that was fundamental and evangelical; so on my Sundays off I went to the Alliance church where Pastor Luck was the minister. I soon made friends in this small church and I was very impressed by a man who used to bring flowers and place them on the communion table each Sunday. I thought what a nice gesture for a gentleman to do, as this was usually done by a deaconess. I found out that Mr. Davis grew the flowers himself. As time went by our pastor announced that we were to visit the homes in our immediate vicinity. Appropriate literature was provided and a date set for this program. The purpose was to invite people to come to our church to help build up the congregation. I don't know why, but only two people came on this occasion apart from the minister and his wife. Who should they be but Mr. Albert Davis and myself? So we were thrown together in a visitation program. I got to know a little about this gentleman, who was a widower of four years and rather lonely. I remember that he was shy at knocking on doors and so I had to make the advances at this time. The outcome was he wasn't too shy to invite me to go with him to other meetings at an Alliance Camp Grounds in Nyack, New York, at a future time. I remember he drove his car and we stayed over for the special meetings. I had trouble with one of my knees and we had a healing service when the Lord saw fit to heal me.

We became very good friends in a short time. We seemed to have the same interests in life and were soon discussing the probability of marriage. He was very frank with me about this because of his financial status. He had been a self-employed man and had no pension or social security. He had owned and operated a small milkman's business in Morristown. At one time he had owned his own cows and plant, but owing to regulations, had to abandon his plant and buy his milk from another farmer. The cost to build new cow stalls was prohibitive for him.

5
My First Marriage

I was forty-six years of age at this time and Albert was seventy-six. The difference in ages didn't seem to matter and we agreed that we could manage financially as I was earning a fairly good salary at the time. Dear Albert had spent most of his life savings on his daughter's education, and she and her family were living in his home, so we planned to live apart from his family. He had sufficient money in the bank to buy me a small engagement ring and the only income he had was the rent from his house, which his family sent monthly. It was a small amount, too. However, this did not deter us from going ahead with our future plans. Things worked out in our favor. Albert saw a house for sale in the local paper. The place was in chancery and was to be sold at a low price. We went to see it and I fell in love with this lovely old house, which was situated at 76 Western Avenue. It had three stories and a basement. The first floor was rented, as well as the one room and bath in the basement. The first floor had five rooms and a good-sized porch. The next floor we decided to use ourselves. It had four rooms and a small veranda. The top floor was a four-room apartment under the roof. We rented this to a doctor who was interning in the local hospital. He was from Germany and had a wife and one son. The whole house and gardens were in disrepair. The property had been the main residence of a large estate on the side of a hill called Fort Nonsense and there was a driveway through our property to the next house, which was a right-of-way for the next-door neighbors.

The estate agent already had a mortgage set up for the buyer, so that was no problem. Albert was excited about getting the place in order, and I was able to provide a down payment, so we bought the house. Albert was able to furnish it from his own house. There were a few things we did not know about the property which caused us a few headaches. One was there was rent control, and another was we had to supply the whole house with heat and hot water. However, we were excited and in love and I was sure that God had supplied a need in both of our lives. We kept everything secret till after the wedding. We were married on December 23, 1952, at the Christian and Missionary Alliance church. This was a first marriage for me and I was happy and excited. The nurses in the nurses' home wondered what was the matter with me, and, although I tried to show off my engagement ring, they did not notice it for sometime. They found out at last, and Minna quickly went around and collected money from the girls and bought me a set of towels for a wedding gift. I was so surprised, as I hadn't thought about wedding gifts. We arranged to have time off for a short honeymoon, and also to get our wedding pictures taken. The pastor's wife planned a small reception in the parsonage. It was just her family and a special nurse friend, Miss Elizabeth Muchmore, who was there to be a witness to the marriage. I had quite some influence in encouraging this friend to go to a mission field. She applied and was accepted by the Sudan Interior Mission, and where she worked for the Lord in Liberia, Africa. Elizabeth has taken early retirement to take care of her brother, but she is still on call as a nurse at Park of the Palms which is a Christian conference center where they now live.

All this happened to me within three months after I returned from England. I had not been back to visit my aunt and uncle so I wrote and told them I was getting married and that we could come and spend Christmas with them. This was arranged, and the whole family was there to meet the new bridegroom, as well as the Whitelaws, who were close friends of us all. I think it was at this time I managed to take the rest of my belongings back with us. I no longer needed a home with my aunt and uncle.

I must mention here that my aunt had written a letter to my sister while I was back in England asking her to persuade me to stay in England, as she did not want the responsibility of me in America. This was due to my severe illness with flu, and I was so debilitated afterwards. She herself had been in the hospital with a heart condition and I did not know about it. I mention this here because I can see the hand of God at work in all these circumstances, taking care of me and directing my life. My sister did not tell me about this letter she got from our aunt till sometime later. God supplied my need just at the right time. I am sure that Aunt Hilda was happy for me and approved of our marriage. My health improved from then on also.

Albert, although retired, was still very active and got busy making our house habitable. I continued nursing on the three-to-eleven shift and

Albert used to meet me every evening with his car. Needless to say, we had our problems making ends meet. My money was frozen in England so I could only get one thousand pounds per year. However, we both worked hard and were able to pay for our house in three years' time.

Morristown is a beautiful city and historical. It was the headquarters of Gen. George Washington during the early days of American history. There was a large fort built by the soldiers at that time to keep them from freezing to death; that is how the place got its name, "Fort Nonsense." This is where our house was situated, and we could see the countryside a long way off. I remember the autumn scenes so well, and Albert would take me to many places of interest while we lived there. A trip to Deposit, New York, was delightful. The Lucks had moved from Morristown to there so we were invited to stay with them.

Albert was proud of his new bride and arranged to spend our first vacation with some first cousins in Wisconsin. These two ladies were known as the Davis girls and had been teachers in Madison University—they had never married, but were so very hospitable and had spent much time making their home especially presentable for this occasion. Rheumatoid arthritis was a real problem for them both. On our way to see them we stayed in Chicago, and Albert left his wedding ring in the hotel bathroom. Fortunately, it was sent on to us. My husband was a devout Christian who, like his father, Thomas Davis, was a faithful worker in his church. He carried out the duties of Sunday school superintendent and elder in the church. His first wife Harriet had been the organist also.

Albert always spoke well of his mother, and among his belongings I found a beautiful write-up of his, which he wrote on Mother's Day 1943, and which I think is well worth recording here.

> In 2 Timothy 1:5 we have immortalized the names of a mother and grandmother of whom almost nothing—and yet everything that matters—is said. Speaking to a young man, a coming man in his church, a foreign missionary of proved worth, a companion close to Paul as a son, Paul writes: "I call to remembrance the unfeigned faith that is in thee, which dwelt first in thy grandmother Lois and thy mother Eunice." How little we know of this mother Eunice, whose name is impressionable because of what she did as a mother. We are told in Acts 16:1 that she was a Jewess who believed but was married to a Greek (presumably a pagan). And in 2 Timothy 3:15 she taught her little boy the Holy Scriptures which were able to make him wise unto Salvation through faith which is in Christ Jesus.

Did the problems which fill the mind of so many, particularly the younger mothers today, confront this Eunice of 1900 years ago? Stylish clothes, modish hair-dressing, cosmetics, keeping up her end—entertaining, cultivating the right people. Pushing her husband to make a better living for her and for their son? We just don't know. Eunice was a woman and a mother. She had her personal problems and interests too. These aren't recorded. What *is* recorded is what she measured up to—her outstanding responsibility as a mother. She taught her son the Holy Scriptures and through them the way to Salvation and discipleship. And that is the All-Important work of a mother in any age or land. That is her work that will endure because it is owned and blest of God. All have had mothers. Not all of us can *be* mothers, but all of us have had mothers. And from these mothers of ours we have received a common heritage: their examples; and what a rich heritage when that example is a life of Faith and of love of God as with Lois and Eunice. Mother cannot pass on to Son or Daughter her own disciplined Christian character. That is non-transferable. That, each must develop for himself. But, mother's example is our heritage to possess and strive to pass on. Not only our own mother's example. We inherit the examples of a long line of outstanding mothers through the centuries. And how these help us! Think back sixteen centuries to that mother Monica; whose wayward son Augustine caused her such sorrow, but whose deep faith and tenacious prayers brought him at last into that way of salvation. Timothy learned as a child. Her example encouraged many another mother to continue in prayer until the wayward child is saved.

Then every Methodist thinks of Susannah Wesley; mother of Charles and John and seventeen other children, less well known. What an example she has given us of courage, and active concern for the spiritual life of her children—what a counselor she was, following her grown-up children with advice, praise or blame. Helping them keep up their courage. Yes, we have a rich heritage of examples handed down by these mothers of old. But let us remember, "To whom much is given of him shall much be required."

What kind of example are we passing on to our little ones? Are we teaching them the way of Salvation as Lois and Eunice did? Are we surrounding with prayer, prevailing prayer, those not in the kingdom, as Monica did, for St. Augustine? Do we let our children know we are actively concerned for their spiritual life as Susannah Wesley did? The examples of all good mothers are given us to profit by. May we be more diligent ourselves in the *ONE* thing that matters: the training of our children in the nurture and admonition of the Lord. To the mothers whose children are grown up out into this dangerous and troubled world, let me leave a message of comfort from an outstanding Christian mother of today, Grace Noll Crowell.

Our church congregation was informed of our marriage while we were on our honeymoon. They were all very surprised, as we had not been seen together. It was our turn to be surprised on our return as they had planned a shower party for us. They were happy for us and they gave us some very nice and useful gifts.

Albert had a strong faith in God especially as Healer. He told me about an instantaneous healing when he had acute hepatitis. He was in very severe pain—gallstones passing into the gallbladder cause one of the most excruciating pains one can endure. His first thoughts were to call the elders of the church, which he did. He was anointed with oil and prayer was offered on his behalf according to St. James and he was healed immediately.

While nursing at the Morristown Memorial Hospital I took care of what was, at the time, the world's second-smallest baby in medical history. She was born on my shift. The doctor, who was an intern, brought her to the nursery and placed her in an incubator. He thought she would die before morning; however, she continued to thrive and lived to be a fine young lady. She was only seventeen and three-quarter ounces at birth and just viable. She was born March 30, 1954. I used to do the monthly write-up in the *Memoscope*, the hospital newspaper for our department. I kept these notes about Debra Anice Newton and will relate here as they appear in the "Pink and Blue Notes," which indicates the Newborn Nursery News.

Our Celebrity Nursery
by (vacationing!) Vera Davis

> The Nursery is well in the limelight this month, and I am sure everyone will be waiting for news of our little celebrity, Debra Anice Newton. Saturday, March 20th, was the great day when this infant made her debut. "She" was rushed into the nursery by Dr. Kuvin Pikaart, at 6:05 P.M. She is so tiny, but such a perfect little individual, with an olive skin, black hair and such beady black eyes that seem to look at you very cutely. The sight is not there yet, but we hope that she will grow up with good eyesight and everything else about her will be normal! We who watch her daily cannot tell if she has grown very much (she is thirteen days old as I write these notes) but yesterday my observations were that she appeared longer and not so fat, and her features seemed more defined. If this is so, I can account for it because she stretches, yawns so much and with such graceful movements. She fancies she is on Miami Beach, maybe! She finally rests with one hand under her chin. She really is a cute little baby, and appears almost grown up in some of her gestures. She has many attributes of a pretty little girl, and seems perfectly happy in her

> own little home, the "Isolette." She looks forward to her two hourly feedings of Alacta formula. To prove she is a normal baby, I've seen her get into a real tantrum when near feeding time. Perhaps you won't believe it, but she actually poked her tongue out at me one day!

Debra was discharged home on May 28, 1954, sixty-nine days old—weight, a hefty five pounds and four ounces, condition good. She was brought back to the hospital each year on her birthday as far as I know for at least three years where the doctors and nurses celebrated with a birthday cake in her honor. I often wonder if Debra is grown-up with children of her own. I did hear that she had a brother after three years who weighed six pounds and five ounces.

My life with Albert in Morristown was happily spent. Albert improved our property immensely; by the time the bushes and trees were trimmed back we had a lovely yard back and front. We discovered a sidewalk in front of the house also. It was covered with mud and debris from years of neglect. I was not very conversant with some of the beautiful trees we had and was anxious to know the name of one especially tall tree which had large blooms in the spring, so I sent away to Kew Botanical Gardens to find out. They kindly informed me it was a tulip tree, and that it was native to the area. There were pretty red-leafed foliage and very tall cherry trees in back. We had squirrels which were a nuisance, I remember. They would play around and climb to the top of the trees, enter and nest under the roof. This cost us money to get rid of them. Another problem we had was roaches. I am afraid to say our first floor tenants were careless and left food around and complained about this pest to us. I tried to rid them by painting the wainscoting myself with an antipesticide but had little results, so we had to get an exterminator in on a monthly basis before this was eradicated. Thus we managed to keep going and pay our way, but without making any money for our trouble. However, we enjoyed living here and found it a very pleasant place. Albert used to keep the garden planted at his old home, so we were supplied with fresh vegetables and concord grapes with which we were able to make jam.

While living in Morristown I became friendly with Dolly and Willard Pierson. We would visit each other from time to time. Dolly worked as a district nurse; I met her in the hospital on private duty. She lived with her brother who worked from their home as a private gardener. They had a rambling old house and Dolly loved to entertain. We were invited on special occasions. They were both food faddists and always looked thin and wiry but both lived to be in their eighties. Neither of them married and Willard outlived Dolly, who was deaf for a number of years. I kept in touch with them for a long time and was able to stay in their home after we left Morristown. I especially recall how Dolly loved to decorate her home at Christmastime. They were members of the Presbyterian church and were friends of Libby Muchmore who belonged to the same church as they did. It was she who stood up for us at our marriage.

Although Albert and his immediately family were by no means wealthy, some of his ancestors were, for he told me that they had financed Mr. Thomas Edison, the well-known scientist who died in 1931 at age eighty-four. This man's inventions, over one thousand of them, helped flood the world with light, music, and moving pictures. We owned a small oil painting at the time which my husband said was of the place Edison used to work and study. It was a small, low building on the edge of a stream in West Orange, New Jersey. According to a write-up in the *Tallahassee Democrat* on Sunday, February 11, 1979, when his 132nd birthday was celebrated, he did have one of his laboratories in this place.

As time progressed, Albert had a short illness; it was pneumonia. He was able to get into the hospital but was soon better with the good care he received and was home within a week.

I was due for a vacation in June 1955, and the state inspector for nurses came around and spoke to me one day and reminded me that it would be necessary for me to take the New Jersey state board examinations. About the same time my husband had expressed his desire to retire to St. Petersburg. He had been there once and had always dreamed of retiring there. After talking things over we decided to go to St. Petersburg for our vacation. The main purpose of going would be to look for a house in which to retire. So this is what we did. We left by car and stayed at a motel overnight and went around with an estate agent looking at various homes that were up for sale.

We found an Alliance church the next day and went to the Sunday morning service. We got acquainted with a lady named Mrs. Driscoll, who was a member there. She was able to put us up for the rest of our vacation. Her rooming house was in a nice neighborhood and on the corner of the same street as the main hospital. This lady became one of our friends and was interested in the work of child evangelism. I would often go and visit her after this. She was glad to have company, as she was kept busy at home with people whom she boarded. I remember spending one Christmas with her; she was very hospitable. This must have been after Albert had passed on.

One interesting thing she told me about was that she had owned property in Nyack, New York. She had sold it to the Alliance College, as it was an adjoining property, so it is a part of the church campus now.

I heard that this dear lady was suffering with cancer and being nursed by her daughter-in-law. She left Child Evangelism Fellowship (C.E.F.) one thousand dollars in her will. This we received with gratitude as there was a great need at the time.

Nothing took our fancy until we came upon the one we chose at 3176 Eleventh Avenue North. This house was built on two lots—it had been the home of the builder for this subdivision. It was beautifully laid out with sub-tropical plants and trees. It was a two-bedroom house with a long, front closed-in porch. It had a small back porch also, where we were able to eat some of our meals. The front boasted two lovely royal palm trees on the sidewalk. There was a kapok tree on one side of the property, along with a mimosa tree and special kind of pine tree. Another feature which was pleasing to us was a laundry room built adjoining the garage, with a long driveway on the side leading to this extra building at the back of the house. This was it! It was situated just one block from a new main highway which was being constructed at the time. The area was almost like a park and we decided right away that this was for us. We made a down payment and told the agent we would take possession in three months. How excited we were! This was to begin another episode in our lives.

There was much to be done on our return. We decided not to move our furniture but would rent our apartment furnished. In order to buy our St. Petersburg home, Albert was going to sell the old homestead. This was no problem to sell, as big business firms were looking for property, and this was a valuable site for a large factory—a corner property also. A

My Florida dream home

friend of Albert's offered to buy his place for a nominal sum and he let it go without looking around. This man immediately sold it again for a lot more money. Poor Albert was not a businessman. This deal upset his son Albert and daughter Gladys and family because they had to move. They bought a new home in Morris Plains, which they enjoyed for many years and continued to live there till her daughter married.

Our next door neighbor was interested in selling real estate and so we arranged with her to keep the place rented and cared for. She was to keep a certain percentage of the rents and send us the balance. It didn't work out to our advantage, and she wanted to sell the house soon after we left. Being so far away, we let her do this. I guess this was the best thing to do considering the circumstances.

Our going away was a little sad as we had to leave our friends. There was a going away party given us by the church friends. We had to take as many of our personal things as possible by car and ship the chinaware. Albert was still doing the driving. It so happened that the house we were buying was completely empty—the family were moving to another section of the city. We knew this and so we arranged to have a bedroom suite moved into our home on the day we arrived so we had somewhere to sleep. We purchased this on the way down; stopping in Tampa, we bought a blond-colored bedroom suite which we thought more appropriate for Florida. After this we finished furnishing our "dream house" gradually by going to auction sales which were popular in Florida at this time. We arrived in St. Petersburg in September 1955. I remember on the day we arrived we found people digging up our plants and the grass was nearly a foot high. Also, because we had been rather a long time letting them know, they had given up the idea of us coming. They decided to decorate the house in their own taste. Well, it suited us very well. The color scheme was good. The outside was pale green and white and exactly what I would have chosen. This saved us a lot of work. They charged us extra for the decorating, which was in order.

On our way down I remember we met an elderly couple, Mr. and Mrs. Sanborn, with whom we exchanged addresses. They were the owners of a well-known coffee business. The lady sent me some pretty material to cover a footstool that we had. I thought how kind she was to do this for a perfect stranger.

We were kept busy putting our home in order. Albert loved to work in the yard. I found out that I could work here as a registered nurse by reciprocity from Great Britain. It was the first state in the Union that I had applied to that offered this courtesy, so I set to work getting my credentials and references from England. This was no easy matter as I previously stated I left school at an early age and we were not given certificates for general education. However, I did have my nursing certificates. It so happened that I had a registered mental nurse certificate and one for midwifery, both of which were required besides general nursing. Otherwise, I would have been required to take examinations for these two subjects or at least an obstetrics course (not midwifery). While waiting to hear from all these people I took a part-time job at Grants in their toy department. I had toy guns to sell and I hated to see little children with guns, so I never pushed these when helping to choose toys for them. Mr. and Mrs. Brown, church friends in Morristown, wrote to us one day asking us if we could put up a lady temporarily in our home. She was coming as director of C.E.F. and needed a place to stay till she had time to look around for a place of her own. She was a great person and soon got me interested in this work. She directed the work in this area for many years till she retired. I became one of her voluntary teachers and had a neighborhood Good News Club for children on my porch once a week. I also joined about thirty other women for a weekly training class. Later, several of us used to go into the black schools for their religious training program and I taught two classes each week. The city authorities wondered why crime was not found amongst the black community but was rife amongst the white children. We could tell them why!

Mr. Brown and his wife came to visit us at our home also, and they invited us to their place on Lake Tomerhawk, Black Mountain, North Carolina. This we enjoyed and must relate here the story of some ducks. We were watching the ducks on the lake one day when a lady stopped us and begged Mrs. Brown to adopt her duck as she was going away. She did so and was expected to take this duck into her home at night. I think she kept it in the yard in the daytime. One day we decided to go to a Ben Lippen conference where Reverend Epp of *Back to the Bible* was to lecture. We wondered what to do with the duck, so Mrs. Brown put him down in the cellar. When we came back she went down to fetch the duck and found that he had bitten or chewed up all of the watermelons that she had bought the previous day.

Along now my registration for nursing came through and I was able to do private duty nursing from a registry. I did a night shift at this time so I could continue to work with the children. I was walking down our street one day when I saw a moving van, and I was interested to know who our new neighbor was. I soon got acquainted with Reverend and Mrs. Roy McNutt. These folks became longtime friends of mine. They were a precious couple. Roy had served as a chaplain in a mission in

Chicago and Rose had been converted in adulthood from Catholicism. I found her to be a very fine Christian and it was not long before she was working in C.E.F. with the children. She loved the work and was a real help and blessing. Her daughter, who was converted at the same time as her mother, married Fred Jarvis, a well-known missionary. Roy and Rose loved to go to the beaches and knew several people who like to do so as well. We were invited also and we used to have beach parties at Gulfport and some of the beautiful beaches around that way. I must say the swimming is excellent in these places. We used to fish sometimes from the Million Dollar Pier. This pier has long since been changed, but we liked it better as it was before. Also, the famous green benches had been painted various odd colors. I hope they decide to change them back to green.

We were getting well settled in our new home. We purchased a lovely old oak desk which someone had painted green and then decided to remove the paint again and then got tired of doing it, so we busied ourselves and removed all the paint. It was a long and tedious job, but we had a treasure when it was finished. We furnished the other bedroom with the same blond-colored furniture and so were soon able to invite our friends to stay with us.

My sister was one of the first to come. She spent a few weeks with us. She first made a trip to Pittsburgh to see Aunt Hilda and Uncle Alf. Queenie was Aunt Hilda's godchild. She enjoyed her first stay in Florida very much. I remember how she loved to go down to the pier and feed the gulls and pelicans. She loves to go to the beaches wherever possible. I think at this time she was not too happy with her husband, and Victor was worried about her going away. When she did return he had planned a big welcome back for her.

It was wonderful how God supplied our needs during these years. I did not mind working in the homes of patients and, one case that I took care of for a few weeks was a terminal case. The man was the same build as Albert and after he died his wife offered me his whole wardrobe. There were some beautiful clothes which suited and fitted Albert without alteration. She was glad to pass them on to someone who could use them and refused any payment for them.

It was early spring 1959, when Gladys Anderson, my stepdaughter, wrote and told us that Margy, her only daughter, was to be married and invited us to come to the wedding. Gladys' husband had died recently so they asked a relative on the bride's father's side to give her away. I had hoped that Albert would have done this but we were not asked, and they may have had doubts about us being able to come in any case. We were happy to make this journey for this very special occasion to be at the granddaughter's wedding. Soon they were to be Mr. and Mrs Samuel Terpstra. We liked Sam very much and they made a very happy couple. It was during this visit with Gladys that she made us really welcome and a rather strained relationship was mended. When we arrived, and before the wedding, Gladys made a point of thanking me for all that I had done for her father in making his life happy. He really was a changed man. Gladys was away at work in the daytime and so he was lonely before he met me. From then on we were good friends. Gladys came to visit us after this and bought us a nice gift for our home which has proved useful throughout the years. It was a kitchen chair with fold-up steps attached.

Albert's health began to fail. He loved to go for long walks, which was good for him, but he had arteriosclerosis which affected him by sudden lapses of memory. Sometimes he would walk long distances and would have one of these spells and would forget his way home again. He was being treated by our doctor with blood thinner. On such occasions he would get exhausted, and his facial color would become gray. I knew how to treat him. I would give him hot or warm coffee to restore him. When he went walking he always wore a hat so we put his name and address inside the crown. A couple of times we had to rely on the police to locate him. I was nursing a lady in a hospital one time when she asked me to go home with her and take care of her for a few days. I told her I had a husband to care for, so she said, "Bring him along with you. I have a separate guest room you can use." So we moved in with her. I remember she liked to have dinner midday. We were near the beach on the south side of the city. So Albert used to take his walk as usual and was out of the way in the mornings. One day he was late coming back so I went down to the beach and hunted up and down a few streets nearby. At last he came along the road looking very haggard and ill. He managed to get to the dining room and sat down exhausted and collapsed onto the floor. I had never seen Albert like this. I rushed next door for help and fortunately there were two men available. Albert was a dead weight and by all appearances a dead person. His face was gray and he was cold and clammy all over. We almost dragged him to the bedroom, which was on the same floor, and we were able to get him onto the bed. I set to work to get all the heat I could to his body—hot water bottles and hot blanket bath, etc. There was no pulse at first but gradually he came back to life again and was able to take some hot fluids. I had sent for the doctor in the meantime, but he did not come till evening; by then Albert had recovered and the doctor couldn't find anything wrong with him. A blood clot must have caused this trouble. He had no aftereffects and lived two more years after this.

During the summer, the C.E.F. used to sponsor a children's camp in Tampa at the Southern Baptist Campgrounds and we used it for two weeks. A number of the teachers used to go as counselors. On this particular occasion I was asked to be the camp nurse, so Albert and I had a room in the administration building. It was a lot of fun and they called Albert "Uncle Al." He was a good sport and one day we were told to do everything backwards for the dinner meal and a prize was offered for the funniest couple. We won the prize by exchanging dresses. Albert appeared as nurse and I was his partner. There were roars of laughter.

In order to get the campgrounds we had to take a certain number of children from a school or orphanage in Tampa. I had to check them in and found so many with enlarged tonsils and sore throats, some of whom had to be sent back as we could not accept them into the camp with the well children. The rest enjoyed this respite and had a lot of fun together. One day I saw a bunch of these kids coming towards the administration building. When they reached me I found they were holding a long snake, and they said, "Nurse, we want you to take his temperature." Camp days were very busy but happy days, and many dear children accepted the Lord Jesus as their Savior.

Another harvest of souls was reaped when we had a chapel on wheels at the state fair in Tampa during the fall. We teachers would take turns telling gospel stories, and then we would follow them up, and many were placed in Sunday schools and churches of their choice.

Another yearly event was a big rally, when each of the Good News Clubs assembled in one of the largest churches. Sometimes as many as thirty or forty clubs took part in this celebration. We had to limit the time to just a few minutes each, but it was well organized and each club was able to perform in some way. Special honors were given to winners of best clubs—attendance, best performance, and other things chosen by the committee. How happy they were to take home a banner with words written on them for whatever they had won.

I enjoyed the fellowship we had with the teachers. Sometimes we would get together and make visual aides or backgrounds for our Bible stories. We had some gifted women who were Spirit-filled. Margaret Kornhi and I used to work together quite often. Lucille arranged to have workshops for us at the center, and there was a dear lady who was an artist who used to help us make beautiful backgrounds. We used cotton flannelette and drew our pictures with a quality crayon called Crayonex. A library of backgrounds and cutouts were made available to us in time for those who needed them.

Albert and I knew a number of people in St. Petersburg by now and so discussed the idea of having a Bible study group for adults in our home. I canvassed the area and found people who were interested. What was surprising to us was the fact that just around the corner we found a gentleman, Bill Henderson, who belonged to another Brethren church than ours and who, in the past, had attended Billy Graham's mother's Bible classes in North Carolina. He was also a trained Bible teacher who was willing to teach our class, and so this is how the Lord provided a teacher for our study group. We became known as the "Berean Bible Club of Floral Villas." This was enjoyed in our home for a number of years.

One day I noticed that Albert was jaundiced, so we made a visit to the doctor. He said that he either had a gallbladder infection or cancer of the pancreas. Also, an operation would be necessary to find out. You will remember that Albert had been instantaneously healed of a severe and painful gallbladder condition many years previously, so it was no surprise to me when the doctor told us he had cancer of the pancreas. When the surgeon operated he found the gallbladder completely shriveled up. This happened when he was healed in his home many years ago. Fortunately this was not a painful illness, but of course he was incapacitated and weak. I nursed him in the hospital, and then six months at home. He was very patient and accepted this terminal illness as from the Lord. He was ready to go home to be with his Savior and Lord.

I did not leave him alone. My special friend Rose McNutt, who lived in the same avenue, would often come in and relieve me so I could do the shopping. People in the church and Sunday school were very kind and sent him a fellowship basket which contained some little gifts, one for each day, lasting a week or longer. He was much loved by them and had earned a certificate for regular attendance in Sunday school in the church.

Albert had his eighty-sixth birthday on July 6 and was still able to sit up in a chair for short periods. We had some friendly neighbors, so I asked some of them in for a little party. This he appreciated. He had done the same for me when I was fifty years of age—I didn't know it called for a special occasion, but he did. He sprung a surprise party for me and invited all the neighbors in at that time.

Albert died September 3, 1962. My friend Rose was there with me and helped take care of things at the end. A day or so beforehand he asked me what I was going to do when he was gone. God had told me very clearly one day as I was reading the Bible. I was reading the Great Commission from Mark 16:15, "Go ye into all the world and preach the Gospel to every creature." It seemed like God spoke these words to me personally at that time—so much so that I answered out loud, "Do you mean me, Lord?" I had no idea what he wanted me to do at the time, but I kept the experience in mind and was able to tell my husband about this, and it made him very happy.

After he died we had a memorial service for him in Simmons Funeral Home. We requested no flowers, but to send memorial gifts to our church reconstruction fund. I took his body back to New Jersey, where his son and daughter arranged a big funeral for him, and his body was buried with his first wife in Evergreen Cemetery, Morristown, New Jersey. I received a memorial book from Simmons in which we have placed some of the family records.

Albert's father	Thomas J. Davis
Albert's mother	Sarah Bailey Davis
Their son, now deceased (my husband)	Albert Lindsley Davis
His children	Albert Lindsley Davis Jr.
	Gladys Pierson D. Anderson

He had three grandchildren and eight great-grandchildren at the time of his death. His marriage records are:

First marriage to Harriet Pierson in Morris Plains, New Jersey, October 25, 1899.

Second marriage to Vera Dorothy Steers in Morristown, New Jersey, December 23, 1952.

Good News Club

6
The Years Between

On my return to St. Petersburg and after settling things pertaining to the funeral I began to wait upon the Lord regarding my future plans for missionary service. It is quite a story in itself how I was led where to go. I wrote to two mission boards. Both of these were sending representatives into St. Petersburg shortly; I continued private duty nursing. One day I had a phone call from the secretary of my church. She wanted to know if I had made any decision for my future. I told her I had not done so as yet. She went on to tell me that there was an emergency at our own Red Bird Mission in Kentucky. She wanted me to apply and gave me the name of our mission headquarters. About this time the representative from one of the boards to which I had applied came to see me and wanted me to go to a small hospital in Ecuador and pay my own expenses on a three-month trial basis. This I did not feel led to do. I told our secretary that I was still waiting to hear from another mission board; however, I would write to Red Bird Mission, which I did. I got an application form to fill out and had to send a brief record of myself. I was accepted, and told to be ready to leave when I heard from the mission. I was to travel by bus to a small town called Pineville, Kentucky. I was to be met by a member of the staff there and continue the journey with her to the mission hospital.

A couple of weeks or more passed and I thought their emergency must have passed because I did not hear and I still had to see Mr. Holmes, the representative of the American Sunday School Union, who was to visit me. I was in church one Sunday evening when this same gentleman was giving a lecture about the work of this mission. He was showing slides of the mountainous area where nurses worked amongst the poor people and also opened up closed churches as Sunday schools for the children. After the service I made myself known to him. I asked him if it was he who was to see me. I had been impressed by what I had seen on the screen, and thought that this type of work I was suited for, and wondered if God wanted me to go and serve in this capacity. I wanted to be quite sure that I was in God's will before going to Pineville. He looked in his notebook and said, "Yes, I was coming to see you on Tuesday morning." I told him that my own church was expecting me to go to their mission, but I was waiting to hear from them and why not interview me this evening? I had a friend with me and we could go together. He said, "I want to bring my wife with me." She was not with him that evening, so we left it till then. However, God had planned where He wanted me to go and made it very clear. I received a letter from the Red Bird Mission the next morning asking me to come at once. The delay in letting me know was because they were isolated due to bad weather. I was met by the director of nurses in her car and we had to travel over Red Bird Mountain on icy roads to reach Queensdale, where the hospital was situated. I was there for three months and then returned to get some of my belongings and take my little car. I assisted them for another nine months while the emergency lasted. A missionary friend, Miss Shirley Butler, who was on furlough from India, moved into my house and took care of things for me while I was away. She lived rent-free.

At Red Bird Mission, Kentucky

There are lots of interesting things to talk about this mission, which is situated in the foothills of the Appalachian Range. The mountain people are descended from the English, Scotch, Irish, and French, and no blacks are to be found at all. They are a shy, reserved people. The people have intermarried and there are only a few surnames amongst them. Here are a few: Hoskins, Saylor, Helton, Asher, Brock, Collett, Fee, and Sizemore. When they were admitted to the hospital we used their first names for identity, as there may have been three patients of the same last name. The new hospital was a modern structure with nurses' home to match. The average number of patients at one time was about twenty-four, but we could take thirty-one. There was an intercom system installed also. They served a radius of fifty square miles. There were two doctors and one lab technician. Doctors Slothour and Schaeffer were very dedicated to their job, as was the head nurse. Sometimes they were up night and day working. Nurses were called to help in the operating room at anytime also. The nurses worked a ten-hour shift when on duty and would have to take care of pediatrics, mothers and babies, medical and surgical cases, everything except the outpatient department. The head nurse, Miss Smith, and Miss Reitz worked in the clinic. There was one nurse and one aide on each shift; sometimes two nurses on the day shift. Sometimes we did not get our day off at all. When there was an epidemic of flu the patients were brought into this hospital for safety measures.

There are whiskey stills to be found in the area in isolated places although this is illegal. The mission has schools for the children and a high school at Beverly. Over forty of the children are boarded and over one hundred lunches are served daily. The classrooms are spacious and there is a very large hall for receptions and ball games. I saw my first ball game there. You should have seen their cheerleaders! The mission also has nine outposts with small churches and a variety of projects to help these people.

I must tell you that my Child Evangelism Fellowship work came in useful while at Red Bird. I had my visual aides with me and so was able to help in the Bible school in the summer.

On my day off I would often go into the nearest town of Pineville. There was not much to do there and I was glad if one of the other nurses could accompany me. I made friends with the assistant cook. She arrived at the mission one month before I did. She was waiting for a job as a teacher so was not there very long, but we kept in touch with each other. Jessie Bouquin, Lucia Knutson, and I sometimes managed to get off together, which was a treat for all of us; otherwise, it was a lonely life for us. Sometimes we would visit the homes of the people nearby and explore the countryside and take a picnic lunch. It was not unusual to find the local people riding the creeks in their cars or bicycles, as there were no roads to get to where they wanted to go.

The mission also helped the local people by establishing crafts and small businesses and farming. I visited the sorghum plant one day where cane sugar was being refined and bottled for distribution. I also saw the field nearby where the sugar cane was harvested and prepared for the plant.

The people experienced severe weather conditions. Every year there were periods when they were hemmed in with snow drifts or floods; some were worse off than others. Woods fires were another hazard we experienced. We were told that these fires were deliberately started but the culprits were never found.

Some of my readers may have heard of a group of nurses or read the book called *Nurses on Horseback* by Ernest Poole, published in 1932. These same nurses still operate in the Kentucky mountains. My friends by the name of Corby, who lived in Margate, England, told me about these nurses many years before. The original nurse who established this Nursing Association was a distant relative of the family, if I remember correctly. I made it my business to go and find them. I discovered their headquarters not too far distant from our mission. I was invited in for a meal. I remember a long dining hall and polished oak table and nurses around the table and the original stately, elderly nurse sitting at the head of the table. Nurses excused themselves and went off to attend their business, not on horseback but on motor scooters.

I became friendly with some girls in another mission, one of whom I met in our hospital who was a patient at the time. She invited me to visit them, which I did. I stayed overnight and in the morning there was a light snowfall. I had no snow tires, so it was dangerous for me to travel through the mountains. However, I felt compelled to go back, knowing how shorthanded we were at the hospital. I managed to get back in calling distance to the mission and skidded into a cleft in the road, fortunately not on the other side, which had a precipice. Someone got a message to the mission, and, after waiting and getting colder by the minute, the rescue party came and pulled me out of my precarious position on this mountain pass.

There were opportunities to witness in the hospital, in the homes, and along the roads. People who use the *Upper Room* devotional should remember there is a little group of nurses who meet in the chapel in Red Bird Hospital before going on duty.

The hospital was just three years old when I first went there and the work has grown since. I heard a new clinic has been built there since.

Miss Smith, who was head nurse at the time, worked every day in the clinic except when she took a day off. It was a blessing when someone like Miss Hagen, missionary from Nigeria, came to help with the office work. Our lab technician was a preacher also and gave a short devotional over the intercom each morning so that all of the patients were served this way. There was a quick turnover of patients. Sometimes we were busier with fewer patients.

One thing I especially enjoyed at Red Bird was the comfortable private room I was given in the nurses' home. After long hours on duty it was very inviting. I had brought back some lounge chairs which we used out of doors. We were able to enjoy the scenic view and get adequate rest a few hundred yards from the hospital. My special friends there were Lucia Knutson, Jessie Bouquin, and Vivian Slothour. We remained friends for a long time; in fact, Jessie will appear in my life history records again shortly. She left us at Red Bird for a position as missionary-teacher in a small school in New Mexico, but she was very unhappy there and lonely. She had a boyfriend in St. Petersburg and missed him very much. She went back to her home in time and at my suggestion applied for training in Child Evangelism Fellowship Institute.

I eventually went back to St. Petersburg where I started nursing again. As a returned missionary for my church, I showed color slides and told about "Life in the Kentucky Mountains" on Sunday evening, February 14, 1965. I had been unable to get reciprocity with the Kentucky State Board of Nursing.

Full-time with C.E.F.

I got a job as charge nurse on the second floor of the biggest nursing home in St. Petersburg, named Swanholm. I worked in the three-to-eleven shift. This again was a hard job with about thirty patients to care for. However, I did have a little more help, as there was a male aide who worked between the three floors to help with lifting, etc. This was strictly nursing of senior citizens, some of whom were ambulatory. I was able to start a little religious service here for those able or willing to attend. We had singing of hymns and Bible study and it was very much enjoyed by the patients. On the whole most of them were bedfast or mentally unable to attend.

My first experience of teaching nursing was here, as I was expected to give the aides lectures on nursing techniques, etc. It was not easy to get them to attend on their time off.

I was in this job ten months, and one of the aides had said I had stayed longer than any of the other registered nurses. It was here that I encountered another nurse who worked on the first floor, which was the admitting ward, and who was jealous of me. She wanted my job and was determined to get it. I guess she thought it might be easier to run. One day as I was going on duty I was called into the office by the director of nurses, who told me she no longer required my services. She had a long list of grievances against me which were all lies. These she had acquired from no other person than the nurse who wanted my job. When I scanned the list I could see it was things of which she herself was guilty. I was given a check for two weeks salary and dismissed with no opportunity to defend myself. Needless to say, this was a miserable experience for me, but God has to put us through "deep waters" sometimes in order to show us his will for our lives. I left this place almost heartbroken. Nothing like this had ever happened to me before. I was visiting there a week later and I learned that there was a big rumpus after I left as the aides had enjoyed working with me. The male nurse who had worked between the floors was the one who had reported what he knew about this nurse who gave me so much trouble, and I heard that she was fired the next week also. God doesn't promise us that life will be a bed of roses, and this experience shattered me.

The first thing I wanted to do was to share my dilemma with a friend, so I made my way to Mrs. Shade's home, who you may remember was the director of C.E.F. of Pinellas County. She was home, and I just broke down and wept on her doorstep. She was the very person to help me. After I had poured out my heart to her she said to me, "Vera, I've been praying for you, because I believe God can use you full-time in C.E.F." Well, I couldn't believe this could be possible, but I said, "If the Lord wants me in this work full time, I will have to be accepted by the school of training, which is not very likely at my age and without any formal Bible school education behind me." However, she urged me to apply and the outcome was I was accepted for the three months summer school. I might add here that Bible school training is now required before entering this institute. There was a period of time before going to Muskegan, Michigan, so I busied myself helping Mrs. Shade and learning from her all that I could of what to do as a county director.

I changed my car, but the tires were not good and I had two blowouts on the way there; but I must have had my guardian angel keeping a good lookout for me, as both times someone was at hand to take care of it for me. I also advertised for a travel companion in the local paper and a lady answered who wanted to go to Detroit, which was on the way. I also got a good itinerary for the trip from my motor club. We decided to take about five days so as to make it a leisurely trip. My travel companion practiced driving my car beforehand, but I did most of the driving myself. I arrived in time for the opening of school and was glad I had my little car with me. It proved very useful and almost necessary to get around.

We had a house mother in the rooming house for us singles, so we got acquainted with one another on arrival and found Miss Husenetter to be a pleasant person. Our rooms were small but adequate, so we arranged our rooms and went around the grounds known as Wolf Lake Campus. It was quite pleasant and right on the lake with woods area. The married couples had apartments dotted around campus. The classroom was rather small for our extra large group—it was over fifty students this summer, the biggest class they had ever had. The campus is now moved to another location, a lovely place in Missouri which used to be a Catholic monastery.

Next morning we met the dean and were assigned certain chores to do each day. This was to help pay for our training. At this get-acquainted session the dean and director, Mr. Roland Gerdes, asked if there was a nurse in the group and I was the only one, so I was assigned another job as nurse for over fifty people. You can imagine my dismay to have this extra work thrust upon me and I was an older student and not used to a heavy schedule of studies like some of the others. So I had to set up a first-aid center and I had a number of calls by students and their children. One couple had a month-old baby who had green stools. Having just had my midwifery training I was able to give the advice needed and so saved them a doctor's bill. There were some whom I had to take to see a doctor and others who just needed a laxative. One evening I was in my room when they wanted me urgently on the tennis court—someone had put his leg out of joint. There was a rule in our house that we could not go out into the grounds with our hair in curlers and here I was in this situation, and I honestly didn't know what I could do in this case; anyway, the next thing was someone followed the other person to say the leg was okay. They had put it back themselves. What a relief that was for me!

Everyone who takes this three-month course agrees that it is a hard course of studies. I recommend it for every missionary, especially children's missionaries. It is a very thorough training and given by dedicated people.

Most of the academic studies we pursued during the first eight weeks, and then we were sent out in pairs to various places for our practical work. After class work we had plenty of homework to do. There were twelve textbooks to be studied and tests at the end of each week. Twenty-two subjects were covered, with credits for three others. Included were various Bible doctrines, art and background making, organization and administration, teacher training, cults, visual aides—preparation and presentation. I managed to graduate and pass the examinations. Halfway through the course a girl named Viola New came to retake certain subjects needed to graduate. She was closer to my age and I found we could study well together. Her home was in Colorado and we kept up a friendship for a number of years.

A disgraceful thing happened during our training period. We had students come in from several different countries, amongst whom was one from England. Not to mention names, this girl was found out to be a lesbian. I knew nothing about her; however, knowing she was from my homeland I wanted to make her feel at home. I guess some of you may know about the custom we have of taking early morning tea. I made tea and took it to her room before breakfast. This continued while she was with us. I noticed that one of the younger students was with her and I just presumed they were studying together. Someone discovered them behaving unseemly at the lakeside and reported them. After being reprimanded, the English girl was dismissed and sent back home. The thing that was unpleasant for me was the fact that suspicion was cast upon me as I had been seen going to her room in the early mornings. I could not believe that anything like this could occur amongst Christian people, but it was true. Miss Husenetta was "on the ball" and broke into Miss Viola New's room where we were studying

Vera with her friend Myrtle Campbell on Myrtle's farm

Our house on Beverly Court, Tallahassee

together to make sure no one else was involved, I suppose. This girl who had to leave came to me to ask me to get her to the airport as she had no way of getting there. I gladly did this for her and counseled with her on the way. I relate this incident because it is part of my life history and to show others how sin creeps into the lives of people of all walks of life. I guess many other people will have similar experiences. Satan is harder at work amongst those who are serving the Lord Jesus than with others.

While I was in Muskegan I had frequent letters from my missionary friend, the Reverend Williams, to whom I am devoting a special chapter, and who was one of my St. Petersburg friends. He was one of my prayer warriors. Also the C.E.F. folks were praying for me each week at their prayer meetings. I was somewhat elated to receive a telegram from them on the day of graduation.

We had a banquet the day before graduation arranged by the students themselves. The class history was written by Audrey Reid—a poem I have kept. It was very clever and summed us up admirably. The Reids are doing a fine job in Spain and still work for C.E.F. After serving in C.E.F. as teacher of teachers, Myra Laird is still using her skills teaching children in Liberia. It would be interesting to know what each one is doing at present. We graduated on August 27, 1965.

I went home alone and on my way I had an accident involving two other cars and my own. This was not my fault, but there were no witnesses, so I had to bear the brunt of it. I was going through a small, sleepy town in Alabama when a young driver stopped in front of me without warning. To avoid hitting him I turned to the right and hit one car, and that car hit the one in front. Both were stationary cars. The result of this was my insurance company dropped me. I had to stay overnight to get my own car fixed enough to get home.

I had a waiting period after this of three months as my friend Jessie Bouquin was taking her training at the C.E.F. Institute. It was sometime before headquarters could decide where to send us, as we had asked to work together. Tallahassee was needing a director. Jessie finished in November. At last a decision was made to send us to Tallahassee, Florida. That is how I came to live here, and am still here at the time of this writing.

A Clear Call to Missionary Service

I was asked to lead the midweek prayer meeting at the Evangelical United Brethren Church meeting in St. Petersburg, after Albert Davis, my husband, had died. It was as follows:

> I always enjoy going to our midweek prayer meetings; the songs, the prayers and messages from God-inspired people are uplifting and speak to my heart. I was so glad to hear the testimony of our Brother George Schapmier last week and to know how the Lord saved him. I rejoiced with him as a fellow Christian that the Lord had saved me too, and I hoped also that everyone in our meeting had shared this experience and received this wonderful salvation which is free to everyone who will receive it.

We in America have such a wonderful opportunity to hear the Gospel preached either in churches or by radio or television and we have our Bibles to read, so there is no excuse if we have not responded to God's call for complete surrender of our lives to Him.

I think it would be fitting here to give my own testimony briefly and tell you how God saved a sinner like myself. "For all have sinned and come short of the glory of God." He surely had His Hand on me. When I decided to train to become a nurse, I was 29 years old, so of course it wasn't too easy for me as all the other nurses were younger than I was. But I am sure it was all a part of God's plan for my life because it was through the influence of Christian nurses that I became saved. I had always been religious, a good church member, Sunday school teacher for years, and had even been sent by my church for specialized training for leadership, but I had no teaching about salvation as I attended a liberal church. Therefore I had been no good "witness" for my Savior. How I missed reading about it in God's Word, I do not know, but it's true. I am sure Satan blinded me. At any rate, it was when I was doing some specialized training for midwifery at the Salvation Army Hospital that I found out I was not saved. As Jesus told the rich young ruler, "Except a man be born again, he cannot see the Kingdom of God." This is not a reformation of the old nature, but a creative act of the Holy Spirit.

I watched certain nurses and the whole atmosphere of the hospital was saturated with the Christian influence of these girls and women who came to "train" in this hospital and most of whom became missionaries later. They had Bible study in each other's rooms and gave testimonies and helped with the devotions in the wards for the patients. I am sincerely thankful to God that He led me away from home to find salvation for my soul and to learn the true Christian way of life.

It was at this time during my training that my father died (my mother had passed on several years previous to this) and my sister married soon afterwards. In the circumstances, I decided to change my plans and instead of becoming a village house-midwife, I came over to America at the request of an aunt to start life anew in more ways than one!

How precious the Lord was in those early days in Pittsburgh. I was able to make a complete break with the "old life" which clung to worldly things and God led me to a church where I was taught to pray and witness for my Savior. I was baptized and found work to do in the church and Jesus has been very precious to me ever since. Time will not permit me to tell you other instances where God showed me how to completely trust Him in difficult circumstances. The following verses were particularly helpful to me on one occasion:

> Trust in the Lord with all thine heart, and lean not to thine own understanding. In all thy ways acknowledge Him and He shall direct thy paths. —Proverbs 3:5–6

If there is anyone here who has not come to the Knowledge of Jesus as Savior, I urge you to do so . . . "There is no other Name under Heaven by which you must be Saved." In Acts 16:31 Paul says, "Believe on the Lord Jesus Christ and thou shalt be saved and thy house." That last phrase gives me much hope for my loved ones. I believe God will save those of our households who have gone on without the full light of the Gospel if we are faithful who know the Truth . . .

This Is My Testimony, Folks!

Now I want to spend a little time in speaking on a subject which is a burden on my heart: the need for missionaries in the foreign field! It was when I got home from prayer meeting that night (last Wednesday) that I picked up a missionary magazine. I was looking at a sub-heading "Everybody ought to know."—"Everybody ought to know what?" Who Jesus is! Brothers and sisters in Christ, who is to give out the gospel or Good News of Jesus? His disciples and followers have this responsibility. We haven't got to leave it to the pastor to do all the work. He is the shepherd of the flock and we must uphold him with our prayers and gifts to support in every way possible, but we who profess to be followers of Jesus—US! . . . blood-bought sinners—we are the ones who must be His witnesses too! Jesus said to His disciples on the Mount before leaving this earth, "Go ye therefore and teach all nations, baptizing them in the name of the Father, and of the Son and of the Holy Ghost, teaching them to observe all things whatsoever I have commanded you, and lo I am with you always, even unto the end of the world" (Matt. 28:19–20).

Now if the followers of Jesus had been faithful throughout the ages until this time, I believe the world would be evangelized today! But the fact remains, only a small percentage of the world knows Jesus. Oh yes, a lot of people know about Him and are called Christians and even profess to be His followers, but comparatively few know Him!

Everybody ought to *know* Jesus! Who is it who ought to know him? Is it just a few chosen ones scattered across the nations? Does it mean a few who happen to wander into our churches? Red and yellow, black and white, *all* are precious in His sight. This is the black children's favorite song. They always ask for this song if we give them a choice. So this wonderful gospel and our wonderful Jesus must be made known to all peoples of the earth:

> To the Jew first, to the Stone Age people in New Guinea, the Tibetan people and the Communist Chinese who were at war with them. The Moslems and Persians, the Buddhists of India and the cultured people of Japan, who believe in ancestral worship, and the poor, ignorant Africans in the jungles who worship evil spirits and imagine the spirits lurk under every bush and stone. These all need Jesus and need release from the captivity of their soul to the freedom and joy of the new life in Christ Jesus.

How Jesus changes lives completely is seen in the radiant faces of new converts in any community or race of people. And, "*Whosoever shall call upon the name of the Lord shall be saved.*" How then shall they call on Him of whom they have not heard? And, how shall they believe in Him of whom they have not heard? And, how shall they hear without a preacher? And, how shall they preach except they be sent as it is written: "How beautiful are the feet of them that preach the gospel of peace and bring glad tidings of good things!" (Rom. 10:13–15).

A new convert in Cambodia was faced with many questions when he returned to his home. He was able to answer many questions but this one he couldn't. It was this: "If Jesus Christ is the true God, then why have we not heard before?" The missionary was faced with the question as the convert returned to him. It was a burning question for him to answer. Here I quote from my *Missionary Magazine*: "Who is at fault?" and "Where shall we place the responsibility?" I believe we can say without wavering, the full responsibility rests squarely on the Church of Jesus Christ . . . *you* and *me!* They have not heard because we have not reached them with the *truth.* Is Jesus Christ the true God? Is He the Son of God? Is He the one who died for their sins? Is He the one who can bring satisfaction to searching, longing hearts? If He is, then "*everybody ought to know!*"

If "*everybody ought to know,*" who shall go? You may say we haven't enough trained personnel for our own churches; this is true as we have learned recently, but, after all, we do still have many churches and the need is far greater in the foreign field where some have not even heard the name of Jesus yet. After all, Jesus did say, "Go into *all the world,*" and He did die for *all* who would believe in His name.

I was reading an article recently which explained that the shortage of trained personnel for the foreign missionary field is entirely due to our modern trend of life. Lots of students will volunteer for missionary service, scores, even hundreds of them, but few ever reach their goal! This article written by Wesley L. Gustafson is published by *Inter Varsity Christian Fellowship* and is entitled "Called, but not Going." The article goes on to state that, "If all of those who have volunteered since 1900 had gone to the mission field, this generation would be evangelized!" But, the truth is, only a small fraction ever reach the foreign field. Here are a few of the reasons:

1. A wrong conception of missionary work. Many believe that missionary work is not for talented, able men and women. Well-meaning friends suggest that the candidate is the type needed at home—good brains, initiative, personality, etc. He feels he has advanced a notch beyond missionary work. The vision is dimmed, and soon lost.

2. Indifference and disobedience to Christ's clear command: "Lift up your eyes and look on the fields." If each candidate in obedience to Christ's command would read articles and books presenting the needs of the foreign field, we would be much more active in encouraging others to go; we would be much slower in accepting advice from well-meaning people that would turn us away from the field.

"Pray ye therefore the Lord of the harvest that He would send forth laborers into His harvest!" One pastor, asking his people to pray fifteen minutes a day for foreign missions, warned that it would be very dangerous. Asked why, he explained, "It cost William Carey his life." A man would urge people to go to the unmanned parts if he were praying to God to send them out. Everyone he met who was considering the mission field would be an answer to his prayers for laborers. And many people would find themselves urgently trying to get to regions beyond if they were regularly, intelligently, and honestly praying that God sent forth laborers.

3. "Health" is a foe that robs God and needy places of promising workers. Many times the loss is absolutely unnecessary. During high school, college, and seminary years, candles burn at both ends! Some get by for awhile. All pay a price eventually. The Christian body is the

temple of the Holy Spirit. So whatever your situation, take care of your body. You will never have another one while here on earth. On the day that we meet Christ face to face, we are going to give account for what we have done in the body, whether it be good or bad. One need not and should not shirk using our bodies strenuously, but should be wise and careful. Living souls pass into the next life without hearing of Christ because some young people will not care for their physical health and thus make themselves ineligible for foreign service.

4. Marriage or engagement is also a bitter enemy of fulfilling Christ's will that all should learn of Him. Marriage is God-given, but, when it becomes a barrier to God's will, it is misused. We could name many, both men and women, who have had a definite call to the foreign field and never got there because associates held them back. It is possible that those who held back were also in God's plan to go but were not surrendered. The ones who married those not obedient to God's will were out of God's will, too. Nothing, not even the God-given blessing of a life mate, must hinder God's purpose for one's life. Jesus said, "Whosoever he be of you that forsaketh not all that he hath, he cannot be my disciple." Today, thousands of persons die without Christ because loved ones have taken priority over God's will!

An Indian layman who is the general secretary of the Church of South India recently stated: "The old type of missionary, fatherly and yet autocratic, superior, separate and undisguisedly foreign in all his ways, the dispenser of money, jobs and patronage, a spiritual and cultural mentor; the agent of the society which sent him out, and the ambassador of western civilization is no longer needed; but we need, desperately, men and women who would come to us constrained by the love of Christ and aflame with a passion to proclaim Him; men whose motto would be that of St. Paul, 'We preach not ourselves, but Christ Jesus the Lord, and ourselves, your servants for Jesus' sake.'"

The following was written to the homeland by a missionary named Judson in 1816:

> In encouraging young men to come out as missionaries, do use the greatest caution. One strong-headed, conscientiously obstinate man would ruin us! Humble men of sterling talents, quiet, persevering men . . . with some aptitude to acquire language, men of amiable, yielding

> temper, willing to take the lowest place, to be the least of all and servant of all; men who enjoy much "closet religion," who live near to God and are "willing to suffer all things for Christ's sake," without being proud of it . . . these are the men.

Not only in the mission field, but also in our government, is there difficulty finding the right type of young men to fill posts in foreign service; so often we are misrepresented abroad. The type of missionary needed today is not the product of a luxury-indulging, leisure-loving, and undisciplined society. Only the grace of God working in a wholly yielded life produces the ideal missionary. The great foreign missionary, the apostle Paul, knew this when he wrote in 1 Corinthians 9:16–27:

> For I take no special pride in the fact that I preach the gospel. I am under compulsion; for woe is me if I do not preach the gospel. For if I do this voluntarily, I have a reward; but if, against my will, I have a stewardship entrusted to me, what then is my reward? That, when I preach the gospel, I may offer the gospel without charge, so as not to make full use of my right in the more. For though I am free from all men, I have made myself a slave to all, that I might win the more. And to the Jews I became as a Jew, that I might win Jews; to those who are under the Law, though not being myself under the Law, that I might win those who are under the Law. To those who are without law, as without law, though not being without the law of God but under the law of Christ, that I might win those who are without law. To the weak I became weak, that I might win the weak; I have become all things to all men, that I may by all means save some. And I do all things for the sake of the gospel, that I may become a fellow partaker of it. Do you not know that those who run in a race all run, but only one receives the prize? Run in such a way that you may win. And everyone who competes in the games exercises self-control in all things. They then do it to receive a perishable wreath, but we are an imperishable. Therefore I run in such a way, as not without aim; I box in such a way, as not beating the air. But I buffet my body and make it my slave, lest possibly, after I have preached to others, I myself should be disqualified. (ASV)

The objective of Paul's ministry was the salvation of the lost, and, to achieve this goal, he was willing to forfeit personal rights and privileges and to identify himself with the people that he labored among!

I have presented the need in our mission fields of today. What can be done about it, folks? We who are older have a responsibility in this great task of proclaiming the gospel to every creature as well as the young folks. The first thing that every missionary of the Cross asks to do is to pray. Prayer is more vital than anything else; more things are wrought by prayer than this world dreams of, and pray that God will thrust forth missionaries of the right caliber into the field. Secondly, we must encourage our young people with a missionary vision. May we never be guilty of discouraging them or putting obstacles in their way. Let us help them to gain their objective; let us fill them with hope and high aspirations. Thirdly, tell others about our missionaries, get interested in them personally and help them according to their needs. Let's get "missionary-minded"!

I think the last great need will be met if the others are fulfilled. Our missionaries do need our financial support.

What did Paul say at his conversion on the road to Damascus? "I was not disobedient to the heavenly vision." Has God been speaking to your heart tonight? Has anyone here had a call from God to "go"? The fourth thing we can do about it? He may want us to be missionaries at home, but to some He may be speaking to go to faraway lands where the people still sit in darkness. Has God been speaking to your heart to pursue a certain course? Are you following in the path of obedience; are you in the place where God wants you to be? I trust that you are, and that all "born again" believers will be able to say with Paul: "I was not disobedient to the heavenly vision."

God called me to Red Bird Mission after I gave this message!

Missionary Service

Jessie Bouquin came back to St. Petersburg after C.E.F. training. Although this was home for both of us, we had not met until we arrived at Red Bird Mission. As we compared our lives, it was interesting to note the similarities we had. We both had been married later in life and had no children of our own; we both had become widows about the same time; and we both decided to devote our lives to missionary service. Also, we were both members of the Evangelical United Brethren Church, although it is the United Methodist Church now.

It was after Christmas 1964 that word came to us that we were to go as field workers to start a new chapter for C.E.F. in Tallahassee. I think that Jessie had a furnished apartment which she had to give up. I still had my home at Eleventh Avenue North in St. Petersburg and was able to rent it furnished. The day came when we both left together driving our own cars, packed to capacity with our goods and chattels; most important to us were all the teaching aides we had made or procured some way. Neither of us had been in Tallahassee before. I imagined it to be quite different than what it turned out to be like and was pleasantly surprised to find it to be one of the most beautiful cities to which I had ever been.

C.E.F. is a "faith mission," so each worker is responsible for his or her own support. In our case, a certain lady, a teacher who lived in Tampa, had devoted her summer vacation to teaching "Five Day Clubs" in this city of Tallahassee during the summer of 1964, and had pledged her title to support the work for one year. In this she was faithful, and it was the only support we had as we started out. We were given a list of contacts who were Gideons and the address of a lady with whom we could stay overnight, including breakfast for a few days and with much prayer and support I am sure. The first place we arrived was near the Governor's Mansion. Here we stopped to make inquiries as to where we were to go. We were not far from East Tennessee Street, where we met our hostess who welcomed us to our new home-city. The first thing we had to do was to find an apartment so we scanned the *Tallahassee Democrat* and looked around to see what was available. I think it was the second day that we found exactly what we wanted and could afford—Kings Drive was situated just outside the city limits. Here we found a one-story, furnished apartment with two bedrooms, small kitchen with dining space, and a good-sized living room and bathroom. It was reasonably priced, so we rented it. We set up our office between the bedrooms which opened into the living room and consisted of two card tables. We decided as to what each should be in charge; I was made treasurer. We both faithfully sent a tithe of what money we received to the state director. Jessie kept records of statistics.

Here I might tell you briefly about our work. Our aim was to teach children the gospel of the Lord Jesus Christ and to train voluntary workers to teach the Neighborhood Clubs for children ages four to twelve years or older. The winter work is via Good News Clubs and the summer work is with Five Day Clubs. It is interdenominational and international in scope. Our programs are used in schools where religious training is permitted, and also in other places like fairgrounds and shopping centers.

We visited some of the churches and found out that people were interested. One group of people was starting a church themselves and wanted to give money as a mission project for our cause, but the pastor could not go along with them. This caused a split in the church. We did find two or three people from this group willing to serve as committee members and hostesses for Good News Clubs. We were both ardent workers, and, in three months, we had found several women to host our clubs.

In three months, a teacher-training couple named Wanda and Wilma, from headquarters, arranged to come and visit us. We launched our first "all-day" training seminar. We were fortunate in procuring a social room in a bank building on Tennessee Street. The bank provided this facility free with refreshments also. We advertised our conference in the local newspaper and invited all the contacts we could. As I remember, we had a good group that attended. This really encouraged us.

A Day in the Life of Two Field Workers for C.E.F.

Up at 7 A.M.; eat breakfast; listen to the news; wash dishes. Devotions. Phone rings. Someone keeps Jessie forty minutes on the phone telling her life history. Scan the calendar for the day. Find that we must telephone a busy pastor for interview. He says he is still too busy and to please call again beginning of next week. This is Saturday and should be our day off, but we need to prepare a lesson for our Good News Club for Monday; also time must be given to study. Jessie gets busy calling people that we cannot get any other day in the week. Yes, they all agree that we should train the children in their area, or "the whole family has the flu." They know others who may be interested and give her a list of people to call. This is the day we have allocated as "clean-up" day, and to shop for the weekend groceries. On Saturday, we were invited to a Christian Businessmen's dinner. This was a real treat for us!

After this dinner meeting, we spent some time at the pastor's home and got home late. Another Saturday we were trying to study our lesson when Jim comes over. He is a young man we are trying to interest in teaching a Good News Club. While Jim is here, we get to work and cut out paper dolls. (These are figures from Life of Christ Visual Aides.) We find that we need to make more tokens for our clubs. (These are memory verses we give out to the children to learn during the week.)

Back to our routine: Mornings are spent in our office. This is at present a space in our living room. Phone calls are coming and going. At the end of the month, we have a "Monthly Prayer Letter" to get ready and send out at the beginning of the month. Many envelopes have to be addressed by hand and stamps to lick. Also, there are a number of brochures to write up on the backs regarding conference on February 28. We are always anxious to see what the mailman brings. It seems so long waiting for "Memory Verses Visualized" for the Good News Clubs. We have to make these up if they are not available. They arrive at last, just as Jessie has copied hers out to take in the afternoon.

We had a letter one day from Mrs. Shade who gave us the address of the Millers. Mr. Orvis Miller was a retired minister and an accountant. The Millers became great friends of the fellowship and helped us in various ways. They were already doing children's work and had a big Bible Club for their neighborhood children. We were able to present the work in their church, and, as time went on, we were able to sell our literature to several churches and Sunday school groups. We had workshops to show them how to use the material and how to make backgrounds for the "flannel board." We also found out we could have a stall in the annual state fair at the fairgrounds in the fall. Our committee was helpful at such times and would sometimes go to another city to borrow a Chapel-on-Wheels for the Fair Ministry, which was a novel and more effective way of reaching the children for Christ. Everything we did was first brought before our committee. By having a Fair Ministry, we were able to obtain the names and addresses of children for follow-up and thus were able to get many of them into Sunday school and church. Also, we got contacts of those who were interested in our work in other ways. Some of these made their way into our teacher training classes.

One day we had a phone call asking us to come and teach a Good News Club. The Rollins family had heard about us, and, when I arrived, there was a room full of expectant children, all dressed in their Sunday best! This was our first black club and it lasted for years. We discovered a fine black lady, Mrs. Daisye Wells, who was able to give much of her time to the work. Also, she went to the F.E.C. Institute for training and proved a real blessing as she was able to help in the training classes. (I might say here, all our workers were voluntary and had to buy all their materials to work with.)

Jessie and I were willing to teach Bible stories in the schools, and, being near Christmas, we got in touch with the superintendent of schools for permission to do so. He said, "I doubt if you can," and invited us to the next meeting. We tried but were turned down. The result was, we made headlines in the newspaper the next day. However, we had been advised by the superintendent to try the Catholic schools. This we did.

We had our story on a tape recorder and carried our "flannel board" to the rectory. The priest was gracious enough to hear us and, after presenting the story to him, he said, "I want my children to hear this." He instructed us to give the story to kindergarten through fifth grade. We also gave them an invitation to accept Jesus into their hearts and the response was great! It was sometime later that one of these boys saw me in the street and said "Hello." I asked him how he knew me and he said, "You came and taught us in my school." I further inquired of him to know if he had Jesus in his heart. He assured me that he had. I asked him about the others and he said the boys in his class were better behaved now! The seed was sown and God must water it.

In time, we were made codirectors of Leon County. Each of us were teaching five Good News Clubs per week. After one year, we found there still was not enough money coming in to support us, so Jessie got another job as a teacher in a Spanish-speaking school in Tampa. The main support had stopped, so I had to find another place in which to live, as I could not afford the rent. I found a place at 407 St. Francis Street with a lady who needed companionship. I also found office space on Calhoun Street. In a short time, the apartment next door, owned by the same lady, became available, so I moved into that apartment. This was timesaving to me, and expense-wise as I had room for an office.

Mrs. Charleville, my landlady, whom we affectionately called "Charlie," was quite a character with her "likes and dislikes." By living with her, I learned that she had met with some severe tragedies in her life. Her husband and only son had both committed suicide at different times. She used to lie awake at night and go over and over these sad experiences. No doubt God had sent me to help her and be a comfort to her, and assure her that God can wipe away all tears and give peace and forgiveness. She was an elderly lady when I first knew her. Fortunately, she took a fancy to me as I tried to help her all I could. In time, she employed a very capable lady as housekeeper and companion who was very good to her. Also, she was a seamstress and she made clothes for Charlie.

There was a family nearby named Culbreth who was buying some property from Mrs. Charleville at a low price. Somehow, they did not meet with her approval and she later became disgruntled toward them. They were extremely kind to her, and Mrs. Culbreth would often walk over from her place nearby with some homemade goodies and biscuits at suppertime. This lady became an invalid herself later and was unable to walk due to arthritis. Charlie had another kind friend, Mrs. Julie Sutton, whom she made executor of her will. She used to come regularly and make up her checkbook and bring items of groceries that she needed. Charlie's style of living was simple and her needs were few. I kept in touch with this lady until her death. Julie is still a good friend of mine and has died since.

While living on St. Francis Street, I met Mrs. Wanda Blauvelt who had attended some seminars. She lived in Chattahoochee and became interested in this work. She came into Tallahassee occasionally and used to visit me supplying some of my temporal needs. I remember that she bought me a beautiful white bedspread on one occasion! One summer I had arranged to direct a Vacation Bible School for a Presbyterian church in Quincy, Florida. Mrs. Blauvelt, on hearing that I would be there, invited me to teach a Five Day Club in her home. The arrangement was for me to stay overnight with her and travel to Quincy from her place to conduct the Vacation Bible School, then return to her for the Five Day Club in the afternoon, and take dinner with the family in the evening. This worked out very well, and the following year she hosted and taught her own club. Her husband was a chaplain in the correctional institute in Quincy. Later they moved to Tallahassee where they are both teachers of the Bible in the church where they are affiliated. There was one day in July which the Child Evangelism Fellowship called "O" Day. This was devoted to outdoor evangelism. The "O" stood for Overholtzer, the founder of the movement. On this day in July, which is set aside in his memory, many C.E.F. workers go out into the streets of the cities and other places where children can be found and be reached with the gospel. I used the "Hand Method" or "Five Finger" gospel message at such times. John 3:16 was an ideal verse to teach and explain to the kids.

Serving C.E.F. was a very rewarding work, and, although I was kept very busy and used to get tired, I sometimes felt lonely. I had acquired some voluntary teachers by this time, and so we had several clubs each week. I used to teach one at the home of Miss Irene Bowman. This lady became a long-standing friend of mine and a faithful prayer warrior over the years. She had a friend in the city who had died and was a supporter of C.E.F. work. Her husband took over the support that his wife used to give.

One day Irene Bowman asked me to visit this gentleman, as he was lonely and she thought I might be able to keep his interest alive and encourage him to continue to give to the cause. I did so and found Mr. William Ervine living in a big house alone and taking care of everything himself, except for a housekeeper coming in occasionally. He asked me to go out with him for dinner, which I did. I found out that he was quite interested in our work. He realized I had a big job on hand and suggested that I use a tape recorder to record some of my songs. He got busy and helped me by providing a tape recorder and we got a number of messages and songs on tapes. A number of evenings were spent this way and we found we enjoyed each other's company. He took me out to eat regularly, once a week, and finally asked me to marry him. He was much older than I, but somehow I enjoyed his company and our friendship was very real and interests were quite similar, so I consented. He had a nice home to offer me and he was a good Christian man, which was most important to me. We had grown to love each other also. So, this began another phase of my life.

Close Friendship

After dear Albert passed on to be with the Lord, and after my services as a missionary nurse in Pineville, Kentucky, for one year and I was settled again in St. Petersburg, Florida, I made the acquaintance of a widower, the Reverend Walter B. Williams. I often passed his house on the same street where I lived. I noticed he had many artifacts on his porch, and seeing that he was an old gentleman who was living alone, I would stop and talk to him. He was indeed a very interesting person who loved the Lord. I would often sit and listen to his tales about his missionary work in Liberia. At this time he was, I believe, ninety-six years of age and a lively oldster! He loved to eat out and I would use my car. We sometimes would eat meals at a nearby restaurant. All the people knew him and he was loved by them. He was living on the south side of the city.

Walter began to feel the need for close companionship after the death of his wife. When he saw that I was not interested in marriage, he wrote and asked "Jenny," his onetime friend, to come and live with him. So she came as his "housekeeper"; actually, he had to take care of her.

It was along this time that I had my own problems. At the nursing home where I was working, I was exceedingly busy and tired, as I remember. The director of nursing at this place expected one person to do too much, and, it was generally known that there was a big turnover of the staff. It was while I was in training at Muskegon, Michigan, which began my next episode in life to become a missionary director for Child Evangelism Fellowship, and Sir Walter continued to write to me. Here is one of his letters:

> My Dearest Vera,
>
> It is now 12:30 and I am writing in a kind of Christian spirit that may help you to have courage and will power to excel in your tests and without taxing you too much in your efforts. You have a good mind. Your letters show that you write well and in good order and plain to understand. So, don't let things bother you. Do the best you can and let the rest go. And, remember that you have the dear Lord on your side and the Little Knight too. My hands are fairly well fixed with N.Y.C. and the colored boy that I have taken in hand.
>
> I get tired but never really depressed. I have spiritual powers at my command that are never disappointing. Then I have a precious, dear girl called "Vera" to cheer me up at times. And, you certainly do give me a shot in the good life and I am thankful for you. You are such a dear! I send you my warmest greetings and would like to make you a cup of tea and some nice Dundee Raisin Cake, and I have it here just now! I am not far from you in spirit and thought, so Goodbye dear love.
>
> —Your Little Knight,
> Walter
>
> P. S. Remember that you have been set apart the same as I am. . . . We are in Great and Strong Hands. Thank God!

He was very encouraging to me while I was busy studying for this difficult course; what a "grand old man of God" he was! He wrote in a bold handwriting and it appears that he was somewhat in love with me at this great age. He was also a determined old gentleman and his son could do nothing about getting him into a nursing home. I tried when I returned to St. Petersburg and thought I had accomplished the task of finding a very nice place which he liked! . . . He was settling up at the business office and we were taking his belongings into the room assigned to him, and, when he found he had to share a room with another man, he was adamant! He could not be persuaded to stay, so we had to leave. He was also a Mason and was able to get into the retired people's nursing home in St. Petersburg. We went to inquire there, but the same thing applied; he would not share a room with anyone, so he spent his last days at his home.

After my course of training at Muskegan, I became qualified to work for the C.E.F. and was appointed field worker with my friend, Jessie Boquin, in Tallahassee where a summer missionary had paved the way for us. This was during the year of 1964. We came into the city in January 1965. It was during my early days of ministry that I used to run down to St. Petersburg occasionally. I still had a house which I left rented and was able to stay with friends. I could keep watch over my property, and visit the Little Knight.

He was always glad to see me, but I feared for him as he was getting so frail. One of these times when I visited this couple, I found them both weak and unable to care for themselves. Walter was definitely hungry! He was in a hurry for me to take them out to eat, which I did. I did everything I could, while I could, but I had to leave them! I wrote a very "urgent" letter to his son but don't think he responded because he knew his father's determination. I could not stay as I had a job to do. I went back to Tallahassee with a very heavy heart. It was not a surprise when I received a letter about two weeks later from a friend with a newspaper clipping, which told of the tragic death of these two old people. They were both found dead on the floor of their home, starved to death; unable to look after themselves and Walter too proud and stubborn to call for help! I went to the funeral of this Little Knight. It was a grand funeral with full Masonic regalia and I placed a red rose on his coffin. I felt truly sorry that he should have come to such an end in this life. However, I am sure he is with the saints of God and has won a crown of righteousness, which is promised to all those who love His appearing (2 Tim. 4:8).

7
My Second Marriage

We planned a wedding for September 1970. I wanted to be married in the pretty church in St. Petersburg where I had spent so many happy years. My first wedding had been a secret affair and I decided to wear a white dress on this occasion, so I purchased an off-white silk dress, medium length. I managed to find a pair of gold-colored shoes and someone made me a headdress of veiling with green velvet streamers. My friend Wanda Scarborough was my maid of honor. Bill bought her dress. Jessie was put out about this as she thought she should have had this honor. She was away when I had to make the decision and I was unable to reach her; however, she returned in time to be one of our guests. I promised Bill that the wedding party would not be more than nine people at his request, although many more St. Petersburg friends came to the church to see us married. Bill Ervine's son and his wife Ruthie came from Bridgeport, Connecticut, and Bill Jr. offered to be best man at his father's wedding. He was very thoughtful in bringing his camera, so we had some good pictures made which he gave to us in an album as a gift. We had a nice reception in the Quality Inn where we stayed overnight.

The next day we went to Daytona Beach for our honeymoon. We had a delightful vacation there staying at the Sand Castles at their nicest oceanfront beach cottage which looked out over the sea. We visited some of the Florida attractions and were especially pleased with Marineland where we spent some time watching dolphins. These are remarkable and clever creatures, having been trained to do various tricks.

When we came back to Tallahassee, we arranged to have an open house for all the people who could not come to our wedding. We put a notice in the *Tallahassee Democrat* and a good number of friends came along. Although Bill was retired, he was always busy working around the house or in his garage. He had a boat that he had made himself, and one day I consented to go fishing with him. It was the first and last time. It was late afternoon and we had caught nothing. I learned later it was "Ervine's luck" not to catch fish. On this occasion, the motor had stopped and we could not get it going again. Someone in a passing boat asked if we needed help but Bill said no. The trouble was, we had run out of gas! We got back somehow, but it was scary as it was getting dark. Have you ever been out on the sea in an open boat with no one around and darkness falling?

When I moved from St. Francis Street, I had hoped to still rent the apartment from Mrs. Charleville for the C.E.F. office, but this dear lady wanted someone to live there all the time and refused to rent it to us, so again we had to find office space for my work. Bill was very resourceful and came to me with a good idea: Would I like to have a corrugated building? We went to see them and decided to have the largest size with four windows and a good, strong floor. Being an engineer, Bill was able to fix it up and run electricity into it. He also lined it with sheets of white styrofoam to keep it cool. We had enough room for this building behind our two-car garage and it made a good office and a training room as well.

Bill was very thoughtful. One day he brought home two rose trees—one was a standard rose for the garden and the other a rambler rose which he placed at the door of the office to train over the building. I was very happy with this arrangement as I did not have to leave home to get to the office. Our committee used to have their monthly meetings in our home, and, as it was centrally located, it suited everyone to meet with us at 536 Beverly Court.

My husband was a good-looking man with fine physique, a retired engineer who had worked for Florida Power Corporation. He limped a little due to an accident he had had at work. Bill had been a widower for four years; I had been a widow for eight years and was not expecting to remarry. We both needed companionship. He was born in northern Ireland; his father was an Irishman and his mother was a Scotch lady. He had lived in Tallahassee for thirty-seven years at the time when I first knew him and had built this house. He had chosen the best and first sight in the road. It was an extremely well-built Cape Cod-style house.

Bill was a good Christian man, and, when younger, had sought out a few young preachers and encouraged them in their service for the Lord. As I went around to some churches, I discovered several who knew Bill Ervine.

Bill Ervine

He had helped them to get started in their churches and had financed different projects. However, Bill was a Brethren and would not join any church as a member.

Bill's father, Grandpa Ervine, and his wife used to live with the Ervines for a few years in their latter days and they were Brethren also. Bill's father became well-known in Tallahassee as a preacher of the Word. Some of the senior citizens would ask me if I knew Grandpa Ervine, the preacher, as he was a lay preacher who filled-in for some of the pastors at different times. Grandma Ervine was buried in St. Petersburg and we visited her grave at one time. Grandpa Ervine made a trip to England when in his nineties. On his way he visited a Brethren group and was asked to finish the service with prayer, which he did. He sat down and passed on to Glory. He did not reach his earthly destination but found joy in the presence of his Savior whom he loved.

Bill and his younger brother trained to be engineers in Belfast, Ireland, where they grew up. They both helped build the *Titanic* and were chosen to be officers on board the ship for her maiden voyage. Before sailing, it was discovered that two brothers were to sail with the ship. The younger one was chosen to go and Bill lost this privilege, for which his life was spared but his younger brother went down with the ship. If Bill had sailed that day I would never have known him. This was an extremely sad experience and the whole world mourned for the loss of this ship and the many who perished in the icy seas that day. My husband told me that it was the only time he remembered crying in his life, when he heard of the death of his brother and the sinking of the *Titanic*. The following is an excerpt about the sad event:

The Titanic

> "Titanic" means "the strongest of the Gods." The Titanic, White Star Liner was thought to be indestructible, and unsinkable, struck an iceberg on the 15th of April, 1912, and it began to sink immediately. The alarm was given, passengers continued to dance, the Orchestra played. The order was given to "abandon ship" but the first boats went away empty. People dressed in evening clothes couldn't believe they should leave the warmth comfort and luxury of the beautiful ship for the discomfort of, and wetness of a little boat. More than 1500 passengers lost their lives; some because there were not enough boats, some because they wouldn't leave soon enough.

I found my husband was easy to feed; he liked everything I cooked. He was moderate in his habits, a non-smoker, and took no alcoholic beverages. He continued to take me out once a week to eat; usually to Morrisons, and his favorite dish was broiled mackerel. When Leech Rider came to live in our apartment, he used to accompany us. There was a lady living in the apartment when I first moved in who was an unhappy person. She moved and we made improvements, then engaged an agent of find a renter for us. We were happy to get Leech, a retired teacher who was blind in one eye but very capable and took care of himself very well. He had a little black dog as companion and he enjoyed living in our house. We adopted a stray kitten who grew into a beautiful Siamese cat we named "Dinkey." His coloring was chocolate, beige, and white. The animals got along well with each other.

One day Bill asked me if I would be willing to give up my job so I could spend more time at home. I had worked as field worker and C.E.F. director for five years and had applied for my Social Security at age sixty-two. This I applied for early as my income was so small, so it was a blessing to receive this. My home in St. Petersburg brought in a little each month as it was rented furnished. It was rather too much for us to go down periodically to rent it again each time it became vacant. The time came when we decided to sell this home. We put it on the market, and fortunately sold it in a short time so it was off our hands. We always enjoyed these trips down to St. Petersburg as I had many friends there and we both enjoyed driving.

We set out to find someone to take over the work, which was no easy matter as there was no guaranteed salary. One of the committee heard about a young man who had been rejected by the Southern Baptist Association as being unsuitable for the ministry. It was decided that we should try him, so we explained to him the financial situation and that we would give him a fair trial, so he was engaged to pursue the work knowing he would also have to go to the C.E.F. Institute for further training. He found temporary lodging at a bed and breakfast. I was asked to initiate him into his duties. He was very good with children and seemed a good teacher and smart in appearance. He was very anxious to sell our literature and made arrangements to visit pastors, which was fine. However, he set his own prices which were lower than what we were supposed to sell for. (All of our literature is priced at headquarters.) In many ways he was unable to adjust. We found out also he was a divorcé, which was not permitted at this time, so this young man left us. This was the first problem we encountered with getting a new director. I was left to "hold the fort" and to wait on the Lord to know what we should do next. In time, the committee decided we should try to find a suitable place for headquarters. We were truly led by God regarding the choice we made.

At the committee meeting, we were asked to look out for a suitable building. During the following month I discovered a house for sale just outside the city limits, which had a circular driveway and plenty of parking space. Bill and I went to look inside and it seemed to be exactly what we needed. We were excited about it and when we had the next meeting, one of our committee men had discovered the same place and was just as excited as we were! This was not just coincidence but God-directed.

The outcome was that my husband said he would buy this little house and rent it to the C.E.F., which he did. They got it for one dollar per month. There was a lot of work that had to be done and Bill took it upon himself to do it. He rewired the whole electrical system, embedding it in concrete. He repaneled the rooms and made the grounds presentable. The place was so adaptable to our needs. One side could be used as a training center and the other side for whatever was decided or needed. It made comfortable living quarters, as the house had two bathrooms and kitchen. We also furnished it partly from our own house and Bill bought some good classroom chairs for the training room. Now we could offer living quarters for our next director. In the meantime, I acted as director for the Fellowship.

Among the many friendships made while working in C.E.F., Myrtle Campbell was very close. Our friendship began to form through annual southeast regional workshops. She was missionary director for Santa Rosa County and lived in the country on a farm in northwest Florida. Our home was a convenient stopover for her, as most of the state and regional meetings were in southeast Florida. I remember once she brought two carloads of young people who were on their way to receive training to teach Five Day Clubs and "Open Air Work" in the area. We had a huge attic room and could sleep five up there, and we found room all over the house for them to sleep. (The same attic was also used by the previous Mrs. Ervine for army boys on leave during World War II.) Perhaps the most loved ministry that we shared together was the Fair Ministry. Myrtle came over each year and assisted me. We would plan a certain theme and make attractive posters, pass out tracts, and invite the children in to hear missionary and gospel-centered stories.

Another phase of our friendship was the visits I made to her home during holiday seasons. We made the usual little trips to see "Grandma Campbell" on the next farm, and made pleasant walks into the woods and pastures. Milton and Thomas Salter lived across the highway and shared Myrtle's interest in reaching the children. They also contributed toward her three-week missionary trip to Columbia, South America.

My dear husband was a lot of fun, especially around company. He was known for his Irish wit and good humor. I am sure you would enjoy some of his sayings. I was checking the electric blanket to see how high the

Myrtle and Vera at the North Florida Fair, 1971

temperature was set. Bill said, "If you smell something like bacon frying, you will know I had it on high." Again, Bill was ready to leave to work on his house. I said, "How are you today, dear?" He answered, "I'm just sneaking out without paying my rent." Another time I was wanting Bill to get ready to go out to eat. I said, "Do you want me to wash your face for you?" He said, "No, send cat in." One day I asked Bill if he would like a cup of coffee. He said, "Yes, I'll be back in a few minutes." I continued, "Are you going right away? Where are you going?" He said, "I'm not going away, I have a good home."

Bill was talking about selling his small organ and buying a new one. I asked him why he wanted to do that, and he said, "Well, the little church will need an organ, won't they? They can put a memorial on it: 'In Memory of Bill Ervine, the Flying Dutchman.'" He donated a new organ! I related to Bill how the Lord had answered prayer for me one day. He said, "I'm glad you are on speaking terms with the Lord."

We heard about a young couple, the David Hendreys, who had done some training for missionary work. Their special need was a place to live, and, as Bill had finished work on the house, we thought they might be suitable to take over the work of Child Evangelism Fellowship. The committee called them so they moved in; however, they were not trained and were unable to do this. David had a full-time job and could not give the time to it. Peggy tried to teach with the training class, and, after a short period, they moved to a house nearby. They later left the area; they were with us for eleven months.

Around this time, we had established some work amongst the black people. We found an enthusiastic lady named Daisye Wells who went to the C.E.F. Institute and took the leadership training. She was a real asset to us and worked with children and adults. Later she was made assistant director and shared the monies which came to us. We were able to reach children in the nursery schools as well as Good News Clubs.

We did find a little time for recreation. The "Trout Pond" was a delightful place where Bill and I used to go. It was for senior citizens and the handicapped. It was a recreational area with a pool and paved walks for wheelchairs leading through the park area as well as a pond for fishing. We would sometimes take a picnic meal with us. You can find this place on Springhill Road in Tallahassee.

We still needed a director. I had a letter from Shirley Butler who was the missionary friend who had taken care of my home while I was at Red Bird Mission. She worked for her parents and used to solicit funds for their mission in India which was known as Grace Mission India, Inc. She was a good speaker; I had heard her in one of the churches in St. Petersburg. She wrote to say she would like to work in C.E.F. and could I recommend her to serve in this capacity? Bill was very anxious to get someone to direct the work here, so the committee sent her an invitation on October 5 to come and see how she liked it here, and tell her that she must take the training. She came early in October and moved into the new house and office. I showed her what had to be done. Bill paid for her training at the Institute and when the next session started in November, she went to Michigan. She was only with us for two months.

It seemed we were just unable to get or keep anyone to do this children's missionary work. Shirley did an extraordinary thing; she closed the office and had all the mail sent to her at the school. Before long she returned to tell us she was leaving and was going back to her office in Farmington, New Hampshire. She did not tell us why. We discovered later that her religious doctrine was not compatible with the C.E.F.'s standards. Shirley was away at Thanksgiving so we invited our little friend Mrs. Charleville to spend Thanksgiving with us. We enjoyed our time together and took her back to her home in the evening.

Previous to this, a few weeks maybe, Bill had gone to a junkyard and bought a trailer which he was converting into a chapel-on-wheels for the Fellowship. Bill had done this without consulting the C.E.F. committee. For many reasons he should not have done this. He got the go-ahead from Shirley. He was such a hard worker and was replacing some of the floorboards which was much too hard a job for him with his heart condition. I was unable to stop him; the day after Thanksgiving, Bill was back at his work on the trailer and I was working in the office. He drove us home in the evening. I noticed he was not driving straight. A couple of times he veered to the right. That same evening he insisted on cracking pecans, which grew in our yard. He wanted to get the pecans in the mail for his daughter-in-law Ruthie. Early next morning between 4 and 5 A.M., I awoke to the sound of a "thud." Bill had fallen in the doorway at our bedroom. It was his custom to have his devotions early in the morning at about this time. He was returning from his den but had a severe heart attack, falling before he reached his bed. He never recovered. An ambulance was at the house within minutes, but he died on the way to the hospital, November 4, 1973.

It was a very sad time for me especially. My stepson came down immediately and took care of all the funeral arrangements. A memorial fund was set up in lieu of flowers to benefit the C.E.F. organization, and his body was laid to rest at the Rose Lawn Cemetery in Tallahassee.

The following days and weeks were busy and at times very lonesome. My friends were very sympathetic, and I felt a keen comradeship and love amongst them. God is so very good to us at such times. Sympathy cards and letters poured in from distant places, as well as locally. The C.E.F. committeemen had acted as pallbearers at my husband's funeral. My stepson, whom we had called "Billy" to distinguish him from his father, was very helpful but never interfered with any of my plans for the future. I appreciated very much his discretion and helpfulness in the years following.

My husband had made provision for me in his will by leaving me the house in which we were living when he died, after which it was to belong to his son or heirs. Also a sum of money to help me along plus the house on Crawfordville Road which was being used by the C.E.F. of Leon County as office and training center. He thought it would make a place in which I could live. I chose to continue to live in Beverly Court and rent the second story furnished. I had some help from my friend Dorothy Miller, who had lost her husband also. She was always ready to assist me in many different ways. "A friend in need is a friend indeed" is very true of her. She has since died. Together we made the place very nice and habitable. The Lord was good to send suitable tenants to share my home.

The Crawfordville house I deeded over to C.E.F. with the stipulation that it could not be sold, making it a permanent property for the Fellowship. This has proved to be a blessing to them and helpful in many ways. The director who serves at present has made some really fine improvements. Dave Bylsma, with help, enclosed a carport and added a nursery to the building. I thank God for sending faithful and talented people to direct the work here in Tallahassee, and for the people who have given to the support. The Lord sent people like Mr. Foltz who supplied electrical appliances and other useful equipment to improve the property.

In 1975, the Lord provided another director. I was sixty-seven at this time and thankful to pass on the directorship to Violet Haberer, a seasoned worker who desired to live near her aged parents. By this time, we had discovered that our property was zoned for business and that Violet could not live at the center, so we found a very nice trailer park for Violet and her friend to move into. It was a beautiful park but some distance from the office, so when a place became available, they moved to the trailer park on Crawfordville Road, which was within walking distance from the office and very convenient.

Violet, with her vast experience, made a good director, and her companion Dorothy Pettington was a great help in the work. We became friends immediately and this friendship lasted through the years. After three and a half years of faithful service, she found it necessary to move to Dowling Park, Florida, to care for aged relatives.

We had some devoted people on the committee at this time, some of whom had supported C.E.F. for many years. Amongst them were the Puffers. Doris and Frank came to Tallahassee from Miami and soon made themselves available to assist the C.E.F. in many ways. Doris was an excellent teacher of the Word, and so was able to teach a training class when needed, as well as children's classes in her home. Frank was able to do woodwork, etc., and made a beautiful sign for the front of the property. They both became the backbone of the work in various ways, especially where the finances were concerned. We thank the Lord for this fine couple.

In 1976, the C.E.F. Headquarters had procured a beautiful property in Warrington, Missouri. This was a great blessing to them as the need for space was critical at this time.

In July 1977 my friend in Santa Rosa County asked me to join a party to go and visit there. The occasion was their fortieth anniversary. We found several beautiful buildings on campus which included several acres of land. How good the Lord is to supply such a lovely place which now takes care of a training center, a plant for printing the literature, plus housing for students. Previously, they had been using two facilities. I was happy to have had this privilege of visiting the new headquarters. I must state here that we made the trip in a brand new car belonging to Beulah Clark, and we each took turns driving. I was away from home a few days at this time. When we returned, I stayed with Beulah in Milton overnight before going back to Tallahassee. She is a special lady, too, who became interested in working with children and C.E.F., and also applied the knowledge gained to her Sunday school teaching.

In 1976, my little friend Mrs. Charleville was badly in need of care; she was getting feeble and unable to take care of herself, so I arranged to take her into my home. She was ninety-four years of age. She loved to be with me so her lonely life was helped. She was able to go out with me in the car, and we used to go to the meetings at the Christian Life Center on Thursdays, which was Senior Citizens Day. She was no trouble and was able to eat anything I fixed. She was with me for nine months and then the dear soul had to go into a nursing home because she lost the sight of her one good eye, making her totally blind. This was her one fear in life at the time. I can see her now as I was ready to leave the house—she was raising her arms and trying to grope her way to the door. "What is the matter?" I asked. "I cannot see!" she replied. Whatever I was about to do was relinquished and I took Charlie to see her doctor. She had total blindness which could not be corrected. The doctor admitted her to the hospital preliminary to going into a nursing home. The only one available was out of town. We had some problems I remember, and, as soon as one was available, we moved her back into a nursing home in Tallahassee. Problems continued and it was very sad to see her go downhill so fast. She was either unable or had no desire to eat and died on February 4, 1977.

It was only four months after Bill died that I had a long-distance call telling me that Aunt Hilda had passed on to her eternal rest. Aunt Hilda was my closest relative in this country and, with Uncle Alf, had sponsored me here. She had suffered periodically with a heart condition.

It was still rather a shock to hear of her death; she evidently had died in her sleep on March 11, 1974. She was eighty-one years of age. I was free to go to the funeral, so I made the journey by plane to Aliquippa, near Pittsburgh. She was very much loved and respected by the neighbors, and many people attended her funeral besides the immediate family. The day prior to the funeral, the relatives and friends observed a "wake." I had never seen one before. I must say I was impressed by the way this was carried out. No one seemed to be sad. The body of Aunt Hilda was put into a sitting position and she looked beautiful; in fact, I was astounded by how real she looked. She was draped in pretty clothing and mountains of flowers surrounded her! It seemed like there were dozens of people in and out of the funeral home. Personally, I would not desire such an elaborate funeral, but this is what her friends chose to remember her by. I was able to get acquainted with some of the relatives at this time. Cousin Alex and his wife, whom I had not seen for several years, came in from California. I also met some of my second cousins who lived in the Pittsburgh area, and whose parents had passed on some years previously. I was glad to meet these cousins and to know they were making their way in the world on their own. My cousin Margaret and her husband had both died young and left a family of four children, three of whom were still in school. It seems that it takes a death in the family to draw folks together.

Aunt Hilda was a member of the Episcopalian Church; she had been quite a worker in her church and a blessing to many people. My uncle lived alone for many years after that. I had a surprise phone call (a few days ago) from him which I was happy to receive. I do not remember him phoning me before. He was ninety-six years old when he went to be with the Lord.

A Few Thoughts on the Loss of a Loved One

Why is it that our loved ones are taken at such a time as we feel we need them? One reason is that God knows best about it. He is the Creator. He gives life and He can take it away at His own time. It is not for us to question why.

Another reason is that maybe God has some lessons for us to learn. It seems that the void in a person's life is overwhelming at times. Naturally that is so when a person is married. They are one. God has joined them in matrimony. It is especially hard when both are saved Christians. The one left behind has had close fellowship with the partner. How often we see stalwart, brave, and seasoned Christians fighting back the tears and going on bravely, finding new paths open to them for service after they have laid to rest a loved one. They commit their loved one to the Lord and thank Him for the joy and experience that they have been pleased and privileged to share. The memories linger long in the hearts of these dear ones.

This same experience can happen when a mother and child are very devoted. I have a friend, Margaret Kornhi, whose only child died of a childhood disease. This mother was very close to her little girl, and the parting was very hard for her, but when she was approached by well-meaning people about her great loss, she was able to gladly point out that she was with Jesus. He wanted her to be one of His jewels in heaven, and she would see her again one day. Isn't it wonderful to know that the Lord Jesus is our friend, and that one day we shall see Him in all of His glory, even as Peter, James, and John saw Him on the Mount of Transfiguration? I'm looking forward to that day, aren't you, my friends? Another dear friend went through an experience with the loss of a little boy; Mrs. Shade is with the Lord now and no doubt rejoined with her son. Both of these women were led into children's work and, through Child Evangelism Fellowship, have won many dear children to the Lord. So, only good came out of these hard circumstances.

On the other hand, the death of a husband or wife can be a blessing where no "true" love exists. God sometimes takes one to relieve the other. There is little sorrow in this case, but freedom from anxiety.

Other lessons can be learned also. We might ask ourselves: Did we depend too much on our loved one? Or, did we love that one more than our precious Lord Jesus? This may be the case of one who is unable to adjust. Is it possible that the devotion has been too great, and that God has not been put first in their life. It is written, "I, the Lord thy God am a jealous God" (Exod. 20:5). He wants our love and deserves it. We can never love Him enough; that Jesus should die on the cruel cross for my sins is wonderful; it is too wonderful for words, but it's true! So, the Creator of all things, who made us in His own image, wants the love of each of us, which is His due. If we are sorry for ourselves over the loss of a loved one, let us give more thought to Him who first loved us.

Sometimes the outlook is bleak for a wife left with a little family. This is indeed a dark experience, but even in this, God has His plans. He knows all about us. Here is an opportunity for someone else to show practical love for a family so left. And does it not say in God's Word, "My God shall supply all your needs according to His riches in glory by Christ Jesus" (Phil. 4:19).

May these few words be a help or blessing to some bereaved hearts today.

My Sponsored Children

I did not have any children of my own but have sponsored a few since living in the States. It was when I was living with Jessie, my C.E.F. co-worker, that I found out she was sponsoring a child under World Vision, Inc.

I think Yoon Mee of Korea was my first child. She was three years and three months old when she came under my sponsorship. I received regular quarterly letters telling me about her progress. When she was old enough, she wrote me herself. World Vision send me photographs of her at least once a year. Those I placed in an album, and when she left the home in Seoul, Korea, I sent it to her with my love. I received a very appreciative letter by return mail. When I last heard from her, she was in training to become a beautician. It is not possible to keep in touch with children who speak a different language. However, a missionary in Korea, named Reverend Charles Greenwell, took photographs of her for me and I was able to keep in touch for a short time only. Reverend Greenwell returned to the U.S. and so we lost contact.

Other children I have sponsored are Young Ae Jo and Jo Yung Chul, both of whom are now out in the world on their own. Mahmooda Bibi Kutti, under the care of "Compassion," was a Muslim who now believes in Jesus as her Savior. Her aspiration in life was to become a plane hostess. She was nineteen when she left school. She lived in Fiji. Today, I have Fabiola Gaspard, a Negro child living in Haiti under Compassion International. She is eight years old and has sent me a very sweet letter with the help of her teacher. Ahsan Rashidal lives in Bangladesh and is a child needing special education. He is nine years old and is my latest sponsored child. I have to commit these children into God's care and trust that they will give their hearts to the Lord and will grow in grace and the knowledge of Him. Another child with whom I have had special interest is Jessica Hand. Her mother, Jackie Hand, a longtime friend, asked me to be her godmother. This entailed watching over her spiritual life and praying for her. Jessica is now sixteen years of age, a beautiful child of God, and I think ready to join the church. She is a child who has done well in school and looks like she will attain what she hopes to do in life. She is on the National Honor Society roll, is very artistic, musical, and athletic, has a sweet disposition, and I love her. She has now graduated from Leon High School here in Tallahassee.

8
Retirement Years

Soon after we were settled with a director for Child Evangelism Fellowship, I was able to take part in a number of activities of a more leisurely kind.

The First Baptist Church had built a Christian Life Center which was near my home and almost within walking distance. They started oil painting classes which I joined. I thought the volunteer teacher was exceptionally good. We all did a still life and our work was exhibited. The teacher, whose name evades me, was a sick lady and she died in the middle of the first term. Others took her place, some of whom were students from Florida State University (F.S.U.) who were needing experience in teaching before graduation.

Before oil painting, there were other classes which I joined. The significant one for me was the Personal Life History class, which was taught by Claudia Noble, also a student from the university. She, in turn, was a student of Laura Hendricks, Ph.D. This was a lot of fun besides being educational. My story is the outcome of these classes. There were seven other students in this class and I often wonder how many of them have continued to write their personal life history. Robert O. McKenzie began in earnest. He was in a wheelchair and had a good story to tell. I kept in touch with him for a year or two when he was still writing; however, I have lost contact with him. I must say he was a good watch repairman whom I can recommend here in Tallahassee.

I got acquainted with a number of senior citizens at the First Baptist Church; they were from all denominations. Thursday was the day we met. We had a social time early in the day. From 9:00 to 10:00 A.M. we would sit around, socialize and take light refreshments. Some played table games. The men played billiards. This period was followed by some educational classes, travel films, or history of Florida. Some people were interested in making ceramics. They have the largest and best ceramic classes that I have ever seen and produce some beautiful things. Toll painting was taught at one time, and other types of art, also. There was a devotional period at 11:30, and then an excellent luncheon was served at 12:30 in the big dining hall for a nominal fee!

Other planned features were vacations in which I was able to participate. I really enjoyed these, which took us to places that I would never otherwise have gone. I will include a brief account of some of these in my story.

Frances Hyatt was a special friend of mine whom I contacted during my early years in Tallahassee. She belonged to the East Hill Baptist Church, where she was a teacher and departmental leader. It was by advertising our conferences that she got acquainted with us and attended some of our Child Evangelism Fellowship meetings and found joy in serving as a voluntary worker. She took over the work of ordering and replenishing our literature, which was a great help to us. She has been a blessing to us financially also. My husband had the pleasure of knowing Frances, and, through other friends of hers, we were able to participate and enjoy the beach parties once or twice a year at Alligator Point. Frances also hosted a Good News Club in her home for several years, and on such days as I taught, she expected me to stay and eat dinner with her, so our friendship grew to a delightful experience.

My friend's Christian life was the outcome of a sad experience. I will include her own testimony here which will show my readers what God can do to bring glory to Himself through ordinary people like you and me.

Testimony of Frances Hyatt
Accepting the Consequences of Choices

In my position as Reference Librarian at the Florida State University Law Library, I received many telephone calls each day for answers to questions regarding legal matters. But Monday, I had a different type of call. I was very pleased to tell Ray [Ray was her pastor] that I would share with you from my experiences.

In Sunday School this month, the theme of our lesson unit is "Accepting the Consequences of Choices." I want to share with you some of the choices I have made in the last thirteen and one-half years:

Trust God, Thy Will Be Done, Believe

Before December 24, 1959, I was a Christian; one who believed *about* Jesus Christ but one who did not really *know* Him.

The three-car collision on Christmas Eve was the end of a beautiful way of life and the beginning of a new relationship for me . . . alone with God.

Choice 1: Trust vs. Non-Trust. My first "remembered memory" occurred two days after the wreck. The doctor told me of my husband's death. Soon after that, the preacher came and said, "I think of you when I read this." I was too weak to remember the words of the ninety-first Psalm, but the main thought of the second verse became my constant thought all my waking moments: TRUST GOD, TRUST GOD, TRUST GOD. I asked the nurses to re-read this Psalm and the twenty-third Psalm several times each day.

Choice 2: Bitterness vs. Non-Bitterness/Forgiveness. Bitterness toward the young man whose mistake in judgment caused the accident would not bring my husband back, nor would it help me. I chose Non-Bitterness and Forgiveness.

Choice 3: Trust doctors. Along with my choice to trust God within myself, all of these choices are my inward thoughts. I also felt a deep trust toward the two doctors whom I had never met before. Comments from the nurses confirmed their great dedication and high reputation in the community. Now it is hard to believe the near-death criticalness of my injuries; the head injury actually exposed the brain itself (both layers of bone and the membrane covering the brain from the inside corner of my eye to an inch or two in the hairline were split open); or that my little finger (displayed perfect movement) was dangling by the skin; or that my right leg as well as the kneecap were comminuted (the medical term for "crushed"); or that there was great doubt whether I would ever live and, if I did, whether I would walk again.

Choice 4: Believe, patience in waiting. Matthew 21:33 states, "And all things, whatsoever things you ask in prayer, believing, ye shall receive." One and a half weeks after the wreck, before I was again taken to surgery, the nurse heard my prayer "to guide the physician's hands and thy will be done." Hours later when I awoke in my room and was still alive, I simple believed that God's answer to my prayer was that somehow, someday, I didn't know when, all would be all right.

During the next eighteen months, the progress in my recuperation was so full of "challenge and achievement" as exercises and measurements revealed steadily upward improvement. My brother's neighbors and friends shared each setback and each advancement with me; I was drawn into a circle of Christian love and sharing which soothed my wounded spirit.

On June 9, 1960, the doctors released me; on June 10, I CAME HOME! Mama was under doctor's orders to stay only three weeks; then I was alone for the first time in my life.

Choice 5: Exhaustion vs. Strength. In August 1960, my return to the normal routines associated with work revealed a lack of self-confidence in my ability to last through the day and to do the things I used to do because of all I had been through. About this time, I saw the movie King of Kings, and saw with my new awareness of suffering the crucifixion of Jesus. . . . In the days following, I thought of His suffering and it made what I had been through not seem so great. I began to think, "If He can do that for me, I can sit here and do this for Him." When the exhaustion began to overcome me, I noticed with a growing excitement that something inside me seemed to rest me at the most tired spot. As time went on, I learned that Jesus was helping me in a way I had not been aware of before. His Spirit was inside me, strengthening me! I was not alone!

Choice 6: Indecision vs. Decision. But, also during this time, certain decisions I had to make caused me some anxiety because I was unsure of what to decide and when I did decide, maybe the next day I would change my mind, and I worried over what others would think. I was miserable in this respect! Self-doubt and fear of what others would say left me in a state of wavering indecision many times and I was not happy in this state.

Choice 7: Firm Foundation. In 1962, I came to Florida to help my sister-in-law who had cancer. The following year, I returned to work at Florida State University and continued to attend East Hill Baptist Church, which I had visited while she was in Tallahassee Memorial Hospital. My third week there, Ray, the preacher, announced a need for a Sunday school teacher for the nine-year-olds. To my surprise, as I went out the door, I found myself volunteering! As we studied together, again I turned to God for help, asking Him to give me understanding of His Word so that I might teach these little girls as He would have me to. I taught myself most of all! Soon I learned the meaning of "the Sword of the Spirit" as I began to apply the truths from the Bible verses to my daily decisions. What a stabilizing effect on my wavering indecision and worry about what others would think. Well, my decisions became sure based on God's unchanging Word, and I was freed from worry about what others thought, for God's way was the best way.

> On December 24, 1959, I was a Christian who believed *about* Jesus Christ; on June 17, 1973, I am a Christian who has learned to *know* Jesus Christ—His love, His patience, His comfort, His understanding, forgiveness, and strength. As Paul said, I also say, "I can do all things through Christ, which strengtheneth me." I am fortunate here in Tallahassee to be again drawn into a circle of Christian love and sharing. I feel my "spiritual family" helps me mature as a Christian.

Frances is still a friend of mine. She visits people in the health care center at Westminister Oaks Retirement Center for the elderly where I have an apartment at present. I thank God for giving me friends like Frances Hyatt.

I Remember

(This short message was given in church on the twentieth anniversary. I am a charter member of this church.)

It was in 1973 when I first heard that a Christian & Missionary Alliance church was to be built in Tallahassee. I was married to Bill Ervine and we were attending a church group which became Grace Bible Church later. I was much involved with the Child Evangelism Fellowship at the time and my work took me to Quincy and Marianna, Florida.

One day while walking in the street here in Tallahassee, the pastor from Quincy stopped me to "tell me some good news!" He said, "Have you heard there is going to be a Christian Missionary Alliance church built here?" I said I had not heard; however, I was delighted to know about it because I had been a member of this denomination while living in Morristown, New Jersey. It was soon after this encounter that I found out a small group of interested people were to meet in the Northwood Mall in the basement movie hall for Sunday school and church. We later moved to the Sealey School temporarily.

I do not remember about the business side of the proceedings but it was decided by the powers that be to erect two church buildings in different areas of the city. These were to be utility-type which were large enough for young people to play ball and useful for every kind of meeting. The idea was that they would be used temporarily as worship buildings. There was plenty of space for a sanctuary to be built at such time as the congregation was able to do so.

The two buildings were funded by Le Tourneau, a Christian engineering firm. They seemed to go up quickly. My sister was here from

England when we both attended the "ground breaking" ceremony. My husband and I chose to attend the Monroe Street church.

I remember there was a lot of anticipation to start a Christian work in this city and the Word of God was faithfully preached. It was hard going; people never heard of the Alliance Church and many people still are unacquainted with us. Eventually it would be decided to amalgamate the two groups so my husband and I found our way into the Piedmont Park Alliance Church. I remember the day when we all became members but my husband refused membership status because it was not the custom for Brethren people to join a church.

After this, there was a big push by headquarters to forward the work. We were competing with a church in Lima, Peru, which was "growing in leaps and bounds." Many good speakers were brought in and weeklong meetings were held. Reverend Hoover and Reverend Mock were our pastors.

I remember I felt weary of attending so many meetings in those days. There were not too many of us to take on special duties, so as a deaconess, there was much work to be done. I used to prepare the Lord's Supper and provide flowers for the communion table. I was very bold in those days and found a number of people who grew flowers and would share with us, which was quite a saving for the church. Some of us had home Bible studies. Circumstances forced me to leave Tallahassee for two years and I lost touch while living in Ft. Walton Beach, Florida. When I returned in 1983, I found the young people had taken over the duties and it was well organized; also several of them heeded a call for missionary service.

I was indeed glad to be back in Tallahassee and I have been blessed and happy, especially since God has allowed me to see the church grow spiritually and numerically. I thank God for sending so many stalwart Christians to befriend, pray, and encourage us.

We still haven't built the main church building; perhaps God doesn't want us to spend the money in that way. I pray God will bless our present pastor and chosen leaders and keep them all in good health till He comes.

Tallahassee—City of Trees

For my friends and acquaintances and those who do not know Tallahassee, I would like to tell you it is a "City of Trees." I can do this in no better way than to quote from an article by Malcolm B. Johnson.

Old Tallahassee

. . . Where no big trees have ever been cut without a fuss, probably has more trees today than at any time since men of 150 years ago resumed clearing and plowing around long-deserted fields of original Indians.

And more kinds of trees.

Waiting for a service truck to start my stalled car, I counted nineteen kinds of wild trees in the sparse woods without stepping off the pavement . . .

There were sweet gum, black gum, wild cherry, live oak, water oak, magnolia, dogwood, hickory, loblolly pine, spruce, pine camphor, redbud, willow, wild plum, cherry, laurel, persimmon, tung and sparkeberry.

Someone has just cleared most of the small undergrowth from the shallow ravine behind the site, but leave it alone for another couple of years, and any competent naturalist would guarantee to find fifty additional varieties of trees and woody shrubs growing there. Fifty to seventy-five separate varieties to an acre is about normal for any patch of North Florida hardwood stands.

I can call off more than seventy kinds growing on two acres of our Half Hill homesite; . . . no more than fifteen of them planted there by us, and most of those brought from a few miles around.

So varied and so rich are our woodlands here in the Big Bend that we can hope for a fast revival of the native plant wonderland which once was there when we get the land reshaped. And Cascades Park replanted in the Southeast quadrant of the Florida Capital Center.

We have literally hundreds of varieties of trees and shrubs brought in from our surrounding woodlands to re-forest that area, recently recovered from the slums with the kind of flora the pioneers enjoyed for picnics a century and a half ago, an arboretum for us moderns where territorial settlers found species "new" to them.

They'll grow fast. An experienced forester riding around town with us recently agreed that perhaps no more than five percent of the trees now standing in Tallahassee were alive forty years ago!

The Sesquicentennial Committee, the previous year conducted a campaign to "find and mark" as "Patriarch Oaks" the Live Oaks which are

> more than 150 years old. The found only about 60 in Leon County. The most notable of our Live Oaks, the one under which May Parties were held in "May Oak Park, couldn't make the list! It falls some forty years short of being "old enough" to qualify as a "Patriarch."
>
> You can prove by aerial maps that Tallahassee has far more trees today than it had when they started taking systematic pictures in the early 1940s. This is understandable. Up to then, thousands of acres of land extending right into the core of present-day Tallahassee had been cleared for cultivation. Now there are streets lined with trees, and homes nestled under big trees in the landscaping of once-bare subdivisions and every vacant lot which didn't attract a homestead is grown up now with shady trees, by the birds and the winds.
>
> Even the suburban land that hasn't been developed generally is more wooded than it was a generation ago, because row crops have given way to fields of pine, planted or naturally reseeded now for agricultural income.
>
> In such areas, left to go wild, you can find a wide variety of naturalized trees which escaped from yards and farmsteads to become a part of the native woods; crape myrtle, camphor, mimosa, chinaberry, white mulberry, pecan and the like.
>
> They grow right in with the wide variety of oaks, pines, hawthornes, and viburnums that cover the hillsides, ravines and hammocks along with beeches, gums, the varied huckleberry types, and the flowering dogwoods, crab apples, tulip trees, silver bells, azaleas, and elders that paint our woods pink and white in the flowering season. Each then contributes its own color to the pageant of Fall foliage that comes about Thanksgiving time.
>
> A whole lot of these native trees from the woods have come to town over the years to decorate the yards of Tallahassee . . . maybe 75,000 or more specimens of a hundred varieties from our "public plant digs."

We had looked forward to the opening of the Senior Citizens Center in Tallahassee. The food program had been operating for sometime and it was a blessing to many people to be able to get a cooked meal in one of the five centers at midday. I used to go over to the one at Georgia Bell Dickerson Building which was the nearest for me and in walking distance. Not only meals but programs following were a regular feature. Many friendships were made through lonely people meeting together. The Old Armory was procured by the city and became the main center. The grand opening was in May 1978.

I began to attend regularly as many programs were made available to us. I met my friend Ellen there. In July she had unfortunately broken her right wrist and had to wear a cast to her elbow for many weeks. It was because of this accident that she found her way to the Old Armory for meals accompanied by her mother. Johnny Grimes befriended her and proved a great help. The outcome was that they fell in love with each other and were married in January 1979. I imagine this was the first love affair which occurred at the center.

I was able to continue oil painting classes at the center, and the teachers we had were very helpful. Ellen Grimes sold her big library to a dealer in London, and now had room for a few pictures. I was privileged to paint for her from her favorite snapshots, places she and Johnny had visited together. I also did a special one of an old gas station, long since demolished but with historical background. The small, faded picture I worked from was in sepia and white, and, when finished, the owner of the place said it was just like his "old gas station." They proudly displayed it over a newly installed wood fireplace. This picture was also chosen with others to go into the Senior Citizens Calendar for 1981. The calendar has been a feature to help raise funds and has been a means of advertising for the local business people. I enjoyed helping with this project.

The center is also open for sewing classes which I attended. I made some useful clothing which has lasted me over the years. It was a lot of fun when we had an annual fashion show, too! Other classes were ceramics, woodcraft, quilting, crocheting, and knitting—all very useful occupations. I was able to reupholster my dining room chairs, one at a time, over a period of five weeks. I also made picture frames. We were indebted to Mr. Owens for teaching us these woodwork crafts. He is a well-known and respected citizen in our midst. The center continues to be a blessing to our senior citizens.

There are other educational programs being brought into our center which are carried out by F.S.U. students including advice on diets, and remedial classes for poor readers, especially foreign seniors. Those interested in history can attend classes by Dr. Rhodes on Florida history. Another class I rather enjoyed was the speech class, similar to Toast Masters. When a leader was available, we had "Sing-A-Long" times.

This spacious building has been available to other organizations, such as Retired Federal Employees, Retired Teachers, and Disabled Veterans. The

536 Beverly Ct
Tallahassee
Fla. 32301
U.S.A.

Oct 20/78

To The Private Secretary to the Queen
Buckingham Palace
London

Dear Madam:

I am a retired naturalized Citizen of the U.S.A. and former British subject. I left England soon after the last World War at the request of an aunt who desired my company. I have always admired the Royal family, especially Her Majesty the Queen.

I have studied art since retiring from nursing and enjoy oil painting very much. My instructor wanted me to attempt a portrait of Queen Elizabeth II and with her help I have copied the photograph which was on the front page of the beautiful brochure put out for The Queen's Silver Jubilee.

If you deem it worthy I would like for you to place the subject of this letter and the enclosed photographs before her majesty.

Thanking you very much.

Respectfully yours,

Vera D. Ervine

Vera's letter to the Queen

BUCKINGHAM PALACE

27th October, 1978.

Dear Mrs Ervine.

I am commanded by The Queen to write and thank you for your letter and for the photographs of your portrait of Her Majesty which she was interested to see.

The Queen thought it was most kind of you to write to her as you did, and I am to send to you Her Majesty's sincere thanks.

Yours sincerely

Henriette Abel Smith

Lady-in-Waiting.

Mrs. Ervine,
536 Beverly Court,
Tallahassee, Fla. 32301,
U.S.A.

Response from Queen's Lady-in-waiting

American Association of Retired Persons (A.A.R.P.) monthly meetings are held there also. At the suggestion of the people in charge, we started an International Club. I was chairlady for about one year and enjoyed these meetings and made friends in this group also.

The spacious second floor is now used for art exhibits and the like. Quite recently, an elevator has been installed and apartments for the aged are being constructed on the adjacent ground. Also some inexpensive trips have been arranged to nearby places of interest. These have been enjoyed by many people. Before very long, a health clinic will be operated on a regular basis. Volunteer nurses are now working by taking blood pressure and giving advice.

The lovely old home that Bill had left me for a life inheritance was too much for me to manage. There were a lot of expenses and insufficient income; so I was trying to do as much as possible myself, such as house painting and most of the yard work. We had beautiful azaleas and camellias with years of growth on them, which I kept trimmed myself. I had to make a big decision at this time.

A few years back I had met a girl who had been raised in a foster home in Dowling Park, Florida. She attended the same church as I did and used to visit me. One day she invited me to go home with her. Her mother had remarried and now had a home in the same vicinity as Dowling Park. I was very impressed by this beautiful place which had a six-story apartment building for seniors and several villas—homes for needy children scattered over the several hundred acres of parkland. The children's accommodations were for about six or seven children plus house parents, and family-type groups. This village is on the banks of the Suwanee River and is sponsored by the Adventist Church (not Seventh Day Adventist). It probably was in 1978 that I put my name down on a waiting list to enter this retirement home. They wrote and told me another building was going to be built the same size as Dowling House to be named Carter House. It was to join the first building and so make room for a larger number of senior citizens. It was in 1981 that I heard from these people to say the place was almost ready, and to come and choose my apartment. It couldn't have been at a more opportune time, so I had to work fast. First I had to let my stepson know. He had already agreed that we could sell the house and I could have the interest on the investment made. This would continue until such time as I died.

Then I had to tell Leech, my longtime tenant who occupied my four-room apartment. He was unhappy about making a change, but it was a blessing for him as he was older than I and was needing care. Everything was done in a hurry. Fortunately, my roomer was already going away to Europe for a three-month vacation and he always carried everything he owned with him and soon found another prospective place in which to move.

The house was put on the market and as soon as the agent (a church friend) advertised, it sold the next day. I told them I had to have a month to get things ready and to move, which was reasonable and agreeable to the new owner. I took Leech with me to Dowling Park as he had also applied for residence there. They had a lovely ground floor apartment ready for him especially for handicapped people, which looked out onto the Suwanee River. How happy I was for him! Then I had my interview which was not so satisfactory. They first needed a statement of my income and then I was told that it was just over the amount for entrance, as the building was subsidized by the government and only a few apartments were available for people whose income was over a certain amount. At this time, there was not one available for me.

I couldn't believe my ears. Here I was with my house sold and no place to go. However, the Lord was very good and supplied my need in a remarkable way. I had a good friend at the Senior Citizens Center named Faith Peck who loved to travel. She owned an attractive trailer which she kept at a trailer park just outside the city. When she heard of my predicament, she offered me the use of it until I had my own place to live. I was very grateful and accepted her kind offer. Dan Coleman and other church friends were on hand to help me move, and my stepson came from Connecticut and hired the largest U-Haul van he could procure. Things we did not need were stored or given away. We had a "two garage sale." I chose the furniture I thought to be sufficient for me in a small apartment and Bill took the rest. I stored my furniture temporarily and lived in my friend's trailer which was furnished.

During this month of August before moving, I went with two other longtime friends to see about another retirement home. This was situated at Ft. Walton Beach. It had been previously discussed by us as to what each would do when ready to retire. I remember that Edie had made up her mind to go to Westwood and had put one hundred dollars down on an apartment there. Dorothy had already settled with a young family who used to be her tenants. They bought the house from her and then decided to move to a bigger one. They treated her like family and she is altogether happy with them. So these two ladies took me to Westwood to find out about this place. They were still building it and the only apartment finished was on the top floor. I fell in love with it and the view from the window, and I decided to take it. I was expecting Edie to join me so I would have a friend in this place, but she never did give up her little house in DeFuniak Springs. After six weeks time, I was told my new home was ready. This meant another change of address.

Easter 1978

It had been a long, cold winter for Florida as well as for the rest of the country, and we were looking forward to sunshine and a warm Easter, which came early this year. I had continued to attend sewing classes twice a week and was making a three-piece suit in the light pastel shades of aqua-blue. It was almost ready!

On Monday of Easter week I had an unexpected telephone call about 8 A.M. from my friend Myrtle Campbell. "How about spending Easter again with me this year?" she said. I was happy to have the opportunity to go and spend some time in the country as I had spent Easter with her the year before; it was good to have fellowship with a co-worker in the Child Evangelism Fellowship from previous working days. My friend gave me the choice of which day to go, so I suggested Thursday, the day before Good Friday. This meant some busy planning to prepare!

Tuesday, I was busy knitting booties for Karen Sue Morris to sell as Easter gifts (Karen Sue is mentally handicapped). In the afternoon, I went down to the Sunland Hospital to give these to her; however, on the way I had an accident. An elderly man moved out from his parking place and hit the rear corner of my car as I passed him, doing quite some damage. This caused me to have to spend all Wednesday morning getting estimates for repairs. He later paid the bill. I had a hurried lunch and was in the sewing class on time at 2:00 P.M. I had to arrange with my tenant to look after "Dinkey Darling," my Siamese cat, and feed the birds while I was away. Between "whiles," I found time to bake Myrtle a cake.

I eventually got away by 8:30 A.M. Thursday. I took Route 90 to get to Chumukla in North Florida. It was more pleasant to me than driving on Interstate 10. Many people along the roads were trying to get rides. I felt sorry for them so I asked the Lord to meet their needs if they were genuine. I always enjoy these little trips out on the open road. It gives me time to relax and talk with the Lord. I was able to thank God for the beautiful day He had given us, for the many signs of spring in the beauty of the trees, and for the scenery along the way.

I had been on the road for about four hours and was looking for a place to eat my lunch when I came to a place which I thought was

Blackwater Park. It was very similar but turned out to be a large area several miles square in the Blackwater Forest, the Blackwater Environmental Center. Many miles of roads had been cut through the forest and I continued on, hoping to get to the exquisite little park I had visited before. After traveling five or six miles, I came to a directional sign and took the road, as I thought it to be five miles to Route 90 again. I soon came to an open pasture on one side which was on the edge of the forest and had hardly gone a few hundred yards when down I went into a washed-out gully on the side of the road, and there I was stuck with no one around to help me.

I was in a very pleasant spot, however. The sun was still shining, so I decided to eat my lunch here. I spread out a plastic cloth on the ground; it was a bank with barbed wire fenced to keep out the cows. One of them came over to me and "moooo-ed" long and loud! As I was eating, I asked the Lord to send someone along to help me, specifically by the time I was through eating. I had almost finished when a truck came along in the opposite direction. Two young men had been to market to sell baby pigs; they had two left but had sold eighteen. Both Eddie Robinson and Douglas Carter turned out to be mechanics! Ed told me later he fixed up old cars as part of his livelihood. They were a jovial pair and said to me, "You are in some predicament!" and proceeded to see if they could move the car. After trying various ways to either lift out or drive out for about half an hour, we discovered the left wheel was not turning and was sticking out to the left. They asked for a jack which I carried with me and went back to their truck and brought a basket full of tools. They soon discovered the trouble after the car was jacked up. A small part called a "sheath" had snapped. They took the pieces off with a screwdriver and left me to go to Ed's place to get the part (it was almost seven miles away). They were back within an hour but it was the wrong size!

While they were away, I went into the forest and gathered a number of beautiful pine cones which I could use at Christmastime. They suggested I go with them at this time because they would have to go down to Crestview, which was the nearest place for an auto parts' dealer, and seventeen miles from their home. We left the car jacked up and I found myself sitting between the two lads. I had gotten to know a little more about them but now could find out more. One, Eddie, was a farmer in a small way, plus he had the auto business; the other boy had a part-time job in a pharmacy and was studying police photography in school. They left me with Ed's wife while they took off for Crestview. It seemed a long time and by the time they returned, it was well into the afternoon. Ed had picked up a doll for his baby girl who was two years old. It was one that a relative had dressed and sent for the child as an Easter present. He dropped it in the house and went off immediately into the forest to repair my car, to hoist it out of the hole, and get it back to me. How thankful I was to see these two come back and hand me the keys to get on my way. It was almost sundown and I was anxious to go! I called collect to my friends to explain my delay and settled up with the young men. They had done a lot of driving and had done a good deed. They agreed to take fifty dollars between them. The young men advised me to get an alignment done on the car, which I did on the following Monday, the day I was returning to Tallahassee. The Lord had sent them my way in time of need, and how grateful I was!

I was able to witness to these folks; being Easter time, it was easier for me to do so. Ed's young wife was only seventeen and very pretty. She was his second wife and told me she sends the other four children of the former wife to Sunday school.

My friend Myrtle had a brand new car which her husband had bought her and I did not have to use my car until I got home. It was nice to ride with her while I was there. On Good Friday morning, my friend had planned to teach a class at her church to train teachers in the methods of reaching children for Christ, so I went with her and later went out on practical work in a new housing project at Pensacola, reaching boys and girls for Jesus Christ. What a task and what rejoicing in heaven when eight of them were reached for Him; eight children made decisions that day and the church will follow up with them with correspondence courses. One little Catholic lad had only arrived the day before.

Saturday was another nice day, cool but sunny. A special treat had been arranged for us. Myrtle's friends were driving to Bellingrath Gardens in Mobile, Alabama, and we were invited. We took a picnic lunch, and, on the way back, ate our food in a picnic area where the big battleship is anchored. We did not have time to go over the big battleship as our driver had to be back, but it was a delightful day's outing.

Easter Sunday found us in the Baptist church where Myrtle is a member. The pastor was anxious to see souls saved and extended his invitation to folks in need of salvation. I observed a young mother in front of me who was in some distress. She was biting her fingernails and wanting to go forward. I felt the urge to ask her if I could go up with her and she agreed. She was gloriously saved and truly happy afterwards! She was a visitor in the church that day. The pastor said that she should now go back to Massachusetts and "be a missionary for Jesus"!

The next day, I took my car to the Ford Gentry Shop in Milton, Florida, where Myrtle had bought her car and had a long wait there to get an alignment done. I was able to talk to one of the salesmen and found out that he had sold my friend her car. It was midday when my car was ready. I paid the man and was ready to get on my way, having eaten my lunch in the showroom, saving some time this way. I went up the road for a few yards, then discovered the car was worse than when I took it in, so I took it back. The manager informed me that I had a "dent" on one wheel which was the cause of it pulling to the right, and this should be taken care of later, but it was perfectly all right to get me to Tallahassee. However, I got a few miles down the road and it got worse! I could not find a mechanic till I got to Crestview. I literally fell into the garage at the crossroads and a lady called to me and said, "Do you know you have a flat tire?" This had been my problem all along! The man in the garage had let out the air and forgot to inflate it again, I suspect. A dear old garage attendant put air into my tire, and off I went with no more real problems. I arrived in Tallahassee about 5 P.M. and was to have met some other friends for early supper, but they had already eaten. (I was glad, as I did not feel like going out again.) We did meet the next day and had brunch together, then I saw one of them off on the bus to return from her Easter vacation. I had a very eventful and exciting holiday!

Lucy Sanderson

Lucy Sanderson was a very beautiful Filipino girl—tall, dark, and intelligent, but rather strange in some respects. I came to know her through my friend Frances Hyatt who was always looking for ways to befriend others with a need.

Lucy had taken college courses in conservation and agriculture and had tried hard to get a job teaching at Florida State University, but without success. She was willing to do anything and found a position taking care of a lady in a nice section of the city. After being introduced to Lucy, I would meet her on her days off. She loved to visit stores and buy attractive things. We would eat lunch out together. The lady died and so Lucy was out of a job. She couldn't afford to rent an apartment so she bought a lightweight tent from Sears and pitched it on a piece of property, of which she was part owner, just outside the city. She was an outdoor girl, and, before she was divorced, had worked out of doors with her husband. She was not allowed to live out in the woods for long, as when neighbors discovered what she was doing, they called the police.

The next thing I knew, she was on my doorstep accompanied by Frances. Her plea was for me to take her in till she was able to get on her own.

I gave Lucy my attic apartment and she started selling Avon products. She did fairly well as a saleslady but never was able to pay for her keep. She would buy luxury things from the grocery stores with the little money she earned. I was having to be very careful myself to make ends meet at this time, and when Lucy had money to spend, she would buy plants and fertilizer and wanted me to run my car to her property about six miles each way, and I had to wait while she planted these trees and plants. I could see it was all to no avail, as there were no open spaces, but Lucy loved to do this. In time, I discovered that this dear girl was mentally ill. She told me stories about how people in the past had tried to poison her.

I tried to help Lucy all I could. She would come with me to my church sometimes, although she was of a different faith. I was glad she was willing to help me around the house; she even helped me paint my porch and she procured a whole lot of lily bulbs and planted them across the front of my house. She was quite capable in many respects and was kind enough to give me a home permanent. However, Lucy needed psychiatric care and Frances felt responsible for her, so she wrote to her brother who lived in Memphis, Tennessee, and stated the situation. He made arrangements to have his sister Lucy live with him and his family. So I bid Lucy farewell as she left me at midnight, August 31, 1977, on a Greyhound bus. She left behind her most cherished possession, a "family chart" of her ancestry. She had descended from a Filipino queen. It was written on a large piece of cardboard, and she left instructions as to what should be done with it, but this was not practical. It was too large to be accepted by the postal authorities or the U.P.S. I almost forgot about it being hidden in a closet until I was preparing to leave the house myself. I had to inform Lucy that I was packing it and sending it by the only way possible—the Greyhound Bus Lines. Greyhound accepted it for transit. I never heard if she received it safely, as it had to be picked up by her at the bus station in that city.

Our Trip to the Canadian Rockies

It is the morning of July 17, 1979. We are looking forward to a wonderful vacation and many of our friends wanted a space in our suitcases. Everything has been planned for us and, as I write, so far, the services have been super.

I am afraid a bad storm occurred the night before which caused most of us to lose sleep. We had to get up very early this first morning, and most mornings afterwards. However, we all seem in good spirits and excited about this wonderful tour. It seemed we had very little waiting between planes. We boarded our Eastern Airlines Whisper Jet at 7:00 A.M. and were served a light breakfast of sweet roll and coffee. Most of us had already eaten breakfast. My traveling companion, Clara Kobetisch, was ready when I called for her. She had called me by telephone a few minutes before 5 A.M.

We had a rest period in Atlanta and were ushered into Room 40 where they had a sign on the door, "Welcome First Baptist Church of Tallahassee." Here we were served coffee and juice. At 9 A.M. we boarded our DC-8 for Minneapolis, Minnesota. Our flying time will be two hours and fifteen minutes. At this time we are leaving the airport and our captain is talking. We are traveling at an altitude of 33,000 feet. Clear skies are predicted and, at present, the temperature in St. Paul is fifty-nine degrees. The sun is shining and we are now being served another mini-breakfast. Our captain has just told us we are now flying at an altitude of 35,000 feet and at a speed of six hundred miles per hour, which is faster than the speed of a bullet. We land at 10:45 A.M. and the temperature has gone to seventy-five degrees. Captain Raymond hopes we can ride with him again.

We are met by our tour guide immediately, and, after a brief rest, are ushered into our Greyhound bus by Mr. Erickson, who introduces Doug Neimann, our tour guide, and Mike Verbonac, our bus driver. Both prove to be nice fellows and helpful in many ways.

We travel along Highway 494, then on to Highway 94 out of Minneapolis. As we drive out into the country, we notice beautiful banks of wild thyme, and myriads of buttercups in hedgerows. The cloud formations are exceptionally beautiful here. We pass a lake with beautiful reflections. We are soon in the land of "ten thousand lakes." We pass Monticello and come into St. Cloud where we stop for lunch. We continue along many miles of farmland but no cattle are seen. The farms are beautifully kept. We pass an historic place called Lake Battle where Indians fought and divided the land. General impressions here are of lush country; clean well-kept farms; billowy clouds; patches of color and wild flowers; hunting land for deer. We come off the highway at Furgus Falls for rest, and have ice cream at a Dairy Queen. The population of this small town is 12,664. It's quite pretty here and the temperature is superb! As we drive along, the countryside is flatter. We enjoy tape-recorded songs on our way. We are now on our way to Fargo, North Dakota. They grow sugar beets and wheat along here. We leave Moorhead, Minnesota, and come to Red River Valley, one of the most fertile valleys in the North. Red River flows 545 miles into Canada. The Fargo Railway is here, too; it was named after Bill Fargo, who established the city, which has a population of 85,000. All farms are extensive with an average of 900 acres each, and there are around 49,000 farms in North Dakota. We are now going through the wheat fields. There are many more acres of sugar beets grown here also. We come to Valley City where there is a variation in the scenery. It's a very pretty place and hilly. Wells Fargo is famous for its railroad. It is known as the Sioux Indian state with a population of 623,000. It is the seventeenth largest state and the thirty-ninth state to enter the union. The Indians surrendered in 1881. This area is known as the "Bread Basket of America."

We have been climbing very gradually. A sign posted here informs us that we are 1,490 feet above sea level. From time to time along the way, we see a sign which reads, "Farmers, we can't live on peanuts!" (Jimmy Carter was president at this time, as you will remember.)

We come into Jamestown about 7 P.M. This has been a very long day of travel for us. We have dinner here, and then have a grand evening on the bus singing sacred songs and listening to tapes recorded by David Humphries. We watch a glorious sunset at 9:30 P.M. It is still daylight and we are coming into Bismarck, North Dakota. This place is named after a German general and is the capital city of North Dakota. The farms average 12,000 acres here in the "Wheat Belt." The population in Bismarck is 38,000. It is another clean, typical farming city. The Missouri River runs through here. It is about 2,315 miles long.

We start off very early for our second day. We are on the bus by 7 A.M. It is very bright and sunny and the scenery is changing. Mountains are showing in the distance, and it is hilly in places.

Our guide tells us that seventy-eight million barrels of wheat are produced in this area every year. There is also a good grazing area for cows. It is a beautiful, cloudless day. We make a rest stop at Belfield. We are traveling on to I-94. We come to Theodore Roosevelt National Park and stop to view the canyon. There is an area called the "Badlands" along here; in fact, the highest point is 3,400 feet above sea level. There is also a school for boys called "The Home on the Range." We greet the sign on the road, "Welcome to Montana." This is the "Treasure State." Montana means mountainous. It is 14,700 feet above sea level here. We come into Glendive for lunch. We continue along hilly land with cattle grazing here and there. Trees are scarce; the few we see are low ones like Chinese elm and Russian olive. We have a rest stop at Jordan. This is a mining town with a population of five hundred. The main street consists of a dirt road. The shop people are glad to see a few more customers come into their town. The temperature is ninety degrees—the hottest this year, the store owners say. After leaving Jordan, we see an oasis of lovely pines, and, as we get further along, more pines on the slopes of the hills. We are gradually getting higher and the Judith Mountains are in view. We are now approaching Lewistown. We just saw our first vegetable garden. Our ears are "popping" due to the altitude. We have made a stop in Lewistown and gone on the Lewis and Clark Trail. The mountains are surrounding us now. We come into Great Falls. It has a total population of 60,000. This town is noted for its schools for the deaf and blind, and also its Air Force base. We check in at the Holiday Inn. It is a beautiful, modern hotel. We are getting excited now as we are in Montana. Great Falls is a lovely, clean city. We can look over the city from our hotel rooms.

Thursday, July 19. We cross the Missouri River onto I-90, crossing the Sun River, and turn off for Glacier Park. We note a lot of yellow clover as we travel between the foothills, and see many pretty mountain streams. Our guide told us we have nineteen hours of daylight today. We notice a lot of contour or strip farming in this area. We come to Versfield Village, 3,900 feet high. Chateau, Montana, is in the news today. Someone found dinosaur eggs there!

We are now entering the Blackfoot Reservation, which consists of two million acres known as "the land of the bad Indians," population 6000. Snowcapped mountains are in view. We cross Badgers Creek and Two Medicine River, arriving in Browning, which has a population of 2,700. There is a big Indian museum here. This is the "Gateway to Glacier Park." We cross Two Medicine River again and enter East Glacier Park. The park lodge was built in 1910 and is situated on Two Medicine Lake. This is where we lodge, and the most fortunate ones manage to get a beautiful view of the lake and mountains beyond. We are served a gorgeous luncheon after which we check into our rooms. We have the eastern side, which was built later. It is clean and comfortable, with a large, luxurious lobby. We shall never forget the beautiful gardens in front of the lodge. There are herbaceous borders leading to a small railway station. I saw three gardeners working in these gardens. We go for a trip into the park, cross Two Medicine Lake, land on the other side, and enjoy a wooded area. We find numerous wild flowers growing there: wild columbine, sweet yellow clover, lupines, Jacob's Ladder, Indian paintbrush, pyrola (one-sided yellow flower), and double-sided pyrola with pink blossoms.

The park keeper told us the names of these flowers. Some others were fleabane, aster, cow parsnip, and yellow arnica. The keeper said there were as many as one thousand different species in the park. We have an enjoyable time that evening at the lodge—good food, and a folk dance arranged by the staff after dinner.

Friday, July 20. All meals were provided by the lodge. After breakfast we board our motor coach. Today's tour takes us to West Glacier. We come to the largest reservoir in the area. We see the railway on the sides of the mountains, which are trestled to protect the trains. We pass along the Continental Divide. We stop at the memorial and take pictures. We go through Moriah's Pass and see the "Silver Staircase" waterfall.

We are now in the "Flathead" National Forest, named after a man of that name. The Indians here used to have "war dances" and would scalp their victims and steal horses and women! We crossed the railroad and came back into the park. We meet a lovely Christian boy here at a picturesque place called "Walton Goat Lake." We do not see any lake here though. The boy is on his way to Hungry Horse. We cross the Flathead River and pass the Amtrak Train and come to some rapids. A warning sign reads "Keep to the tongue of the rapid." We come to a little place called Belton and have lunch at McDonald's Lake Lodge, after which we take a scenic tour in small coaches. This tour takes us around the lake, around the mountains, and onto the "Going to the Sun Road"; also through Logan Pass and Lunch Creek. Then we see the "Weeping Wall." Our guide tells us many things about the places we visit. We see some beautiful mountain flowers, some growing in patches.

Our guide explains how a glacier is formed. The snow gets packed down and causes ice to form; it melts from underneath and forms waterfalls. We see spaces between the pine trees where the avalanches of snow have fallen, destroying the trees in their wake.

We come to a pretty spot at St. Mary's Lake called Sun Point, from where Wild Goose Island can be seen. It is supposed to be the most photographed spot in the Rockies. We see a mountain sheep here. We stay at the Many Glacier Hotel, which is situated on a lake with the most beautiful vista. They have 380 guests overnight, including eight tour groups. One of the mountains nearby was considered to be a very sacred mountain.

Saturday, July 21. We are soon about to cross into Canada. At 10 A.M. we see the sign, "Welcome to Alberta, Canada." The population of Canada is about nineteen million, with one percent Indian population. We cross the Belly River and come into Waterton Glacier International Park. We arrive in the small town of Waterton. We browse around and do some shopping here. We are amused to see some of the local people going up and down Main Street on tricycle-type vehicles which have sunshades over them. This little town is on a peninsula, as we found out looking down on it from the Prince of Wales Hotel, where we had lunch. There was an excellent meal served by waiters and waitresses in traditional dress. Again, the hotel looked down on a lake with mountains in the distance. After lunch we pass through the Blood Indian Reserve, then cross "Old Man River." After this, we go through many miles of wheat lands. They have big granaries where farmers pool their wheat.

We are now on our way to Calgary, which is 150 square miles. There are 25,000 Americans living here and the population is half a million. It is the largest city in Alberta. We arrive at 4:30 P.M. and have a rest stop at McDonald's. We cross the Elbow River. I see the First Alliance Church along the way. It is a very beautiful structure. We are now on the Glenmore Trail after which we get onto the Bow Trail, which is 4,860 miles long, the world's longest highway. It goes through the length of Canada. The Banff Mountains are coming into view now and then. We see fire on the mountains in the distance. We note the price of gasoline is 16.9 per liter. We see the North Pigeon Mountain and continue along Cline Highway. The mountains are all around us again; they are jagged and Alpine type. We see snow in the left side of the mountains. We are soon in the Banff National Park. This park has two resort areas: Banff and Louise. The area used to cover 10 square miles but now it is 2,564 square miles. We cross the Cascade River and come to the Banff Inn where we are to stay.

Sunday, July 22. We are to stay here for two nights and have to arrange to get all our meals out and there are a number of places to get food. Clara and I took a long walk up the main street last evening and found a store in good time to buy food so we could eat breakfast in our room. This is a very homey place—an electric kettle was supplied and packaged coffee. The only thing we find not so good is the fact that there is no elevator and we are on the third floor! Also, no air-conditioning. It is rarely needed here, but this is their warmest summer in twenty years. It is arranged for us to go to the Community Protestant Church for the morning service. It is very nice and almost the whole congregation is visitors. After church, we go to some place to eat and then take a tour in the afternoon. We first go through a paddock where the wild buffalo are. They are grazing at the foot of the mountain with their two young kids. Bear marks are pointed out to us on the trees. They each have their own territories, we're told.

The next interesting thing we see are some ground squirrels. They have holes in which they live and have burrowed. I must say here that no one is allowed to feed any wild animal in any of the parks. These animals look like rats with short tails and have a tunnel system underground. We view Mount Rundle, which is 7000 feet high. Most of these mountains are 9000 to 10,000 feet high. After this we see Cascade Mountain. We are told to look out for bears. There are two kinds—black bears, which can vary in color but are all called "black" bears, and grizzly bears. We see only one on our trip. We come across some rock formations under a mountain, one of which looks like a bear.

There are many different mountains to be seen. Some are glaciers. Our guide explains again how a glacier is formed. After the snow packs down, it forms ice. It keeps moving and leaves behind rocks and sediment. The rocks "powder," and as they dissolve from underneath, they then carry with them the blue rock which gives the lakes the beautiful aqua-blue color. In the afternoon, we ride around the mountains and look down onto Banff. We see the university in the mountains, consisting mainly of small huts in which the students practice playing flute and other pipe instruments. All the arts are taught here.

We look down on a hotel in the mountains, a castle-like structure built in 1928. It was twice burned out so they rebuilt it out of rocks. Rooms range in price from $56 all the way up to $3000 per night. The hotel has 600 rooms with a capacity of over 1000 guests per night. Banff came into being after the discovery of hot springs nearby. These are from 5000 to 7000 feet up the side of Sulphur Mountain. We see a grand waterfall and the entrance to Upper Hot Springs. The gondolas take us to the top of Sulphur Mountain. Many buses are in the parking lot and everyone who goes up in the gondolas has to line up to do so. We see wild mountain sheep at the top of this mountain. We take pictures of the view and line up to get back. When we are all together, we go on to the next place of interest—the "big hotel" I spoke about. This time we pass close by and see the pretty flower gardens around it. We can see it is close into town, but from the higher level, it appears to be in the middle of a wooded area. We see some matted golden squirrels where they are living in the rocks.

Monday, July 23. It seems a little cooler today. There are rain clouds over the mountains. We start out at 9 A.M. and stay in Banff for an hour. Some do some shopping. We say goodbye to Banff and make our way out into the mountains again. We see the very majestic mountain called Mt. Eisenhower, which once was called "Castle Mountain." We turn onto the Icefields Parkway. We notice more snow on the mountains now as we are climbing higher all the time. We see lots of wild flowers on the roadside, and the mountains are more pointed along here. We make a stop at Bow

Lake. We cross "Mosquito Creek" and continue on between the mountains. We are now approaching the icefields. Our guide informs us that we are in the middle of the blooming season. We stop to take pictures at Cowfoot, Bow Lake, and Bow Glaciers, which are at least five hundred feet thick! Later on we have another rest stop at a little red chalet. We take pictures also by Waterfowl Lake. Then we are on our way again. We cross the Saskatchewan River, which flows into the Hudson Bay. After a very long ride through the mountains, we reach the Columbia Icefields. It is now 1:30 P.M. and an excellent lunch awaits us at the chalet. This is the largest ice field this side of the Arctic Circle. After a very substantial lunch, we take the shuttle buses to the ice field, then on to the snowmobiles. It is a sunny and cloudless day. We have donned our coats in case it is chilly. We are told the ice is 120 feet thick here and 3000 feet thick out on the icefields. It has formed a basin between the mountains. They told us it is moving 120 feet every year, and 2 1/4 inches every day. It loses 30 feet every year. We take a two-mile ride out on the icefield and are actually riding on a glacier!

They have a different road each year for traveling over the icefields. The road on which we traveled at the entrance is at a 40-degree angle—the steepest passenger road in North America, we're told! Our guide told us to shut our eyes if we are scared. We are on our way again. We see an icecap about 359 feet thick, and Mt. Kitchener, which is 11,450 feet high. The water which flows from the glaciers falls in two different directions: one side flows into the Pacific Ocean and one side flows into the Atlantic. We proceed through the Athabasca Valley. Pines and aspen trees are seen along here. The elk eat off the bark of the aspen trees for emergency food in the winter. We pass Athabasca Falls. There is great excitement in the bus—we have seen a black bear! They are very unpredictable and so are dangerous. We are coming into Jasper National Forest and Trading Post. We turn east onto the Yellowstone Highway. Jasper has a population of 2000 and Hinton has a population of 4000. More excitement as we just saw a pack of mountain goats. Also, Lake Jasper is on the left. A train is moving on the other side of the lake. We pass another lake on the right side of the road. Black clouds bring a few rain drops. We have been in two national parks all day and we are now passing out at 6:45 P.M.

We arrive in Hinton, Alberta, in the late afternoon, and put up at the Travel Lodge. I am determined to get a swim during my vacation, so I do just that here! The water is cold and I am the only one who ventured out.

Tuesday, July 24. We are up early and have breakfast in our rooms. We start at 7:45 A.M. after a very disturbed night. Weather is cool and cloudy today. We have devotions on the bus and retrace our journey for some distance. By 8:30, the sun is shining brightly. We are on our way to Lake Maligne (pronounced "Maleen"). We see a pretty sight: a mountain behind a range with the sun on it and a white cloud like smoke at the top! We see a deer and a robin. At a beautiful lake, we see "garbage cans" hanging up. Venison Lake has no natural outlets, it's like a huge sink. It is known as Jaspers Disappearing Lake. Here we see a huge mule deer and more snow on the mountains. We are to take a ride on Maligne Lake. The temperature is thirty-eight degrees in the lake. The Indians were the first people to inhabit this area. They trapped beaver and other animals. Rainbow trout can be found in this lake. We can see it snowing on the mountains again. There is a U-shaped valley formed by the glaciers. Thousands of years ago, these glaciers drained into the lake. There are seven glaciers that feed the lake. Underground streams also feed the lake, which is 350 feet deep.

We board our launch for one of the most beautiful trips of the whole journey. We travel to the end of Maligne Lake. We land on a pretty wooded area where we take pictures. We board our boat again after about half an hour and continue to our starting point. Maligne Glacier, which we viewed closely, is three hundred feet thick and is moving. Charleston Glacier is six hundred feet thick in its main body. The guide told us it takes three hundred feet of snow to produce one inch of ice. The main ingredients of the Maligne range are limestone and shell. The Bow Hills are rounded. It is said they are two hundred million years old. We see great boulders which have been brought down by the glaciers. We move into Jasper Park again. We enjoy our cruise very much, and our guide has told us many interesting things. We go on till we come to Jasper Park Lodge, where a delicious luncheon awaits us. It is within a magnificent park. The luncheon was served English-style in a luxurious setting. There are beautiful arts and crafts exhibited by the local people. We return to the Travel Lodge at Hinton. This is a poor-looking place and a contrast to the scenery we have seen; we spend the evening writing postcards and taking a walk in the area.

Wednesday, July 25. We start off early again today at 7:30 A.M. It is foggy as we leave Hinton, but it soon lifts and the sun shines through. This is to be another special day. We are on our way to beautiful Lake Louise. We have had to retrace our journey back through the mountains and branch off from Iceland Highway for Lake Louise. There is some excitement on the bus when we see a whole herd of deer. As we continue, we see an elk grazing on the side of the road. The mountains along here are very majestic. Mt. Edith Cavell is in this range. It is 11,100 feet high.

We turn off to visit Athabasca Falls. This is a glorious sight! Unfortunately, my snapshot does not do it justice. The falls are fed by a large number of mountains in the area. We are coming back to the Columbia Icefields and have just seen Mt. Kitchener, at 11,400 feet high, and also Angle Falls on Canada 93. We make a rest stop at the foot of the icefield. We notice plaques warning people of the falling ice and moraine. Another plaque says it is likely to rain or snow any day during winter or summer. As we proceed, we climb to an elevation of 6,675 feet. We say goodbye to the Columbia Icefields.

Our guide tells us more about the glaciers. Some are seven hundred feet thick! We are now leaving Jasper National Park and enter Banff National Park again. We come to a place in the mountains where the waters divide north and south. We pass the "Weeping Wall," which is a huge mountain straight up and down; see the Smoke Stack and Castette next to it. The Saskatchewan River now flows east. A big rock is pointed out to us which looks like an Egyptian mummy. A peak called "House Peak" holds the clouds in place. It is 10,973 feet high; Waterfowl Lake is at the foot of it. We see Astaire Mountain, which is 10,100 feet, and a small icefield called Wapta. We come to Bow Summit which is 6,785 feet high. Bow Lake is where we have previously made a rest stop. The water is very blue here; it has a tourists' "coffee house." It is the headwaters of Bow Summit. We see the Crow's Foot Glacier with one foot broken off. We see a cow moose above Lake Louise. We arrive here for lunch at 12:30 P.M. We are told to be on the bus again by 2:30, so we have two hours at this enchanting place. We are served a marvelous lunch "buffet style." Let me make your mouth water: the desserts are especially delicious! There are raspberry and mixed fruit gateaux, cheese cakes, fruit Jello, fruit flans, pies, and fresh fruit to go. The great dining hall is resplendent with chandeliers and beautiful furniture with large windows overlooking the lake and mountains. After lunch, we are free to go around and see the rest of the place. My friend and I choose to go outside to view the lake and mountains. There are lovely gardens laid out and all kinds of beautiful flowers to see, also an excellent band is playing on the lawn. We take some pictures and enjoy the panoramic view. The time passes all too quickly! We hear the sad news before leaving that a grizzly bear has had to be shot in the vicinity. It was too bad as they are few and far between. (Of course, it was in the interest of the public that this one had to be shot.)

We are on our way again and have just passed Paradise Creek and now going to Lake Morraine. This has a beauty of its very own. We have a closer view of the mountains and the lake has a solemn stillness and lovely reflections. Our stay here is short but very worthwhile. After this, we make our way to Calgary where we are to stay for the night. Calgary is noted for its rodeo and annual stampede. It has the world's biggest race; this year, odds are $90,000. We have just missed it, not that any of our group would have gone! The city boasts a tower for observation which is six hundred feet high. We stay at the Sheraton Hotel and are very close to the tower, so some of us go out after settling into our rooms. The tower has a revolving restaurant and circles the landscape as one eats. The rooms in our hotel are very comfortable. We have a good night's rest and enjoy a little balcony with each room.

Thursday, July 26. We have left the mountains behind, although on a very clear day, they can be seen from the Observatory Tower. We start out at 8 A.M., leave the city behind and are out on the plains. We have devotions on the bus, and then some of the folks tell stories and keep us interested. It is another clear, sunny day. The air is very dry and the daylight lasts a long time in this area. We have a rest stop at Brookstown, population 8000. It is clean and neat, and we enjoy coffee here. They have an area roped off for the youth who are going to have cycling races. They are able to practice here for the Olympics.

They raise beef cattle and have a few oil wells here. It is flat country and the Bow River Pipeline is here also. Our guide said they have rich oil fields. We saw many pumps working as we proceeded along the highway. We just saw a herd of antelope. Also, we saw a tree—they are almost nonexistent here! The first natural gas was started here. This is desert or scrubland. A few cattle are seen and there are trucks for well stimulation. A train is moving across the prairie. We arrived at Medicine Hat, on a river located in one of the world's largest natural gas locations. The name of the city was derived from a medicine man who lost his hat in the river. It is a thriving city with several industries, including tiles, cement, and gas refinery. They raise plants and flowers here, too. The population is 33,000. The city is situated on the Saskatchewan River. We have our lunch here and the waitresses seem to have difficulty coping with a large party. We are now in the province of Saskatchewan, the second largest province in Canada. They grow grain here and it is known as Canada's "bread basket." They raise cattle also. It is a historical place—they had a big massacre amongst the Indians in the nineteenth century. We come to a place called "Swift Current" and have a rest stop. The population here is 15,000.

There is more oil drilling here and beef processing. Two-thirds of Canada's wheat is grown here, as well as flax, rye, beef, and milk. We come to Chaplin Lake, a natural reservoir. Moose Jaw is another city we visit with a population of 31,000. Here was North America's space for its largest air show, along with storage space for 5.5 million bushels of wheat. Potash is mined and processed here, too.

We are coming into Regina, the Queen City of the Plains, which has a population of about 140,000. Mostly British people live here, but Indians originally. This city has over 250 industrial plants and import oil refineries. There were 1,600 acres applied to government legislature. Thirty-four types of marble are used in the main building, which is mostly of a yellow stone. A beautiful lake is next to this building. There is a Museum of Natural History and many other interesting and lovely buildings. We arrive at Regina Inn at 6:30 P.M. This is a very nice hotel. Clara and I order our supper in our room and are pleasantly surprised that it does not cost us anymore.

Friday, July 27. We start out early at 7:30 A.M. We are soon on the plains again and take a last look at Canada. We stop at a shopping mall and spend our Canadian money, or get it changed. I buy a leather purse for $3.66 plus tax, which is five cents on the dollar. The grocery store lets me have a banana for 17 cents, which is really 24 cents to use up my Canadian money.

We cross over into the U.S. into North Dakota. We sing songs along the way and Louise Burnette entertains us by reciting a poem she has written. We have a luncheon stop in Minot. The countryside has more trees and waterways now. The cloud formations are very beautiful; wheat and corn are growing along the way. We come to Devil's Lake. The story goes that two bands of Indians fought a battle. The side that won got caught in a storm on the lake and perished! We see fields of sunflowers growing. A good shower of rain comes along the way, the first on the trip, I believe. We cross the river Turtle. Then we come to Grand Forks Air Base and later to the Holiday Inn where a farewell dinner is provided. We enjoy a wonderful meal and make presentations to our driver and guide.

Saturday, July 28. We depart from the Holiday Inn at 7:30 A.M., having devotions on the bus. We pass through the Red River Valley where sugar beets are growing. Last year this was a flooded area. We have been having a few speeches on the bus showing appreciation for different ones. We turn off to the Hector Airport where we leave Mrs. Folsom, and have a rest stop here. We see a field of sheep, the first we've seen on our trip. We cross the Red River into Minnesota. We are back on Route 94 again. Nell Locke entertains us with a poem she has made up about our trip. It is very good. Her husband Red tells us stories and reads a poem.

He leads in singing "Edelweiss," "Bye-Bye Blackbird," and "Singing in the Rain." Louise renders more of her elocution. We are now at the airport where we say goodbye to Clara, where she is staying with her cousin for a few weeks. Our guide and driver see us into the airport where we await our plane. We say goodbye to them and are soon on our way by air to Tallahassee. Our captain has just reported we are flying at 20,000 feet and rising to 29,000 feet. It is a good flying day with fluffy clouds around us. Our stewardess is beginning to serve dinner. We boarded the plane at 3:45 P.M., and now move our watches forward one hour.

There is excitement at Tallahassee when some friends of Jay bring the two children to meet Mommy and Daddy. We are also met by the church bus and we're home at last after a wonderful vacation. We look forward to the next good time together!

Our Trip to Europe

Wednesday, June 25, 1980. Today is a full day of travel. Ethel Brown and I are roommates on a trip with a guide and three hostesses to cover several countries. We have to be up very early to get to Valdosta to meet our party. Fortunately for us, Ernest Mitts, a relative of Ethel, offers to take us there. It turns out to be a wet morning and the rain follows us over to Europe. However, we are comfortable in his Oldsmobile.

After meeting the rest of our party, we ride the church bus with Art and Carol Harris to Jacksonville International Airport. We have some time to wait and have an early lunch in the airport. This helps us feel better, as we have had an early breakfast. There is very little waiting after this and with clearing weather, Flight 156 is soon en route to Kennedy Airport. The flight is perfect—no bumps. We are served a snack at about 5 P.M.—soup, sandwiches, and orange cake, plus a drink. We anticipate a long, drawn-out wait on our next trip via Royal Jordanian, as our overnight flight is not until 11:30 P.M. However, time passes quickly. Before leaving, we take walks to different parts of the Kennedy Airport and watch people of many nationalities. We met a mother with three little children. The oldest is eight and going to India. Also met and spoke with a lonely looking Nigerian who needed help and encouragement. We saw a party of Armenians, the men wearing black suits, hats and beards. The time grows nearer for boarding; we meet up with other groups who are to join our tour, bringing the total to fifty-three in all. We board the Prince Ali of the Royal Jordanian Airlines and are surprised to find it almost full. It has come in from Texas and the rest of our tour group is already on the plane coming from Houston. We rest as best we can and some are able to sleep while others cannot. A late supper and breakfast are served. When we alight at Vienna, we note what a grand plane she has been—a Boeing 747. We are met by our host and driver with a luxurious bus, very nice indeed. We find out later that it was the only one of its kind made in Linz, Austria, fitted with a TV for the driver and guide and with an intercom system. They are downstairs and we are upstairs.

We are taken to our hotel, the Prinz Eugen, which turns out to be a very special place. We all take an afternoon nap and dress for seven o'clock dinner, which consists of six courses with first-class service. In the evening, we go to a musical held on the grounds of a beautiful building called Wiener Waltzer. The evening is perfect for an out-of-door performance. The professional players are in a big bandstand. They only play waltz music. There are two professional couples who dance. The public is invited to join in dancing later. It is well attended by the public. After the performance, we leave to go back and Ethel and I get on the wrong bus. We almost go off with another American tour party.

The next day we do a tour of beautiful Vienna. We see a big city park with English gardens; a monument to Johann Strauss; a famous opera house in the process of being cleaned; the palace park and monument to Mozart; the St. Stephens Hotel; two state museums; a palace; and the rose-colored Parliament buildings. The city hall has a magnificent spire three hundred feet high and a coffee house. The university was founded in the year 1365 and is the second largest German-speaking university in Europe. Some of our party goes in to view the noted white horses at the Spanish Riding School, which is over four hundred years old. The horses are born black, and, at four years of age, they change color. They keep one "black horse" for good luck. In 1945, a Texan came to train the horses and continues to do so. All of the horses come from Florida. They are not scheduled to perform, so Ethel and I go to explore other places. We go through a big archway into the Imperial Apartments where we have a picture taken of us with coach and horses. We pass through a fruit and flower market where we can see Vienna Woods in the distance. Some of our party takes a tour of the woods in the rain. It has a large underground lake, six hundred meters long. Vienna was founded two thousand years ago. Prince Joseph was the ruler for many years. Maria Theresa, his wife, continued to rule after his death in 1916. The palace is now used as a "school for diplomats." In 1857, Prince Joseph tore down the city wall and erected a large and beautiful highway. The city has good transportation with double and triple tram rails on one side of the street. We see

St. Charles Gothic Church near the center. A Russian memorial stands, which the people had to keep in order to get back their freedom.

An afternoon tour takes us to Schonbrum Summer Palace. The first floor is a museum and the second floor is rented to and kept by city officials. Its rooms are very beautiful with decorations of gold leaf and gorgeous Bohemian chandeliers. There are ornate porcelain wood-burning stoves in each room, a billiard room, a reception room for officials, a day room with beautiful ornaments, and the small bedroom of Joseph and his wife. Maria Theresa had sixteen children. Many lovely paintings of the family are on display. A picture of Napoleon's only child, who died at age twenty-one, is shown with his little friend, a bird. The Chinese Room has blue and white ornaments and parquet floor. Another room is full of beautiful mirrors. Maria Theresa did most of the ruling. Her husband was a sportsman and had no political interests. The view from the palace terrace is beautiful. We take pictures of the famous Glorietta Gardens of the palace.

Saturday, June 28. Breakfast of hard rolls, butter, cream cheese, and wiener paste is good. We spend the morning on foot. We also visit St. Stephens Cathedral and St. Joseph's Church, along with the shopping plaza, going by subway and returning by tram car. Continuing our tour, we leave at midday on our luxury bus for Linz, Austria. It is lovely scenery as we go along. We see buttercups, daisies, and other wild flowers which grow in a cooler climate. En route, we stop at a busy restaurant and have lunch. I pay sixteen schillings for soup. We then head for Melk, where there is a famous monastery.

Our guide plays some famous Strauss music. We particularly enjoy the beautiful "Edelweiss." We visit the monastery, a beautiful edifice on the river Danube surrounded by lovely rolling hills. We arrive at our hotel in Linz about 5:30 P.M., the Hotel Turotel, and after refreshing ourselves, report to the Strauss Dining Room for dinner. We sleep well in our feather beds and are up at 6:45 A.M. This city appears to be old in part, modern in part, and prosperous. The houses seem to be the same white-washed pattern with red, sloping roofs.

Sunday, June 29. As we continue our travels today, we see lovely farmlands, hilly and lush meadows, and the distant Austrian Alps with traces of snow on them. Arriving at Salzburg, we visit the home of Mozart, now a museum. It is most interesting and full of small dioramas of his musical works. Traveling on, we come to the place where *The Sound of Music* was produced, set on a lakeside. A castle rises behind it on a hill, the home of the Von Trapps. We stop to take pictures of this beautiful place.

Time for lunch. We go back to Salzburg. The river runs through the town—a pretty place with surrounding hills. We move on our way to Mirable Gardens, but it is too late to visit them and it is raining. On to Munich. We arrive at the Holiday Inn, where we are to stay for two nights. It is a large place with three entrances on the front. Dinner is good. Up early the next morning, there is some confusion as to which dining room we are supposed to use. Many people are served here on vacation like us. The food turns out to be good and plentiful. By 9 A.M. we are on our way to see Munich. It has a population of 1.3 million, with 35 percent young people. It has the fourth largest university in Europe, with 70,000 students. The university library has four million books. Munich is fast growing. The center is where all the banks are and a plaza where people stroll. We come to a church which is of Italian style, built by Italian settlers in 1663 and called the Church of Court Gardens. The front of it was demolished in the war and restored fifty years later. It has an ornate pulpit made of ebony. We take a walk in the Odeon Platz and banking areas, where we exchange some of our money. Back to the bus, we continue our ride, passing the Olympic Village. An English garden crosses over the city. There are many and various buildings to be seen: a Bavarian museum, a monument with an Angel of Peace, a fancy shopping center, the National Theatre, and Rabitan.

All valuable exhibits were taken out of the museums and stored during the war. The main post office was attractive with red and white murals across the top. There is a tremendous technical museum with 313 towers, a covered swimming pool, and a big marketplace. On the outskirts of the city is a summer palace of the Bavarian monarchs, with a collection of porcelain in old patterns, and a hunting lodge. The Olympic Village was built in 1936 and has 182,000 squares of glass over an area of 950,000 square feet. It is now used as condominium apartments. We have no time to visit these, so we return to the hotel for lunch. Some ladies have a converter for the coffee plug, so we have lunch in our room. I must mention here that a cup of coffee outside costs between two and three dollars per cup. We have the afternoon free, so some of the ladies and I decide to go back to visit around the Summer Palace by tram car.

The Summer Palace of Ludwig II is luxurious! One room is elaborate, with raised pilaster ornaments in silver and blue with beautiful Bavarian chandeliers; another room, a bedroom, is in yellow; and another has lovely wallpaper with pheasants and trees on it. The entrance room intrigues us, as there are rounded holes near the floor. We find out that this is the kennel room, right in the lodge. I fall in love with the kitchen.

It has Dutch tiles in blue and white from floor to ceiling, with scattered strips of pink. Some of the tiles were designed as vases of flowers.

We finish our day with a nice dinner at the hotel, and are invited into the conference room, where we are given instructions about our trip to the "Passion Play," and we receive some sad news. One of the hosts, the pastor of East Hill Baptist Church, has received news that his mother has died and already been buried (it was her will not to be embalmed). Pastor Robinson has been sick one day during the tour, so it was unfortunate circumstances.

Tuesday, July 1. Have had another good night's sleep, followed with a good breakfast. The weather is brighter and warmer. At 10:30 A.M., we take off and are soon in the country again. Our first stop is Dachau, the big concentration camp. It has been reconstructed in part. Another set of buildings is a museum of the Nazi atrocities of 1940. Our guide has met a lawyer who told him the story of Hitler. You may have heard it, but I had not. Hitler had hypnotic power, his voice carrying him. He developed wonderful highways throughout Germany, as well as new industries. He closed the value of the mark and instituted one-course meals for economy. The German people consider him a great man still. They say that Hitler slaughtered hundreds of men, women, and children. There is a monument at Dachau—which means "House of No Mercy"—which states "Never Again." It is thought that Hitler was Jewish and that his motive for slaughtering the Jews was to cause a blood bath in order to open up Israel as a nation for the Jews.

We're on our way again, and come to a low "overhead bridge" which our driver cannot get the bus underneath. This makes it necessary for us to return to Munich and take the main Autobahn Highway. We found ourselves viewing beautiful country with lush meadows and rising into the mountains. We were two thousand feet above sea level. Our guide told us about the Alpine cows at Oberau. They graze on the mountains during the summer and the cow that reaches the highest point is given a bunch of growing flowers to wear on her head. She becomes the cows' leader and the others look to her as such. We are now riding high in the mountains, which are covered with trees of different kinds. We have come to Ettal with its famous Benedictine Monastery for training boys. The village is extremely picturesque with pretty murals on the sides of the houses. One has the story of Red Riding Hood in pictures on the sidewalls.

We have a delightful lunch at the cafe in Ettal, visit the church there, and find it very ornate and elaborate. We board the bus and arrive at the inn at Wurmansau where we are scheduled to have supper. From here, we are assigned our lodgings in the homes of the villagers and are met by our hostesses with their carry trucks for our luggage. There is a slight drizzle of rain and the weather has turned cold. This is a pretty village. Ethel and I found ourselves in the home of one of these dear people. It is a farm house with an attached barn. The lady is very pleasant, but cannot speak a word of English. We find our lodgings comfy and attractive. She houses six people in all. After settling in, we make our way back to the Village Inn for supper of soup, roast pork and vegetables, stuffing balls and beans, and apple strudel. We retire early and sleep under the eider-down. We have explored our immediate surroundings beforehand and found an abundance of wild flowers, and a tiny church near our house.

Wednesday, July 2. We have slept well, had the usual breakfast of crusty rolls, batter, and cheese, and boarded our bus. Our driver takes us along to Oberammergau for the long-awaited "Passion Play." It is situated about four and a half miles from where we are staying in a beautiful, mountainous country. Thousands of people are already waiting to go into the theater. We have excellent seats near the front. It is very cold, but the rain keeps off during the first part of the play. Of course, the play is very moving and rendered in German. However, the script is obtainable in English and we are able to follow it very well. It started at 9 A.M. and the first part finished at 11:30 A.M. I lose my party after the performance and they go off for a special dinner at some location unknown to me. I drag around in the rain alone and find a small cafe to eat a light lunch. A cup of soup and a slice of dry toast costs 4 marks, about $2.50 in our money. We all meet again at the theater for the second part of the play. While waiting around, I meet an elderly couple who has come from Wales. They are celebrating their thirtieth wedding anniversary. They seem happy to meet me since I know some of the places they have been. They say this trip has cost them five hundred pounds. The rain continues at intervals but keeps off for the performance, which is an answer to prayer. We enjoy the play immensely. After it is over, we all meet in the Lutheran church where someone is playing the organ. We board our bus when it arrives, and are on our way back to our little homes in Wurmansau.

Thursday, July 3. We pass through Garmasch, a place for winter sports, the highest peak in the range seen from here. It is another cold, dull, wet day, making it impossible to see much of the beautiful scenery. Low clouds and rain obscure the view. The highest peak is five thousand feet. On the longest day in the year, the children climb to the top and light bonfires. Last year it was a washout, they told us. We steadily climb higher into the mountains, which are covered with fir trees here. We reach the Austrian border again at 8 A.M., going back to the village where we stayed two nights earlier. The people there own a few cows each, and, early in the morning, we can hear the farmer taking them up the mountainside to graze. If you meet any cows on the road, they have the right-of-way. Now, three thousand feet above sea level, we enjoy seeing the mountain lakes as we are driving down the hill to Nazareth, Austria. We are making hairpin curves. The dark skies and green trees give a turquoise color to the lakes. This is a pretty village and a holiday resort. People "let" rooms to visitors. There is a grazing area for cattle here. We can view the snowcapped mountains now. We come to the Valley of the Inn. "Innisbrook" means "The Bridge Over the River Inn." We next come to the Village of Landeck where we see a ski lift. Saying goodbye to the end of that range, we pass the highest bridge in Austria; we see a small castle, and from time to time, we see a small grotto, a place for Catholics. Our guide told us about the watchmakers, the chief industry in Switzerland. They make precision parts for the various instruments, and they are put together in other countries. We are traveling through a tunnel now. Switzerland is the oldest democratic republic. Two flags are seen flying together denoting the city and the province respectively. We pass through the famous resort of Arlberg, St. Jakob and, further on, St. Anton, where we stop for a coffee break. A piece of cake cost sixteen shillings and two cups of coffee another sixty shillings. We have a mix-up changing our money here. We have paid in German marks and had change in the Austrian shillings. It is delicious coffee and a lovely cafe. Beautiful snowcapped mountains appear as we move away. The sun peaks out at 10:45 A.M. We go through another tunnel and along a safety ledge. This is the longest tunnel in Europe, nine and a half miles long, and opened less than a year ago. It is 2,200 feet above sea level. We are on the borders of Switzerland and lose one hour in time. It is 10 A.M. there instead of 11 A.M. We save one and a half hours and fuel by coming this way. We see another ski lift and waterfall. This is formed by the melted snow. When it rains below, it snows in the mountains. We are now going through the clouds to another open area and village. We pass through the smallest country in Europe, Liechtenstein. It is ruled by a monarch, Prince Josef, who came to the throne after his father abdicated two years ago. Most of the houses are painted white as in Austria and Switzerland. The main thoroughfares command a beautiful view of the castle which is the residence of the prince and his family. The prince has four brothers and sisters. We are told that they have won gold medals in the winter Olympics. The farm houses have the cowsheds attached to them as they do in Austria. A church very high up was formerly a "fortification." The castle has many tall towers. The sun is shining for us as we visit Liechtenstein. We make a few purchases and enjoy walking around in this pretty place. The flag is not flying today, which indicates that the prince is not in residence. Recently, Queen Elizabeth paid a visit here. She was able to travel around without any escorts or policemen accompanying her.

A local guide enters our bus, a gold medalist in the Olympics! He tells us a little more about Liechtenstein. It is only sixty square miles in size, with two identical political parties—one to say "Yes" and other to say "No." They have an annual "Cow Festival" like Austria in September, when all the cows are brought down from the mountains and the one producing the most milk is honored by being decorated with flowers and designated as the "leading cow" for the next year.

After lunch in Liechtenstein, we are on our way again and enter Switzerland. The farmers have a lot of influence here. Butter is high priced to the housewives, who refuse to use it and get margarine instead. Four languages are spoken here. Swiss-German is spoken but is not written. It is the only country that does this. Anyone who learns to speak Swiss-German can automatically become a Swiss citizen. It is not understood by most people. It is so twisted that it is difficult for anyone to speak it. The Swiss franc is valued at $1.58 at this time.

Crossing the Rhine River, we see beautiful vineyards on the mountain slopes. They make a special white wine with these grapes. Our guide tells us another story about Monaco. He went to the mayor to procure a guide, as this was necessary because of the language barrier. They proceeded to a tent where a woman came out to meet them. She was caring for her children. He noticed her dirty hands and dirty glasses. They were very hospitable and offered him some camel's milk. He had to do some quick thinking, knowing how these people are governed in every way by the Koran with their eating and drinking. He thanked the lady through the interpreter, refusing the drink by stating: "Thank you, but my religion does not allow me to drink camel's milk." He told another story about two men quarreling over a sheep. The rich Arab watching took the sheep and settled the quarrel by stating, "It is God's will." Xavier also said, "The reason for so many marriages failing is that the girl does not marry the best man!"

There are 100,000 farm workers in Switzerland. Previously, any child born there became a citizen automatically. It is not so now. If a foreigner marries a Swiss girl, he can apply for citizenship when he has children. The houses are built with a cowshed on the end, and a loft for hay at the top. The father gives orders to the rest of the family and when he gets too old to work, he gives his house and farm to his eldest son and moves out to a small house on the estate, taking orders from his son. The farmers are rich! They get the rich "cow manure" from the mountains to fertilize their farms. Most of the cows are black and white and are imported from Holland. They have a professional army which consists of only a few hundred. All the young men are given arms and vie with each other in shooting contests. This makes them good marksmen, and therefore they have a trained army available without specialized training schools. We pass through the town of Cham, which means "town of low manners." We see the First Parliament House, a small building through the mountains of Kishnat.

We pass through a small part of Belgium and see the tree where the queen of the country was killed by Lake Lucerne, Switzerland, near the village of Kussnacht. We stop at Lausanne, which is a large, beautiful city. Unfortunately, it is raining the entire time we are there. There is a lovely old covered bridge built there diagonally across the lake. It has many murals and old paintings on the walls and ceiling. There is a casino here but there is a limit to gambling—a person is only allowed five chances. A large jewelry store is located just across from where our bus stops and many tourists are buying watches there. Some of our party buys watches also; in fact, this may be the biggest store in Switzerland. I walk through it to get out of the rain, and they are very busy at small tables demonstrating the watches.

Boarding the bus again, we continue along the lakeside. We have just passed a high class section which is across the lake; this was a favorite place for Winston Churchill to visit. We pass through the village where "Heidi" lived. Passing Lungus Lake, we climb higher and come to Brienz, and then we are getting nearer to Interlaken, which is 2,600 feet above sea level.

Brienz is the center for Swiss woodcarvers. Their carvings are quite different from those we saw and bought in Oberammergau. As we come into Interlaken, the weather seems to clear. We soon arrive at our fancy Hotel Beaurivage, meaning "beautiful river." Our party is divided here, with half of us going across the street to another location where my partner and I are housed. I say to Ethel, "My, Ethel, we've hit the jackpot! I am sure this is the Bridal Suite!" We enjoy it very much. We all go across the street to a bigger and more elaborate hotel for our dinner. Afterwards, being tired, we retire early. It is good to get into a comfortable hotel with every convenience after being two nights in the German village homes.

Friday, July 4. This is a special day for us Americans away from home. We are up early and have our continental breakfast of hard rolls, butter, jam, and coffee. The hotel environment is super; our dining room decor is beautiful—gold and light coffee in color. The Swiss curtains of net and lace add to the beauty. We all meet at the biggest hotel and are led by our guide to the railway station. We are to ascend the mountain to Jungfraujoch, one of the highest Alpine peaks, 11,300 feet above sea level. The day is one of the best weatherwise, and we are glad to see the sun shining. On the lower mountain climb, our train passes herds of goats. Higher, we see myriads of wild flowers. All of the mountain flowers bloom at one time over a period of a few weeks. The edelweiss and gentian are special noted flowers here. There are small villages along the way and the houses are all pretty, with window boxes of flowers. We see a healthy herd of pigs, and of course many cattle grazing. We view an Ice Sphinx from a plateau which is 11,723 feet above sea level. Halfway up, we change trains to another line to reach our destination. We have lunch in a very good restaurant and visit an ice palace. We stop and listen to a man playing his matterhorn and find him still there entertaining the folks when we come back. We have been told that there is a surprise awaiting us when we get back to Interlaken. We arrive in good time and are told to "dress for dinner." A party has been arranged for us by our hosts and hostesses, celebrating the Fourth of July. We gather in the American cocktail lounge at the big hotel. It is a beautiful room. It has a grand piano and is decorated with red, white, and blue streamers. Refreshments of red and white wine with plenty of orange juice and peanuts are served. Two or three of our party are able to play our national songs, to which we sing with gusto, pledging allegiance to the flag at the end. I notice our waiter looking around in amazement as we all say the pledge. Afterwards, we go into the restaurant for a very good dinner of braised beef, mashed potatoes, squash, butter, rolls, and ice cream sundaes. After dinner, most of the party go out for walks and explore the town. Interlaken is one of my favorite towns we visit. Many jewelry shops are there, and they stay open every night until 9 P.M.

Saturday, July 5. We are up at 6 A.M., and after a light breakfast are on the bus ready to travel at 7 A.M. We leave the beautiful city of Interlaken behind and see the two lakes which join together in the center. The scenery is particularly pretty along by the lakes as we branch off toward the capital city of Bern, an old and beautiful city. We approach Bern by coming over a high mountain with exquisite scenery. We look down upon it from our high position. The river Acherer encircles the city, which is built in the hollow. There is a bear pit with several of the animals begging for anything that people might like to give them. We feed them cubed sugar. A bear is incorporated into the Swiss flag. We do not have time to go into the city. We note a cathedral which stands high, and we are able to take pictures. Continuing on our way, we pass through Basel, Switzerland, and are on the borders of Germany and France. The agricultural views are interesting. Wherever grass is grown for fodder, they have special ways of drying it off. This is done in small lots because of the rains. It has to be dried quickly, I presume. We see crops of barley and other plants in varying stages of growth. Leaving this area, we come to a place called Eggberg, named for a huge stone there which is shaped like an egg. Through a tunnel, we come to a flock of black sheep, they are brown really. We now enter Basel on the Rhine in Germany. They fly two flags, one denoting the province and the other the city. This city has light industry and chemical factories. We cross the Rhine into France. More variation in the houses is observed here.

Leaving the mountains behind, we now cross a canal and come to a small town which has a supermarket like in the States. We pass through an avenue of linden trees on our way to Colmar, a medieval city. The designer of our Statue of Liberty, Auguste Bareholdi, was a native of Colmar. We tour this old city and see St. Martin's Cathedral, famous for its fifteenth-century paintings. We go into the museum and see the famous pictures of *The Crucifixion* and *The Entombment*. We are on our way again into Germany.

There is a toll to use the highway called Autobahn. We make an exit and enter the Black Forest. Our guide is playing some good English and Scotch music. He is "luring his tourists" to take a trip in that direction, I guess. A lot of fruit grows in this part of Germany. Beautiful orchards and vineyards are seen on the hillsides. The villages are clean and pretty with flowers growing everywhere. We see many strawberry beds and cherry orchards. It is a hilly country. We pass through the village of Waldrun where everyone is growing cherries. However, the bus does not stop for us to buy any. We leave the Black Forest by crossing the little river Acherer and get back on Autobahn Highway. We pass through Waldorf where the natives in the past got rich trading with American Indians. One man was named Astor, and is associated with New York City where the Waldorf-Astoria Hotel is located, along with many others all over the world. I am impressed with the beautiful highways in Germany. We have just passed a London bus. There is no speed limit for cars and any speed limit posted is advised only. However, a bus is not allowed to overtake a car on the road. We have to trail along for miles because of slow cars on the road.

We pass through the industrial city of Frankfurt on Meinz. There are two Frankfurts in Germany—this one makes champagne. We reach Wiesbaden at about 8 P.M. and are housed at a lovely modern Pinto Hotel. At 8:30 we have dinner of ham, sauerkraut, soup, mashed potatoes, rolls, butter, and a creamy dessert. Two large glasses of water are added to the meal—it is hard to get served water in some places in Europe.

Sunday, July 6. We do not see much of Wiesbaden. Our trip today has taken us to see a castle which is the seat of Mrs. Robinson's ancestors (Mrs. Robinson is one of our hostesses). Going through the country toward the castle, we have our Sunday devotional period on the bus. Xavier Puslowski, our guide, keeps us in stitches throughout the trip with his funny stories. Today he tried to scare us with a tale about Josef Hamner, our driver. He said that Josef has always been quite frightened by "hairpin bends" in the road and "curves in the mountains," so he always closes his eyes so as not to see them until he passes them! We pass through Heidelberg. Xavier tells us a little about the last place visited. It is especially a health resort for various ills. It has mineral springs. The Germans are very health conscious. We see more growing crops. They are mainly sugar beets, asparagus, turnips, and vineyards on the flat grounds. Charlotte Robinson gives us a little talk about the castle we are approaching. She has been there several times and has compiled a chart beginning with 1656, taking thirteen generations. She is really proud of the place. It is one of the smaller castles, beautifully kept on the Rhine River and quite interesting. Charlotte has gone to a lot of trouble for our large group to have a special dinner at the castle.

Heidelberg is a big city of 130,000 people. It has a university of 18,000 students and another big medical university. An interesting tourist attraction is the huge wine vat built by a former king. It holds 55,000 gallons of wine, but is, of course, no longer used for much. The large wine vat brings forth another of Xavier's stories. He tells about an eighty-one-year-old Italian who used to drink twelve bottles of wine a day. Someone changed it to water and the shock killed him.

Many visitors have gathered to see the Heidelberg Castle. Fire destroyed one fortification of it (a turret) in 1714. Big moats surround it. In the prisons, to hold the captives, we note the big iron spikes which could be lowered at the doorways. Heidelberg was not destroyed during the war. We visit a Protestant church built in 1601, with a beautiful painting of John the Baptist in it. The operetta *The Student Prince* uses this city as its setting. The next place we visit is Worms. All of the towns are between two rows of hills, the foothills of the Alps. The farmland is kept beautifully. It is a picture to see, and the Autobahn goes between impressive tracts on both sides. Occasionally, we leave the highway and go through the forest. Today is warmer and we are glad. We have lunch at a tourist stop and then continue on to Schaumburg Schlob. Our driver has some difficulty maneuvering the bus, but we finally make it and climb the steep incline to the Castle Terraces. The courtyard is flagged with squares of black and white cobblestones. The castle, now unoccupied, is owned by the Waldecker family. One wing, built in 1657, is faced with oak bark. Another wing was added in 1855. There are 236 steps to get to the top and I make it all the way and enjoy looking at the distant scenery. The chapel is reached by an iron spiral stairway. It is small with about twelve pews and a gallery. It has a cross of red lights and sixteenth-century stained-glass windows. It is still used for Waldecker weddings and funerals. We have to wear felt slippers over our shoes to tour the castle in order to protect the pretty floors. While we are in the chapel, we all sing "Amazing Grace," and a prayer is said by Charlotte Robinson. We note the seats the prince and his consort would occupy over the chapel doorway; other rooms toured are impressive. A large library which at one time held 41,000 volumes is included; other parts of the tour include a drawing room, Bohemian crystal chandeliers, a room with marble floors, and other rooms with parquet floors. The gray marble was quarried from a local area. We see a desk three hundred years old, and French tapestries which two women spent ten years making. Beautiful paintings are scattered throughout, many of them badly needing repairs and restorations. One room has a huge fish shell weighing fifty-four pounds, and interesting fossils. We see the guest room where Queen Wilhemenia slept—the last guest to use it. Then many of us climb the 236 steps to the top of the castle. The top turret is reached by a winding iron stairway. We can see for many miles around when we finally reach the top. A lovely meal is served later at the castle restaurant. We start back to our hotel about 8 P.M.

Monday, July 7. We get up early and have breakfast by 6:30 A.M. I have time for a walk to see the beautiful flowers and gardens in a park in back of the hotel. We start out at 8:45 A.M. It has rained during the night and is still cloudy, but the sun peeks out a little after 9. We see a little of Weisbaden, a town of 253,000 people, and especially remember the Monument to a Horse. On our way to Bingen on the Rhine River, we see more castles, mostly uninhabited. One the French could not ruin because of a secret passage. A large obelisk on a hill is a monument to a war in 1871. We see more orchards, gardens, and vineyards along this road. No wasteland appears anywhere. Cherry trees are laden with fruit; vineyards cover the hills. We board the *Duseldorf* at Bingen for a relaxing cruise on the Rhine. The ship has three decks. We all find seats at tables with white cloths. Not many go to the decks since it is cold and sprinkling rain occasionally. This seems to be a main resort area since so many people are traveling on this boat. The scenery is beautiful as we cruise along. Beautiful hills are on both sides of the river. We pass a silver mine back in a group of trees. Many castles are seen from time to time. Only one of them is still occupied; they are gradually deteriorating and going to ruin. Everyone seems to enjoy a glass of wine on this trip, with waiters standing ready to serve. I take my first glass of wine, dry white, which is very delicious. We are told that the grapes were grown in this area. We have lunch on the boat and alight at Boppare. The boat trip has taken two and a half hours. Josef drove the bus from Bingen and is still waiting for us when we land. We continue along the riverside for some distance. Roads and railroads parallel the river on both sides with an occasional port for boats. All river traffic is required to dock overnight at a port unless equipped with radar.

We see some churches which have as many as four spires. Germans still call Berlin their capital, but Bonn is where the Parliament meets. Many big conferences meet there also. One of Beethoven's homes is located there. The German flag is black, red, and yellow, and is similar to the Belgian flag.

We head toward Cologne, passing a large oil refinery. This is the home of the famous Eau-de-Cologne which is quite expensive to buy there. The Rhine is wider in this section, but not as pretty. The hills are behind us now. Cologne has a magnificent cathedral, and the hotel we are assigned to is near it. Much construction is going on and our bus has to circle the block to get to a side entrance of the hotel. Some places are not restored since the war. Cologne was almost demolished by the bombing, but the cathedral, the largest Gothic one in Europe, was spared. Hundreds of people are visiting the cathedral. There is a large shopping plaza for pedestrians only. We shop at the famous 4711 Shop, the original place where the Eau-de-Cologne was made. I note a "lottery booth" on the cathedral pavement.

The hotel is unable to feed us, so we all meet at a designated place and walk to an unusual restaurant in the neighborhood of the cathedral. It is a typical German tavern, with a musician playing and singing with a one-man band combination setup. The homestyle meal they serve is good, but the cost of coffee, which is not included in the meal, is exorbitant! Water is not served at such places unless you beg for it. We go back to the hotel and prepare for bed. Ethel and I get a nice corner room. We seem fortunate with our rooms.

Tuesday, July 8. This city of Cologne is known as Klon. It has mineral waters and is a health spa. It is a well-known sports center. Charlemagne, the onetime ruler of all Europe, resided there. We are now on our way to Amsterdam, Holland, a good distance to travel. We leave the Rhine behind and go north on the Autobahn Expressway. We come to the American Square where there is a beautiful fountain.

We tour the Cathedral of Aachan, and also see the Throne of Charlemagne by special permission. He was crowned Emperor of Rome in the year 800. He sat in this "stone" throne to watch thirty "lesser kings" crowned. We see Music Hall and a statue of a horse before reaching the Dutch border.

Holland is a very clean place. Its houses are built slightly different from the ones we have seen in other countries. The varying architecture is especially noticeable in the city of Amsterdam. The parks are very pretty with neatly clipped grass and glowing flower beds. Holland is ruled by a queen, the third successive monarch of her sex. The present queen has a son, and her subjects are happy that a king will finally come to the throne. Holland has a large monetary market, many colonies, and operates one of the largest Merchant Marine fleets in the world. Shell Oil, which originated there, has made the royal family immensely wealthy. The country is largely agricultural.

En route to Holland, we pass through Culpen, where we see the war cemetery and cross the river Mass which starts in France, Basilica of Our Lady of Culpen. This places us in Belgium for a brief stop before heading for Amsterdam. We note the two flags—the Dutch, which is red, white, and blue, and the Belgian, which is black, yellow, and red. Monarchy is a figurehead here. The prime minister has power to make laws. They speak Flemish as well as French. Many famous artists have been produced here. At one time Belgium was under Spanish domination. We go through Bilz and then back onto the motorway on our way to Antwerp. Antwerp has 600,000 inhabitants. Many blocks or large apartment buildings are seen in all directions. At one time Rubens had a home here. It is principally an industrial city. It has one of the biggest cathedrals, which stands 383 feet high. Belgium is the only country which has fog lamps on the highways.

We reach the border of Holland again, have lunch, and change our money into guilders. We continue on into Holland and make a detour through the country, where many pretty homes, gardens, and black and white cows are seen. A tunnel takes us under the river Zudi and we enter a section which seems to be all grazing land. The cows are grouped on familiar spots in the fields waiting for the farmers to milk them. This is done by machines while the animals are fed high-protein fodder. Cattle are sold at the Auction Mart, where prices fluctuate from high to low and back again. Torrential rains are falling when we finally reach our Amsterdam home for two nights at the Euro-Crest Hotel. Fortunately, the rain stops within a few minutes and we settle in comfortably.

After a rest, we go to dinner at 7 P.M. Our hotel is on the outskirts of the city. The meal is especially nice. Everyone is happy to get some salad with it, the first we have been served since we left Vienna.

Wednesday, July 9. Breakfast served at 8 A.M. is different from those we have had in other places. Everything is packaged and put on a tray. There is ham, cheese, jam, butter, and two rolls. Today is dull and cloudy and looks like more rain is coming. Since we are staying here two days, it is nice to get a rest from packing our cases. At 9 A.M., we leave for a tour of the city. The city is laid out with canals and streets on each side with bicycle tracks for cyclists, who have the right-of-way. Houses are varied in styles and in color of bricks. They are built several stories high with plenty of window space. The doors are smaller and it is often necessary to use pulleys to get furniture in through windows. We saw this being done! Housing is expensive—the majority of the apartments rent for one thousand dollars per week, or month. We note that most of the apartments have three windows. Taxes are higher if they have more.

Xavier tells us a story about the two princesses. They stole food from a barrow boy. The queen was informed that they were at the police station. She asked what the punishment was and, when told, asked the officers to double it to teach them a lesson.

The river Amstel gives the city its name. Amsterdam is the capital place for hippies. A square is provided for them near the red-light district where they smoke marijuana and amuse themselves from 9 A.M. to 5 P.M. unmolested. We see the Royal Palace and its worship chapel. A large railroad station has a beautiful front with towers at each end. Many canals are necessary in order to drain the land, which is below sea level.

We visit a diamond factory and see the workers cutting and polishing beautiful gems. A woman gives a lecture on how they estimate their value. Two art museums are visited before lunch. The larger, Wryk Museum, is famous for its collection of Rembrandt paintings. His most famous, *The Nightwatch*, is the center of attraction here. It was encased in glass until the paint was dry after being damaged four times by visitors. All of the European museums were emptied of their art treasures by the Germans during the last war and the art was stored in empty salt mines in Salzburg until peace was established. The Van Gogh Museum contains more modern paintings. We also visit the home of the Jewish girl Anne Frank, who had hidden there during the war for a period of time before being killed by the Nazis. In the afternoon, we leave for Volendam, a picturesque village, considered one of the prettiest in Holland. Royal Delft is sold there. Each Dutch village has its own costumes and women wear them all the time. Some villagers are not allowed to travel on Sundays. En route to Volendam, we stop at a cheese factory and watch them making the cheese which is exported from here. Of course, much cheese is bought by our group and other crowds of visitors.

We are supposed to meet at a certain point where our bus is parked to leave. However, Xavier stops me and asks me to spread the word to be at a different point on the waterfront since he has a surprise for us. The surprise is that he has hired a boat to take us across the "Zuider Zee" to another village. The bus meets us there. Before we reach Maken we make a detour to visit a shop where they make wooden shoes, or sabots, chipped out of varying-sized chunks of wood. We expect to see more windmills in Holland, but few are used now. One is seen in someone's backyard and another tiny one in a field. While crossing the Zuider Zee, the rain keeps off, but after landing, blustery winds and heavy rains cause us to seek hasty shelter until our bus comes along. We are glad to get back to Amsterdam where we are served another delicious, homestyle dinner.

We are all excited over going home now. The news comes that instead of returning Royal Jordanian from Amsterdam, we are to go British Airlines to London and on to the States from there, from Heath Airport. I have the idea that I may be able to visit my sister in London, but since I cannot get through on the telephone, I give up the idea. We retire early trying to defeat possible "jet lag" since we are six hours ahead of New York time. An exciting episode happens at our breakfast table—one of our party loses her handbag, which she has placed at her feet at the table. There is a hustle to find it since we have to leave soon for the airport and the bag contains her passport. They have to contact passport officials at the American Embassy and just as plans are being made for rushing a duplicate, police officials report that the bag has been found on the street and has been run over by a vehicle. Money was taken and her glasses smashed, but the passport, so badly needed at this time, is intact.

We have a pleasant trip to London on British Airways. A large restaurant in the airport provides us an ample lunch. We board our plane at 3 P.M. and are off toward New York by 3:45. We are served afternoon tea soon after departing, and a full-course dinner before landing. We pass the time away by watching a "cowboy film" starring Robert Redford. The journey is comfortable and time passes quickly with daylight all the way to New York. After custom checks, we decide to stay overnight in the International Airport Hotel and are soon in bed, tired and worn-out. It is good to see the sun shining again in the good old U.S.A. The temperature is just right. We wonder how we will get any sleep since big airliners buzz over our heads every few minutes, but are surprised that we do sleep well. We make our own coffee and breakfast in our hotel room. After a walk around the flower beds, we join our group at the restaurant, say goodbye to the others, and start on our return home to Tallahassee.

We are shocked to enter the heat wave which meets us in Florida and feel sorry for other members of our party returning to Texas where it is even hotter! This is the end of our exciting vacation to Europe.

9
Life at Westwood Retirement Center

I had been at Westwood for one year and enjoyed the new environment very much. It was so completely different from living in Tallahassee. Here I had someone to cook for me and clean my apartment. However, I was really too young to retire (I was seventy-six years old at the time). There were sports to engage in and I joined the shuffleboard group and went in for the tournaments, but I did not win any of them. Then there was the putt-putt golf on another day. It was nice to do these things for a change of occupation. Once a week, some of us did volunteer work as host or hostess in the front lobby and Sundry Shop. This was a pleasant pastime also. I found many friends while living in this complex. From time to time someone would have to go to the hospital, and, since it was next door, it was easy to go visit them, so this was one of the things I did. Also, we visited each other in our apartments. I found one lady who enjoyed a game of Lexicon, and we often met and played a couple of games on Saturday evenings. We were promised a swimming pool, but it did not materialize until shortly before I moved. I did get to go in the pool a few times.

The experience of being at Westwood has enriched my life. I must mention some of my close friends. There was Hertha Steiner. She fell in the dining room one day and broke her arm. Needless to say, this drew us closer and we would get together for lunch; this meal we ate in our own place, while breakfast and dinner were included in our fees. Poor Hertha needed a lot of care so her folks decided that she should go into the health care center where she still is. I also got acquainted with Esther Apple. She was a longtime resident in the city and knew the area well. She is a remarkable lady, very self-sufficient, active, and dressed impeccably. I found out Esther was a Christian lady, and, although eighty-three years old, she was living for the Lord and was helping others who needed help, too! She had a big Lincoln automobile and was always running to and from transporting others. Esther unfortunately fell and broke her right wrist. She was somewhat helpless for a few weeks, so I was able to help her with bathing and taking her to the doctor. We became friends and I was invited to go to her church where I later became a member.

While I was at Westwood, it was time for my sister Queenie to visit me, and, although we were in close quarters for six weeks, we managed very well. It was Esther who helped me to get Queenie from the Pensacola Airport. It was good to visit with each other after an absence of two years. We had previously tried to visit each other every second year. I had paid for some of her visits to me because I preferred to stay here, and Queenie was agreeable and enjoyed visiting different parts of the States. While my sister was here, Esther took us out to eat in Destin, Florida. That was a new experience as, while we ate, the restaurant quietly and imperceptibly moved around so we could see with advantage the surrounding view and eat our meal at the same time. Queenie and I enjoyed going to the beach almost every day. Her visit ended far too soon.

The Methodist church I joined was in Valparaiso, about ten miles from our residence. I liked it there because it was a small church and I could see there was a need to help build it—that is, try to get more people to come. We had a very Spirit-filled pastor who was doing a wonderful job. Since joining, I had the honor of being elected to the church board and my job was chairperson of evangelism and missions. While I was at Westwood, I was also elected to the board of the Residents' Council, and I represented the art class. A few of the folks enjoyed learning to draw and paint. We kept our painting to watercolors, and several of the students did some very nice work which they have framed. I continued to teach this class once a week, until I left Westwood.

There were many interesting people at Westwood, too numerous to mention but a few. Grace Jewitt was a lovely person, quiet and unassuming. She took it upon herself to send "get well" cards to all those who went into the hospital. She was in her nineties. Ethel Van Horne was a charming lady who may have been the oldest at Westwood at the time. She was a poet and was always seen smiling. She could write up a poem at any time and for any occasion. Her poems were often seen in our monthly newspaper. Louise Rohrer was my friend who liked to play Lexicon with me. She was a gifted musician and had been trained to play theatrical music on an organ. She often entertained the other residents on the piano in the dining room. I often tried to get Louise to attend church with me. She was somewhat bitter toward God because her only daughter, who was married and had two daughters, had died at an early age. She claimed to be a Christian and said one day she would start going to church.

I was living on the sixth floor and did not have any neighbors on either side. One day I heard someone next door, so I went to find out who it was. A young man came to the door of the two-bedroom apartment. I introduced myself and found out he was getting the place ready for his mother and aunt, who were coming in from Chicago soon. They arrived and we became good friends. These two became known as the "two sisters in white," as they seemed to wear white all the time.

Mr. and Mrs. Dick Naylor lived on the first floor. Beth was a very faithful wife to her husband. He had previously been an attorney and had had a stroke which disabled him. It was really hard on Beth to wait on him in so many ways. She would be seen at every mealtime walking him by the hand very, very slowly. Although physically handicapped, he was voted to be the president of our Residents' Council. I heard that he was an atheist, so one day I offered him a book by Billy Graham entitled *What the Bible Is All About*, which he graciously took and promised to read.

At the end of the year, all of our rents went up. Mine increased to $630 for my efficiency apartment. Of course, this included many things—two meals a day, light and heat, bi-monthly maid service, linens if required, and transportation to stores. There were organized sports, a swimming pool, and an atrium. Emergency facilities relayed from our apartments to the health care center. I never had to use it.

Well, all this spelled luxury for me, so I decided to move. My income was flexible, and the trust fund that was set up for me by my stepson and through the sale of our house is reduced every year, as I receive the interest only on the money invested. We took a mortgage on the house, so I think I made a wise move at the right time. It was while my application was being processed for a one-bedroom apartment amongst some new town houses in Valparaiso that I heard about a job that carried an apartment with it. I definitely felt it was in God's will for me to take this job. It involved caring for an elderly woman, Stella Thomas. I thought it would be something that I could manage and I applied and got the job. I worked at my new address for one week before moving. This was to get initiated and learn the routine. The two women who had been caring for Mrs. Thomas were leaving to go back to Greece.

Ann Streit obligingly moved her mother's furniture to make room for mine. The few large pieces that were left blended very nicely with mine. The first week I was in the house, I was kept awake by the chimes and tunes of her beautiful grandfather clock. I was very happy with the arrangements, though, and had beautiful accommodations with private bath, big closets, and a pleasant view from my windows. It was about two months since I first came, and I found myself quite busy but not overly so. I enjoyed looking after this dear lady who was extremely deaf and the victim of several strokes, which had caused much brain damage with loss of memory. In spite of it all, she had a sweet disposition.

I was wondering what I might be doing for Christmas that year when an invitation came in the mail from some Tallahassee friends. I did not get too excited about it at first because I did not know what the relatives of my patient Mrs. Thomas were doing. Next day I caught Ann on the telephone and asked for the time off. I was surprised when she said we might arrange for me to be off for three days. I continued to stay busy and put up my small, artificial tree and other decorations I use each year. It all looked so pretty, and I was hoping to have a few friends in to celebrate, but no one came. All were too busy.

A week before Christmas, George Selby Thomas arrived in Ft. Walton Beach especially to visit his mother. This was a nice change for my lady. He ate all his meals with us except breakfast. He played Santa Claus the first night he came. He gave us both a Sony Walkman radio.

I began to get excited about Christmas now as I counted Tallahassee as my home. I have many friends there in the Christian and Missionary Alliance church and amongst the senior citizens. Ellen and Johnny Grimes were special and I am always welcome to stay there, if they are home. I was counting on leaving Ft. Walton Beach after lunch, but Ann suggested I go early. I bathed Stella, and, with breakfast over, I took her down to her daughter Ann's house (a few doors away on the same street). She was happy to be spending Christmas with Ann. I was given a check to cover salary and housekeeping, so I thought it best to put it in the bank before leaving town. It had been raining all night and all day, so the roads were very slippery. I remember asking the Lord to give me "journey mercies." I had gone a couple of blocks and was turning a corner when my car went into a spin. I was traveling slowly so did not lose control, but it was scary. A car behind me and one in front both saw my predicament and came to a halt. I was able to get righted and continue. This was the first accident I avoided on my trip!

As I drove into Tallahassee, I went to see Janina Lipcious, my Polish friend. Janina is a nurse and was off duty, so we had a nice visit. Then I called my little friend Louise Day, who had been very unwell and was waiting to go into the hospital for surgery. After a brief visit with Louise, I met my other friends for lunch. They have a delightful home and everything for convenience and comfort. They had bought a new motor home since I last saw them, so after our meal, they were happy to show me this miracle home of the road. I am honored to have four of my paintings hung in their house. These friends were in early retirement years and enjoyed the out-of-doors, going away for weekends or longer on fishing trips.

It was Christmas Eve and we had arranged to go to a candlelight service at my hostess' church, St. Paul's Methodist. We had agreed to visit their church together that night, and they were coming to mine on Sunday morning. We had a beautiful Christmas Day. We picked up another citizen, Irene Boman, who spent the day with us. We ate a good deal of turkey, stuffing, vegetables, and delicious pies. The weather was beautiful and we were able to sit outdoors. My wonderful friends arranged for some other friends to come over and visit in the afternoon. I appreciated this immensely, as it saved my running around so much to see them. It was a lovely reunion, and Ellen and Johnny made some new friends that day also. I was especially happy to accidentally meet four friends on Christmas Eve, all of whom were members of a speech club I used to belong to.

After church on Sunday, I bade farewell to Ellen and Johnny. Several of us met at McDonald's for lunch. Dorothy Miller was able to come along also. Little Louise was very emotional, wondering if she would ever see me again, facing two major operations. It was time to part. Traffic was heavy but the weather was fine. We had gotten along well and people seemed to be obeying the speed limit. Suddenly, about halfway home, a new truck came upon me from the rear and passed me on the wrong side. This really was scary, as there was so little space for him to pass. I slowed up a little and moved to the right to make room for him. He went to the middle of the road and, for a moment, I thought he was going to stop. However, he was gone in a jiffy. I don't know what he was up to, but I do know this: I thanked God for protecting me from a second accident on this trip. I really believe God has guardian angels watching over us. I also thank Him for this opportunity to visit with my friends again and for a safe trip home.

Living with Stella

Since Christmas 1982, plans were made for my lady Mrs. Stella Thomas to have cataracts removed; a lot of her disinterest in life could be contributed to the fact she had had cataracts growing on both eyes for the past several years. Also, she was deaf in both ears. This condition was much relieved when she used her hearing aides, but she hated wearing them. She said she enjoyed the quietness. Her doctor operated on one eye at a time. She had the first operation on March 15, 1983, and it was very successful. I contribute this to much prayer being offered on her behalf. She said she was able to see better than she had ever been able to see before, and was anxious for the other eye to be done, the date for which was set for July 27. Now she had a new lens in her glasses, and with the implant was able to read the newspaper with her one good eye. She could even see out-of-doors in the distance! We learned to love each other and Stella seemed so much happier than when I first came to take care of her.

I planned to go and visit my sister Queenie in England that spring, so I made preparations for this trip. I love England in the spring, and it had been eight years since I was there, but I did see my sister every other year since she had been coming over here to see me. I knew very well that we would need someone to take care of Stella, and I felt confident that the Lord would provide. So I began praying about this and in a very short time we heard about a lady who lived on the next street who needed this kind of work. She had just come in from California and appeared to be the perfect one for the job. Peggy Horsley was willing to give up other jobs so she could relieve me for the six weeks I planned to be in England.

I trusted all the wet weather Queenie told me they were having in England would be over when I got there. My sister was getting lonely since she moved into her bungalow home on Mission Lane. However, it was easier for her as she did not have the steps to go up and down since she broke her hip before Christmas. Also, she was much nearer the shops.

I was happy to have my own apartment which gave me privacy, and I had my own personal things around me. Living alone can enable us to draw closer to the Lord and give more time for Bible study and devotions without distractions or annoyances. The area here was quiet and we liked the neighborhood. Also, migratory birds lived here and were often seen in great flocks taking off for cooler climate, returning in the winter. The ducks and water fowl flew back here in the spring after wintering in the South, also. While living with Stella, I got to know Sherry Reily, who lived next door to us. Her mother co-owned a restaurant with Ann Streit,

Stella's daughter. Sherry was unfortunately born with spina bifida, but had been trained to take care of herself, which she did very well. She was left alone each day except for her little dog, who became her faithful friend. She lived in a waterfront home with beautiful lawns reaching down to the water's edge. Sherry had a few hobbies, one of which was knitting lap robes of various colors. Her mother was able to sell these in the gift shop at the restaurant. This was an encouragement to her, and helped her to become more self-reliant. One day, her mother approached me and asked if I could go and stay with her overnight for two weeks while she was away on vacation. This I was happy to do. While living next door for awhile, I got to know Sherry. She voiced her desire to learn to paint, so she engaged in this new art. She became quite proficient and enjoyed watercolors.

Since leaving the area, I have kept in touch with Sherry, and one day a pack of her watercolor paintings came through the mail to me. She was very proud of her work and, of course, I encouraged her. We keep in touch for birthdays and special days during the year. She is in her thirties now and is doing well for a child who is so handicapped. She is unable to walk, but scoots around in her wheelchair.

Vacation to England, May–June 1983

Monday, May 10, was a busy day for me. All the last-minute things had to be done. I took Stella to Westwood Health Care Center where she would be taken care of until my return six weeks later. "Charlie" was safely away with his new mistress and doggie friend down the road from us. Clothing had to be tagged and packed for Stella, plants placed out-of-doors, food disposed of. It had been somewhat of a hassle because last-minute arrangements were different. We had planned to have Peggy in to take care of Stella, but she turned out to be an alcoholic, so we could not have her in the house. We had to help her get readjusted, also, a day or two before. So, feeling somewhat relieved of my responsibilities, I left the house fairly early on Tuesday morning, May 11. I spent a quiet day with my friend Myrtle on her farm in Milton.

Wednesday, May 12. I planned to travel via Pensacola to England. It was a blessing that I had to change planes only once. Atlanta and Gatwick was the route our DC-10 took. I left my car at Myrtle's place and she was to pick me up and drive me to the airport. The journey was pleasant. I always enjoy travel by air. I was especially impressed by the good service shown me at Atlanta.

An officer met the plane and had a conveyance which was to carry me and two others to the International Airport. The time seemed to pass quickly and we were on our way across the Atlantic Ocean. It was exciting for me to arrive in the land of my birth. I was met by my sister Queenie, Grace and Fred Allen, and Grace's sister Violet. We were soon speeding through the English countryside. (Yes, they drive faster than we do!) We found a wayside place along the road and stopped for coffee. This was of course the next day, as I had gained six hours along the way. We rested on arrival and I must have slept some to make up for the loss of sleep on the plane. Queenie's home is near her church, and, happily for us, the senior citizens were having their monthly dinner party. We were able to get our dinner by the carry-out method as a concession. Carry-out meals are quite popular over there now.

The next day it was time to start a round of visits, and, as Jan and Dudley Patterson lived close by, we went to see them first. We found they were ready to go to Portsmouth, so we went with them. We had to take every opportunity to go places, as Queenie has no car and does not drive. We visited the shopping area and marketplace. I had to go to bed that afternoon, as "jet lag" was catching up with me; then we just had a good talking session in the evening. Saturday turned out a nice, sunny day, so we got busy in the little garden, cutting grass and such. I just saw that the folks here had been blessed with rain for the last thirty days. We had a nice dinner and went to visit Flora Stone, who prepared a typical English tea for us. Sunday was still cold, and I was feeling the change of climate; however, the warmth of the Evangelical Reformed church was a real blessing for me. They had a visiting pastor who preached splendidly both morning and evening, and the music of the choir touched our hearts.

The sun came out in the afternoon and we went for a walk in the Queen's Enclosure—a beautiful, wooded area. We could not enter too far in because of the mud underfoot. We invited some of the church friends in for coffee after church. We had an invitation to their place at Waterlooville the following Sunday.

Monday, May 17. We had to go to Waterlooville for times of coaches and fares. Lydia France, who was living at Horndean and leaving for Australia in a few days, was arranging to have all of her friends for farewell visits, so Queenie and I were invited for tea in the afternoon.

Tuesday, May 18. Today was the Senior Citizens Arts and Crafts Class at Wecock, another village nearby. We passed a pleasant afternoon with these ladies and learned a new craft. Every second week, the church has family Bible study and prayer meetings in the homes of several of the members. This was the night for this meeting. I was impressed by the good attendance and quality of the studies. This seems to be a feature which has helped build the church.

Wednesday, May 19. We went to Waterlooville shopping. They have a freezer shop there, and Queenie can stock up and buy a little cheaper at this store. A new thing to me was the way that the shopping areas are cut off so that no traffic is allowed through. They are called "precincts." The roads are paved for walking, and seats are placed for rest. Also things are made more pleasant for shoppers, as there are more and better restaurants and coffee shops. The Women's Fellowship was well attended in the afternoon. The Tea and Biscuit seems to be a drawing card; and the women love to get together.

Thursday, May 20. Proved to be a pleasant day. Queenie took care of her garden. She has some beautiful flowers and bushes, as well as flowering cactus growing in her small conservatory. I did some shopping in the village in the meantime. Being a fine day, we decided to take a bus ride to Petersfield. This is an interesting place and very historical. It was early closing day, so we could not do much in the way of purchases. However, we found a good book shop which sold art supplies and made one purchase for one of my students. We had a two-hour wait for a return bus, so we found a good coffee and tea shop open called the Punch and Judy Restaurant. A large, old church was near the bus stop, so we visited there also. As we went around, we found that all these old churches were badly in need of funds and were selling literature and cards to help with finances. I am sorry to say that most of these old church buildings are monuments rather than places of worship.

Friday, May 21. Friday proved to be a very wet day, so we had a quiet day at home. My sister has many friends and had planned in her schedule "set times" to visit with them. In fact, they visit back and forth quite regularly. So today (Saturday) was the day for her friend Joyce Tucker to come. She arrived at 10 A.M. and Lydia, who was leaving for Australia, came later and in time for a lovely roast dinner followed later by sumptuous tea.

Sunday, May 23. This was Whitsunday or Pentecost, a special day in the church calendar. It was a very enjoyable day at the church. Also it was the day we went over to visit our friends, the Ritchies. Pat is a wonderful hostess and wanted to do her utmost to entertain us. It was the first time that Queenie had been to her home, too, as it was newly built and they were just about settled into it. Well, that meal was unforgettable! After dinner we were shown the wedding of Prince Charles and Lady Diana by video tape. I enjoyed that very much as I had not seen it before.

Monday, May 24. It had been previously arranged for our friends, Eileen and Ron James, to come and stay with us for a few days. They arrived after lunch and Queenie had cooked one of their favorite meals: Sausage-Toad-in-the-Hole, peas, and french fries. We reminisced, looked at the garden, and read some of my notes.

Tuesday was a nice day and Ron had a car, so he took us for a ride, first to Southsea, our nearest seaside place. There were lady gardeners laying out carpet gardens on the seafront. Eventually they looked very beautiful. We were treated to a lovely dinner in a restaurant on the seafront.

After our midday dinner, Ron proceeded to take us into the country after viewing Portsmouth from the highest point around that area. The country lanes were narrow and pretty. We saw several thatched cottages and homes. White and mauve lilacs were in bloom. The horse chestnut trees were blooming also. These were white and red. I had not remembered red ones before. The gardens were so pretty, all the flowers were out—laburnums, tulips, clematis, and various rock flowers. There were fields of yellow mustard or some plant grown for its oil. Suddenly Ron came to a stop. There was a gorgeous cock pheasant, a fine bird taking its time to cross in front of us in a narrow lane.

While we were on the seafront, we were able to watch the hovercraft come in and leave every few minutes and take off for the Isle of Wight. We spent our evening looking at old photographs. It was an enjoyable day.

Wednesday, May 26. Ron, Eileen, and I went for a long walk and viewed the new blocks of apartments going up. We studied the nice gardens of the people who were already in residence. Queenie had a lovely roast chicken dinner ready for us by the time we returned. My sister and I had previously arranged to go on an afternoon coach trip with her club members. It was a mystery trip in the Meon Valley and on to Bognor Regis. We had a very nice tea on the seafront and returned a different and faster way. We spent our evening all together and did knitting. Our friends went home today, Thursday. We all went to Waterlooville to buy a garden ornament; came home and had fish-and-chips, and went to Horndean with our friends, where we parted.

Tony and Simone were caretakers of a senior citizens' apartment complex. Being friends of Queenie, they invited us to come and have a cup of tea and they showed us around the buildings. These were beautiful places for the elderly to spend their last days. Tony took us home and we spent the evening watching a cup final at Wemberly Stadium.

Saturday was Joyce's return visit, so we made our way over in the morning. She gave us excellent meals, typically English. She served Shepherd's Pie with peas and carrots, rhubarb pie and ice cream. High tea later consisted of ham and salad, bread and butter, Bakewell tart, whipped cream and fruitcake. Her home was very nice. She had sliding-glass doors to the living room and separate dining room and two bedrooms. We had to walk home as there was no evening bus on the weekends. We watched an opera from Covent Gardens Opera House, and the weather was cold and showery.

Sunday continued to be cold and showery. We went to church, both morning and evening. Flora came in to visit with us and stayed for supper. We watched a good film on a team climbing Mt. Everest and they reached the top. Monday was their spring bank holiday. It was sunny and cool most of the day; Joyce came for dinner and tea. Queenie cooked a special roast pork with applesauce, beans, peas, and roast potatoes, followed by Christmas pudding and cream. The whole dinner was too rich for me. I had a stomach upset. Joyce and Queenie worked on the baby coat I had started, and got it finished. I wrote two airmail letters. The cactus in the conservatory were now in full bloom and a beautiful sight.

Tuesday was a nice day. We had a coach outing in the afternoon with some club members. We went to some small villages in the Meon Valley. We saw a stone monument in Hambledon in a cricket field where the first match was played in 1750. A single match is played for charity there once every year and the players dress in the original costumes of the players, which consisted of red and white striped costumes and straw boaters. We passed through Mercury, the Naval Defense Headquarters, and came through Old Winchester Hill, a national nature reserve. We got a lovely view from here. We stopped to take pictures of Cole's Gardens and went on to Oxenbourne Farm where we were expected for tea. They served a full High tea with strawberry jam, scones, and clotted cream. This was in West Meon Valley. The farm here was noted for its piggeries. We went around and saw the pigs in different stages of growth.

We had a severe storm Wednesday night but I slept through it. My sister prepared for summer as it was June 1. Very little summer yet. She cleaned up the conservatory and opened the living room doors; she put certain plants out-of-doors, discovered a bloom on a Christmas cactus, and found more cacti in bloom. Several people came in to see the cactus. We took a walk to Flora's home.

Thursday, June 3. We spent another quiet day; visited Allen and Dudley. I finished my baby coat and did some fancy work; saw a good film on the coronation of Queen Elizabeth in 1953, which included all the preparations for it. It was an old film in black-and-white, and millions saw this event for the first time all over the world; in fact, there was a two-mile procession. People came from all of her colonies. People took part in the program telling of their impressions at the time. A lady-in-waiting showed us a close-up of the dress the queen wore. She had ten fittings for it. It was made by the queen's dressmaker, Norman Hartnell. The Right Honorable Dr. Ramsey took part and told us his impressions. It was a cold and wet day. When the queen was anointed, a canopy was placed over her. Prince Charles was a tiny tot and was seen on the balcony of the palace when the royal party returned from Westminster Abbey.

Friday, June 4. We went to Waterlooville Travel Agent to arrange a weekend in Paris. (However, this did not materialize.) We came home and Queenie did some baking.

Saturday, June 5. It's the best day so far, and it's beginning to feel like summer. It was fun to watch people change into summer clothes quickly. We were able to do a little sunbathing and reading in the garden. Our friend Mr. Allen came around to do a little job for Queenie and he invited us back for tea, which we accepted. They had a lovely home and terraced garden; tea was served out of doors. In the evening we went to church for a missionary evening, when two young people told about the field to which they had gone. Sue and Andy worked for the Church Missionary Society. One of the neighbors, Mrs. Simpson, invited us in to see her collection of dolls.

Sunday, June 6. We enjoyed going to church morning and evening, and the Communion was served in the evening. The pastor in church gave a good message on the second coming of Christ. It was a very stormy day and we had a freak storm in the afternoon with hailstones as big as golf balls. Some homes were flooded nearby. We also had a scare when some people behind us made a bonfire and clouds of smoke arose. David, next door, said his fish pond was overflowing. We watched a good film in the evening about St. David's Day, by a priest from the Canterbury Cathedral who took us into Wales with his story.

Monday, June 7. I went to Joyce Tucker's for the day. She made a nice curry and rice dinner. Queenie went to the hospital for her final checkup and X-rays on her leg and the doctor discharged her. She lost her diary and tickets for our trip to Bournemouth. She had a call from the hospital to say her lost things were handed in to them, so the next day we went to Hillsea. Flora was with us this time. Queenie broke her journey to pick up her things and we all met and went to the bus station to make bookings for other outings. We went to Wecock Farm Village Arts and Crafts Center in the afternoon, where we worked on making some pictures. A new craft was done on glass with use of aluminum foil. One of the neighbors took us and picked us up later. We had cold lamb and mint sauce and salad for dinner, herrings on toast and salad served for tea, with sliced peaches and cream for dessert. We finished our day by going to fellowship prayer meeting; the theme was on worship from the Book of Psalms.

Wednesday, June 9. This was a very special day on our calendar. The Allens took us out in their car. On our way into the country, we passed through many small villages—Fyning, East and South Harting. We found art students were out drawing here. We stopped to eat our lunch by Buriton Pond and fed the ducks. We came to a very old inn which had been kept in good repair. The Red Lion Inn had just had a new thatched roof, at a cost of 30,000 pounds, and is situated in the village of Chalton between the South Downs and Portsmouth. The building dates to A.D. 1147 and is mentioned in *Domesday Book*. It was originally used as a workshop by craftsmen who were rebuilding St. Michael and All Angels Church which stands opposite the inn. The original church was a Saxon building. It is believed that from about 1503, the workshop changed its role to that of an inn. It was built on solid chalk; its cellars were cool and ideally situated. In recent years, a lounge and new toilets have been added to the half-timbered, thatched building.

Our next stop was at the Church in a Field at Idsworth, built in A.D. 1053. This was badly in need of a new roof. We went on to Milland where we saw another very old Church in the Woods. It was in the process of being restored. It had an old heater and original beams, a font on the wall, and the original wooden pulpit. We went on to Chichester Cathedral and Old Cross at the end of the main street where a precinct had been built. Many of these precincts can be seen in England now. (They make safe shopping places, as no traffic is allowed in them.) On the way home, we came to Bosham and the tide was out, leaving many little sailing boats stranded in the mud. We found another interesting old church here. There is the tomb of an eight-year-old child in this church, which is thought to be the daughter of King Canute. There was also a sundial in the courtyard dedicated to Eugene Gerald Marcuse, the "radio pioneer" and dated June 4, 1886, to April 6, 1961. He was the first person to transmit by "short wave." He sent programs to the Commonwealth in 1927. There were records on this dial and mileage to various places—for example, to California was 5500 miles. We came to Fyning Hill and saw the "Golden Gates." There were rhododendrons growing profusely along the main roads. These were in various colors but mostly pale mauve. We arrived back in Cowplain about 5 P.M. and we went home for a rest. The Allens invited us to go back to their home and they were to take us out for dinner. We went to the Bat and Ball, a restaurant in a historical building that is built in two villages, Clanfield and Hambledon. There is a white line running through the building to mark the division between the two villages.

Thursday, June 10. This was Polling Day. There had been much advertising of each party on the airwaves, but it seemed that most people were in favor of putting Mrs. Thatcher back in office as prime minister. She did get in by a good majority. Today was also the fortnightly Friendship Dinner served at the church, so we went along and enjoyed that. In the evening, the same group had a lecture on the use of herbs; they even showed us how to make a "poor man's pizza" by use of split wiener rolls, cheese, and herbs.

Friday, June 11. We went out early with a picnic lunch on a bus to Southsea. We spent some time in the Rose Gardens, ate our lunch, fed the birds, and did some knitting. We walked towards the pier and found a restaurant which served "pots" of tea; afterwards, we sat on the pier in the sun for the rest of the day. We arrived home about 6 P.M., when Queenie prepared dinner, and we spent the evening watching television.

Saturday, June 12. It was cold and windy with sunny intervals. I wrote cards and letters. Fred came and did a job for Queenie. We watched the "Trooping of the Colors" on television. It was so much better than going to London and getting into all those crowds. We had dinner and then went to a Bible conference. Some ladies in the church called for us and took us to Milland. The speaker for the morning session was Mr. Oram of "Back to the Bible Broadcast," and Mr. Duncan in the evening. We had a lovely tea between meetings and some time was spent looking around in the tents, housing and literature. We came home and watched Liberace conducting the Philharmonic Symphony Orchestra.

Sunday, June 13. This was a sunny but cool day. We enjoyed both church services in which young people took part. The evening service was followed by a fellowship period and a talk by someone about Prison

Fellowship Organization which is headed by Chuck Colson.

Monday, June 14. We had a quiet day, and got ready for our trip to Bournemouth. Queenie tended the garden. We went to a friend's home for tea. Daisy is a sweet senior citizen, and she and her sister Audrey had made much preparation before we arrived. We had salmon and salad, fruit flan, and coffee sponge for our meal.

Tuesday, June 15. We were up early so that a friend could take us to Portsmouth to catch the coach for Bournemouth. We were there an hour early, so we watched the Hovercraft coming in and going out. Many business folks go over to the island every day. Our trip took us one and three-quarters hours. Cousin Doris was very happy to see us; it was eight years since I had seen her. She had a nice meal ready for us, after which we took a walk to Hengistbury Head, about a mile away. This was a long walk for Doris, who was eighty-three years of age. Our cousin was determined to make the best of our short visit and planned to go with us the next day to a place called Mudeford. We again walked to the Head in short stages. We took the little train to Mudeford and looked around, then decided to take the ferry to Mudeford Quay, where we were able to get the best fish-and-chips dinner. We sat on one of the many seats along the seafront and watched the swans, about a hundred of them. We had ice cream in the afternoon and then returned by ferry to the little train to home. We spent the evening reminiscing and went to bed at 12:40 A.M. We enjoyed our visit very much.

Wednesday, June 16. We prepared to go back home; went for a walk in the morning towards Bournemouth along the seafront, then had coffee along the cliffs, and arrived back at 12:45 for a nice dinner which Doris had prepared. We pruned Doris' fruit trees before leaving, and Doris gave Queenie more plants for her garden, then she saw us off on the bus.

Friday, June 18. We went by the London coach to Richmond; the driver was new to this route and took us miles out of our way, but we eventually got there. Flora was with us this time and we had planned to stay at a hotel called "The Quinns" for two nights. We had lunch in our room and all went to Kew Gardens in the afternoon. We took a bus to Brentford, our old hometown and birthplace. It was almost unrecognizable. There were so many alterations—many "high-rises" had gone up instead of the small cottages of olden days. The house in which I was born was not there anymore, and blocks of flats were there instead. We visited Mabel Malone, a blind friend of my sister. She did not know that we were going to see her but was delighted, and busied herself getting us a cup of tea. I was impressed by this sweet person who was very cheerful and glad to have us visit her.

Saturday, June 19. We had a nice breakfast served by the hotel. Flora went on her way to visit friends and we decided to go to Hampton Court. It was a beautiful day; the flowers in the Palace Gardens were magnificent everywhere. The Pond Garden was especially pretty. Just nearby was the famous "Grapevine" planted in 1768. The girth of the stem at ground level is seven feet one inch, and above the ground level it is six feet two inches. Measurements were taken in 1962. The small gardens are laid out in seventeenth-century style. The outer walls of the palace date from the sixteenth century. We sat in the gardens for a long while as it was so pleasant and warm. Since it was such a nice day, we did not spend much time in the palace and courtyards, but one thing that I wanted to see that I had not seen before was the indoor tennis courts built by King Henry VIII in 1530. They are said to be the oldest tennis courts still in use. They are somewhat smaller than our conventional tennis courts today.

We did tour the Tudor Kitchens and found them very interesting. We also ran into a bridal party who were being married in the Palace Chapel. The bride was in white and the groom wore tails and a top hat. There were four attendants in powder blue taffeta, plus two child attendants. The photographer took a few pictures, they were ushered into the chapel, and then the doors were closed. Queenie and I were mistaken for some of the bridal party as we were hurrying along that way!

After this, we made our way to Bushey Park, which is directly opposite the main entrance to the palace. It is a beautiful sight to see the main road through the park which has horse chestnut trees on both sides of the road. We had lunch here and fed the ducks in the round pond. There was a children's playground closed off on one side which was new to me. I remember that this was the place where we used to scramble for sweets (candy which was wrapped) when we came here for our Sunday school outings nearly every year. We tried to find a place for tea and settled for ice cream instead. We walked down to the Thames Riverside walk and found that many people were taking advantage of the sunny day, either walking or sitting on the grass. There were some regular boat rides, too, so we noted the time of the last one back in London. We re-entered the gardens and found a cafeteria where we were able to get tea. We also discovered some beautiful rose gardens. We made our way to the river again and waited for the *Thames Queen* and boarded her to take us back to Richmond instead of going by buses the way we came. This was a very pleasant ride back and much longer trip than we had anticipated. It took almost two hours.

Sunday, June 20. This was another beautiful day. We had planned to go to visit our childhood home church. First of all, we found it had changed its denomination. It was called United Reformed Church, and used to be a Congregational church. The church was bombed during the Second World War, so the lovely gallery was done away with and a new roof affixed. A lovely feature added was a stained-glass window of Jesus and the children placed high up in front of the building. A new organ was placed up front on the left-hand side and two new commemorative chairs behind the communion table. One of these chairs was given by my sister in "loving memory of my father" who was a deacon in the church and to other members of our family who died about the same period. The little church had no pastor of its own, so it had one assigned from headquarters each week. The congregation is so very small they cannot afford a regular pastor, but the building has been kept up very well. This Sunday was Fellowship Sunday, which they have once a month. Most of these people come in from out of town. We had told Mary Lynch, an old member whom we knew many years ago that we were visiting, so she phoned around to some of the oldsters telling them we were coming. It was a joy to visit with these dear people. We had coffee and cookies in the church hall and then went home with Mary to Chiswick in her friend Margaret's car. She had a delicious meal prepared for us of chicken and salad, and Margaret had supplied the dessert which was strawberries and ice cream. After awhile, Margaret took us back to Richmond. We wanted to go up to the famous Richmond Hill before leaving. She took us to the top of the hill and we enjoyed looking down onto the river Thames and walking along the terraces. We walked back to the hotel, checked out, and were soon on our way to the bus stop and driving back to Cowplain. We were back in time to water the garden and go to bed early.

Monday promised to be another nice day. It was cool but sunny in the morning. We did a little shopping and again met Flora, who was to accompany us on an excursion trip to Windsor Castle.

We got away by 11 A.M. Our trip there was delightful. We saw more of the beautiful English countryside. Our driver was a congenial young man who explained things along the way. We stopped at a place called the Wooden Bridge for a coffee break. We were taken right up to the castle and given three hours to explore the vicinity and do what we wanted to do. The queen was in residence so we could not go into the State Apartments, so we went onto the terraces and viewed the scenery. Also, we spent a long time in St. George's Chapel. It was exquisitely beautiful and something not to be missed by visitors going to Windsor. The ceilings and architecture are magnificent, along with the carvings and statuary. One should also look for the famous "Treacle Bible," encased in glass. It is written in Old English with artistic lettering. The Bible is open to where it reads about "The Balm of Gilead" and reads "The Treacle of Gilead." We next went to see the "Changing of the Guard" and many children were out on a trip with a school group. They were really excited to see these guards in their bear skins and red uniforms. We made our way back into town and to a restaurant where we just had time to get some tea and then back to our stopping and pick-up place. We were away by 3:45 P.M., having had an enjoyable time in Windsor.

Tuesday, June 22. We had a quiet day at home. We learned from our next door neighbor that her brother had died, whom she had nursed in the house for some weeks. Queenie cut the grass and made dinner for us. She loves to cook. We went out mid-morning and had a coffee break with Janet. We went to the Arts and Crafts Club and worked on our pictures. This craft is done with black enamel paint and colored foil. We finished our day at the fellowship Bible study group.

Wednesday, June 23. Wednesday means it is coming to the end of my vacation. We both had our hair done, visited Flora, and went to the ladies meeting at the church. They asked me to say a few words to the group, so I gave my testimony of how God had led and guided me throughout my lifetime. Jesus is all the world to me, and I wish that everyone else would accept Him as Savior, too.

We found it convenient to speak with Mrs. Currie who had lost her brother, and we made a few phone calls to bid goodbye, packed my case, and helped Queenie in the garden.

Thursday, June 24. This was the day I would return after a lovely holiday with my sister. We were up at 5:30 A.M. We had a good breakfast and were ready to leave at 6:45 A.M. Our friends the Allens were here to take us to the airport. It was a pleasant trip and I saw the last of the English countryside for a time, at least. We had a cup of tea and boarded the plane at 10 A.M.

I was on my way to the U.S.A. by 10:30 via a Caledonian plane arriving in Atlanta by 1:30 P.M. that same day, but was five hours behind English time. I had a rough time from then on until I was safely in my friend Myrtle's care. It was a joy to meet her and to get to her home. I was truly glad of the next day to recover from jet lag.

My Beloved Sister

I am very blessed to have one sister alive, although I have two others who passed on to the afterlife.

Queenie may sound like an odd name in this country, but it is her "given" name. We grew up together in England, and she is three years younger than I. Strange to say, I do not remember too much fellowship with her, or the rest of the family. I do know we do have much the same interests in life.

Queenie has a lot of determination and accomplishments. During the Second World War, she was called into a factory by a well-known firm called Sperry's, became head of her section, and was able to train others in work that was secret at that time.

I have noted during our adult years that she has found satisfaction in various occupations pertaining to handicrafts and the arts. There was a period in her life when she learned some nursing skills under the Red Cross, and she became a beloved nurse aide at the Portsmouth General Hospital.

In her retirement years, she has joined art classes and is painting in oils and watercolors. She is clever at drawing, also. Her latest skill is making toys in her spare time which look professionally made. She was honored by having a "write-up" in the local paper.

Queenie is a very proficient and useful person in life, caring for people who are in need. She loves to travel, so we have been able to see one another for a few weeks once a year. I am truly thankful and proud of my sister Queenie.

10
Life at Westminister Oaks

After this wonderful vacation in England, life had another change for me—I bid my friend Myrtle goodbye for perhaps another year—the usual amount of time before we saw one another again. I then made my way back to Ft. Walton Beach where I was living at that time.

My little apartment was quite inviting and I was anxious to learn how my companion was faring. I must remind my readers I was living with Stella Thomas at this time, and I was a paid companion-housekeeper. For the last six weeks, she had been boarding out at the Westwood Health Care Center. I phoned her daughter to find out when we should get her back into her home. She casually said, "We'll wait a few days."

I set to work to make ready for Stella's return. Eventually I called again. This time Ann Streit, her daughter, had gained courage to tell me the truth. She said, "Mother has been very happy at the nursing home and has decided to stay." This is exactly what the relatives had wanted but did not want to go against their mother's wishes, as she had asked them previously not to put her in a nursing home. They did not want to tell me that my services would not be required anymore. But I could see that I must make plans to move again. I was able to take my time, and so, in looking ahead, this should be my final move for retirement. I remembered the beautiful retirement home, Westminister Oaks, in Tallahassee. Also the happy times I had with friends in that city living there. I did not have the means previously to enter this facility. By working a little longer, this obstacle had been overcome. I therefore wrote to my friends the Grimes, asking them if I could come and stay for a weekend, and, of course, I was more than welcome. I had made an appointment for an interview in hopes of entering this lovely retirement center. Ellen was happy to accompany me, so we made our way to find out if there was an available apartment. One requirement was a down payment or entrance fee; I was happy to find that I was financially able to meet this need. The salesperson at the time was a gentleman who gave me the choice of two apartments, and the one I chose was on the top floor of the main building, where I have been happily settled for the last ten years. I had a friend in my Tallahassee church, the Christian and Missionary Alliance Church, who was very kind in helping people to move; I was no exception! When he heard I was to return to Tallahassee, Dan Coleman came with his truck to move me. I was truly glad to be settled in this beautiful city again. I was not enamored with Ft. Walton Beach. I had enjoyed my two homes there, but to me, the layout of the city was not very inviting. It was a struggling mass of homes and shopping centers leading out to a concourse with the Atlantic Ocean on one side and the Gulf of Mexico on the other. I must say that this concourse, after a few miles, led to a beautiful seaside resort. Destin was a real gem, drawing many "holiday makers" to its beautiful, white, sandy beaches. I will always remember the exquisite colors of the Gulf seas—turquoise, green, and blue. Also the sailboats which turned out on weekends by the dozens. The sand dunes and scrubland on the beaches added to the beauty of this place. The long concourse leading out to Destin is owned by Eglin Air Force Base and so is protected.

Westminister Oaks is a beautiful facility built in ninety-six acres of park land. South Oaks is where most of the residents reside. The administration building and the first floor above which is the health center were the first two buildings erected. The large kitchen and dining rooms are also on the first floor, where we all take at least one meal a day. We early residents have watched other floors go up and we now have four floors in the Parry Building. These last floors house patients who need some extra care. One is known as "Assistant Living" and the other is especially for Alzheimer's patients. We are adequately staffed and our needs are met as they arise. Many new buildings have gone up since I first came to reside here. These are built to meet the needs of various types of retirees—some wealthy and others not so wealthy. There is the village for people who are independent and they can take a few meals as they choose to do so. We also have the Chason Gardens. A large donation from the First Baptist Church made this three-story building possible. People who like lots of plants and flowers enjoy their specially designed windows. There are other homes being built called "cluster homes." There is a walking trail which encircles the whole grounds. Not many walk this trail, but I have done so many times. There used to be a blackberry patch and some of us have taken advantage of it. I still have jam from the berries I picked. We even had a blackberry cobbler made from some of them.

Our gardeners are hardworking men who keep the grounds in good condition. Our Residents' Council oversees the planting of flower beds and some who like gardening do some of the work entailed. Various committees are formed and headed up or supervised by directors of activities, so there are quite a few things in which we can engage. There are two buses available for shopping and doctor appointments and occasional outings. We have four parking lots available for those who still drive their cars.

As I was getting settled into the Oaks, I had a number of large oil paintings which I could not hang in my apartment, so I asked for permission to hang them in the corridor. This was granted. At the same time, the faculty asked me if I would like to teach a painting class here. At the time, there were a few people interested, so I became their mentor. We have since had a set time each week for a painting class and have a very nice room in the basement which is appropriate for this. Each year we have had an art show which has been open for residents and employees to enter their work. I have continued to be the coordinator for this. The class has dwindled to about two or three at present. Two of the men who participated left the class because their spouses became a care to them. I should mention that one of these who showed his watercolors has recently departed from this life. Ike McCarty was a beloved resident whose chief aspiration in the painting class was to make "beautiful sunsets." I remember his perseverance in attaining his desired effects. We remember him also as a tenor who entertained us frequently in the Gallery (our auditorium) with Cy Cowden, Earl Armstrong, and Ed Griswold. Several dear saints of God have joined him in the great beyond where we hope to see them again. I remember the last time I saw Ike. It was at his death bed, and he asked me to pray for him. He introduced me to his two daughters Beverly and Judy. He said, "This is Vera, my painting teacher." I may have helped him artistically in some way, but he launched out on his own. When he went away on vacations, he came back with materials, which his family had given him, for his favorite hobby and pastime.

Other members of the art class have included Walter Mochel, Nan Shaw, Marge Smith, and a few others. Marge has been a faithful one and has done some beautiful watercolors and oil paintings. In fact, she turned a small kitchen into an art studio. Her apartment allows for this because she shared a double apartment with a friend. She has won prizes in the Senior Citizens Art Shows and takes further instructions at their institute. Nan is a ninety-three year old and accompanies Marge each Thursday morning to the Old Armory where they paint in watercolors. Walter paints in watercolors, also. His recent cataract surgery has revealed the true colors of his work and so he hopes to improve; however, he has exhibited some beautiful paintings. He has since procured a computer and is more interested in learning to use it.

About a year ago, our activities director wanted a whole wall of her office painted with a mural. This was accomplished with the help of a young man who was directing a class in ceramics. The scene depicted was a lake with distant scenery on the horizon with masses of azaleas in the foreground. It truly brightened the office, which is situated in the basement of our building. I was involved in this project, also.

There are many ways in which we seniors can use our gifts and share our time with the rest of the community. Even those who feel unable to do too much can serve the rest on one of the various committees which have been set up to meet the needs and interests of the rest of us. Then there is the store, mostly food necessities, which is a help to many and a convenience to others who run out of some commodity. This store is run entirely by residents who volunteer their time for two hours a day. There is no profit to be made. The "Thrift Shop" is next door in the basement; Doris Ahrens was in charge of this facility for a number of years; Margaret Crumpton is now in charge. It is amazing the things people donate to this shop for resale and others enjoy using again. The employees, staff, and residents may be found browsing on Mondays hunting for bargains. What is one man's trash is another's treasure.

There was a time when a well-meaning person suggested that the Oaks should have a Bible study group to meet at a certain time each week. At the appointed time, quite a number turned up and the activities director in the health center brought down a number of patients from there to participate. The first meeting disintegrated because the teacher did not come. Also, a few people objected to the patients from the second floor sharing this study with them. Finally, I saw a need for the health center patients to have their own Bible study, and after seeking God in prayer concerning this, I became the leader for them. I have been doing this for a number of years.

Recently, the Chason Gardens have produced a good teacher of the Word and have a regular study of the Bible each week. Margaret Roane was the teacher of this group which is open for anyone to join. I am indebted to Mrs. Lorraine Simmons for teaching my class at such times as I am unable to do so. This lady is also a musician and does many good deeds for the Oaks' residents. May Schaeffer plays the piano for the hymns, also. We have chapel service each week and the music committee helps with their talent by playing piano and organ preludes before each service. Waver Schenller was an outstanding musician. She has recently departed this life. She used to play one of our organs. It was a delight to listen to her, as she would put her heart and soul into playing this instrument. We all loved her and miss her very much.

Some Friends I Have Made in Westminister Oaks

Dorothy Harper was a remarkable little lady of ninety-two years of age. She emigrated from England when she was sixteen years old. She lived at the Oaks on the fifth floor where I resided for three and a half years. Because of her English background, we quickly became friends. Dorothy was a "talker," and she loved to reminisce about her life in England and France. When in France, she lived on the coast and loved to go shrimping. Her parents were interdenominational missionaries. At one time they lived in a rambling Old English house where they cared for sick people. She used to help her parents at the mission by playing the piano for their hymns. She told about living in Ramsgate, England, at a girls' boarding school. One elderly teacher had an "ear trumpet," and it caused some amusement for the girls. She remembered the good times when she would be taken over the cliff to a tea shop where they were served cream cakes and delicious strawberry cream teas; I spent four years of my life later at Margate, the next town along the coast.

Dorothy was married early in life and had three children, all still living. Her youngest son Bobby is a curator and director of the St. Augustine Museum. Her daughter Joyce has married one of the directors of I.B.M. Her other son is a retired engineer. Many and varied were her jobs in life. Both she and her husband were the owners and operators of a general grocery store and lost money during the depression period when they had so many creditors who never paid back what they owed. She was also the local postmistress of a township in Florida. Both she and her husband were retired state workers.

She told with pride about the time she went to Mexico as a missionary for the First Baptist Church, where she was a member. She was eighty years of age at that time. She painted railings around the compound for several hours every day. She had also been a leader for international students at her church and so had made many friends over the years.

Virginia Leukel, also known as "Ginny," is very special. This dear soul is completely deaf and has tunnel vision only. She is my next door neighbor and has lived here nine and a half years. Her chief occupation is walking; she can be seen traversing the new walkway recently installed, which extends through the woods to the entrance of our facility. She walks in all kinds of weather and will dress accordingly, taking complete charge of herself. She is remarkable in that she keeps her balance with the aid of a cane. I have only known her to fall once, but she was not seriously hurt. She has no inner ear apparatus to help keep her balance. She walks for two hours or longer every day. When weather permits, she spends much time on our Northeast Porch where she is never idle. She knits the most beautiful sweaters, caps, and scarves, all done in intricate designs and colors. She also sews other clothing which she wears and all are exceedingly well made. She takes pride in her apartment. Recently, she had a new carpet installed and bought new pieces of furniture. She is unable to speak, so we communicate by writing notes. She is very sympathetic when she finds out someone may be sick. Her writing is clear and legible. This is a sample of what she writes to me:

> Hi, Vera. I'm glad that your operation was successful. I did pray for you; please take care of yourself. I love you. How is Queenie [my sister]?
>
> Ginny

We frequently have birthday parties for Ginny and it is a joy to see how much she enjoys these occasions. She has moved to another floor now, as she is needing more help, but she is still a happy resident.

We here at Westminister Oaks all pay for one meal a day with our service fee, and we can choose to eat this meal whenever we like—breakfast, lunch, or dinner. I have chosen to eat my main meal in the evening. I have a few friends with whom I eat in the dining room. We have been close to each other for a long time, so we take one another out for a meal on birthdays. We also have "Birthday Luncheons" served for all residents about the middle of each month, and this is done in party fashion. The activities director and kitchen supervisor make this special using decorations and introducing games or competitions, thus making it a fun time for everyone involved.

Agnes Harrison was one of our residents whom we came to love and admire, so I feel led to include something about her in my personal history. Her artistic works are well-known to many. Her ability to enjoy life and use her talents is well laid out in this obituary of her from the *Democrat Staff Report*:

> Agnes Carter Harrison, 90, longtime local artist, dies: Local artist Agnes Carter Harrison, 90, of 4449 Meandering Way, died Wednesday at Tallahassee Memorial Regional Medical Center.
>
> Harrison was born in Columbus, Ga., and operated a dancing school there. In the 1930's, she moved to New York City where she graduated with Honors from the New York School of Design. She worked in Textile Design in New York until moving to Tallahassee in 1942.
>
> To support herself, she learned mechanical drawing at Lively Vocational School, then worked for Southeastern Telephone Co. as Chief Draftsman, drawing Plat Maps of the City and County, but she once said ever since childhood, she'd had a paint box and brush in hand, and her first love was painting.
>
> After studying art at Florida State University with Karl Zerbe, Florence Kawa and others, Harrison became well-known for her watercolors, as well as for works using a variety of other mediums and techniques. She was best known nationally for her paintings of native southern flowers, such as camellias and magnolias.
>
> Her works were exhibited in New York City and throughout the South. She was a Charter Member of LeMoyne Art Foundation, which offered a retrospective exhibit in 1984 of her work from 1964 to 1972.
>
> In later years, Harrison painted many of Tallahassee's old landmarks before they were remodeled, including the Columns, Old Union Bank, first Leon County Courthouse, and the original First National Bank Building. Various prominent Tallahassee families own many of her paintings, which captured the history and flavor of the area.

Harrison was active in many civic organizations, including the Tallahassee Memorial Hospital Auxiliary, Tallahassee Little Theater, LeMoyne Art Foundation, Tallahassee Garden Club, and the Colonial Dames.

Westminister Oaks Chapel Service

It is the custom at the Oaks to have weekly chapel services, some of which are conducted by our own residents. I would like to include one such message in my narrative by the Reverend Frank Elvery. We all admired Frank very much; his wife, also, has been a great community worker. Frank often took part in the Communion services and funeral memorial services. He was such a blessing to those who lose loved ones in this life. The following discourse is a story about himself.

The Parable of the Wheel

When I was a boy, my father was an accountant for a lumber company which cut the pine forest south of Venice, Florida. We did not live in the lumber camp but my brother and I were sometimes permitted to visit there. The men around the sawmill were always very kind to us and told us many tales; some I believed and some I did not believe. One that I did not believe was about the occasion when the governor on a steam-engine stuck and the flywheel accelerated until it broke up. Imagine my surprise when I studied physics to learn that such things could and did happen. When a wheel turns, two opposing forces exist: Centrifugal force exerts an outward pull and Centripetal force exerts an inward pull. The faster a wheel rotates, the greater the Centrifugal force becomes and when it exceeds the Centripetal force, the wheel may rupture. The wheel is a revealing modern parable which tells us a number of interesting things. It says something about our bodies. Cells are constantly being destroyed, germs multiply, and viruses are ever about their dirty work. But new cells are created, white corpuscles devour germs, and viruses are being tamed by other forces. As long as the building forces more than match the destructive forces, we are healthy; but when they lose the battle, we become ill.

It says something about our spiritual welfare. Unfortunately we are never able to banish many negative aspects of our character. We carry the taint of pride, selfishness and resentment all of our lives. There is a constant struggle between good and evil in the heart of every person. Through the grace and forgiveness of God, we can triumph over the negative aspects of character and lead Christian lives.

It tells us about our nation. There is ample evidence of the destructive forces at work in our country. We observe criminals and law breakers tearing the fabric of our nation. We read that if the government were able to collect all of the income tax legally due, there would not be a budgetary deficit. Dishonest citizens are mortgaging the future of our grandchildren and threatening the Social Security System on which many of us depend. The one thing that keeps the nation moving forward is the fact that there are more honest, hard-working, and law abiding citizens than indifferent law breakers; but if the time ever comes that this is no longer true, chaos will result in America.

The wheel reveals a truth about the family. The alarming rate of the break-up of American families is well known; and in the brief time at our disposal, we cannot try to isolate and discuss the problems which contribute to the tragedy, but we can safely say that the failure of the family is the failure of persons. Where persons are more interested in what they can "get" than what they can "give," and are not willing to control their emotions, and to discipline themselves, disruption is inevitable. There is no substitute for love, forbearance, mutual goals, and Christian Love. Where these exist, the greatest joy may be found.

The wheel may be helpful in considering the Westminister Oaks Community. Here we share characteristics of both the State and the Family. We are a corporate community where the welfare of all is dependent upon the welfare of each one. We are bound together in a bundle of life. Before we came here, we lived in homes where the concerns of one or two persons existed. Here the needs of more than a hundred persons must be given due consideration. It is a temptation to measure every decision made by the Residents' Council or the Administration by how it affects me. Before the decision is criticized, we should find out why it was done; and when we do, it will likely be a fair and just policy which serves the greatest good for the Community. You might even find out that other people are well pleased and that you are the exception. Here too, there are always contrasting forces at work breaking down and building the Community. Some of the negative things that may occur are judgement without full knowledge; being inconsiderate of others; failure to share in the life of the Community; constant criticism of residents and those who serve you; spreading rumors; and flaunting a negative attitude. That's a beginning, and you can likely think of others. But, there are many positive forces at work here. Friendliness, concern for others, identifying with the spiritual and social life of the home, and a desire to make this a better place because you live here. We should all have a genuine pride in Westminister Oaks and strive to make it the best home in the world.

A lot of experience and knowledge dwell here. If our average age is 75 years, there are over 8,000 years of experience on which we can draw and share.

Sharing is the most effective way that people can grow closer together. I learned that while in a stalled elevator! A number of years ago, a committee on which I was serving was deadlocked. We adjourned for dinner and then went back to work on the task again. Seven of us entered an elevator and the elevator became stuck between floors. We rang the alarm and nothing happened. Then we realized that it was Friday night and no one would be back in the building until Monday. After finding that we could not get out of the "escape hatch" in the top of the elevator, we decided to try and jar the elevator by "jumping in unison." One of the men sang "Shall We Gather at the River" and we jumped in time to the music. Suddenly the door opened about six inches and then closed. We took a rod from the ceiling and repeated our jumping. When the door opened a little, the rod was inserted and we were able to force the door open and get out.

When we went back to work, we discovered that our deadlock had disappeared because we had been drawn together by our common experience. This is what can happen at Westminister Oaks as we share the experience of living together and helping each other.

We can rejoice that there are many wonderful persons who exert the kind of influences that recognize the worth of every individual and the dignity of God's beloved children. Let us make sure that we contribute to the continual strengthening of the benevolent force.

—From the sermon given at chapel service March 15, 1984,
by the Reverend Frank Elvery
(Our beloved Frank Elvery had a period of ill health and died in April of 1993.)

An Illness Takes Over

A few years have elapsed since I last wrote of my life's experiences. I was reminded only yesterday that my "life story" could become a reality. It was not the only time either! My neighbor Mary Davis said she would like to hear my whole story. Getting into the swing of things again will take effort and to accomplish something worthwhile, an unfinished task, I must make the time to do it! However, I shall be going on vacation in one week's time. England being the place where I was born, is a natural place for me to return occasionally.

My family has almost died out and my only sister Queenie Glineur is the only close relative that I have now. We have wondered if the trip would be made possible, but the Lord has given us favor in providing me with health and strength to do so.

It was in the middle of May 1987 that I came down with an attack of sciatica, which kept me bedfast for three weeks! I have been a remarkably well person, and, needless to say, I was sort of worried for myself. It certainly made me aware of the ills of other people. After a series of forced bed rest, doctor visits, including a neurology specialist, medications, and exercises, I was diagnosed as having a pinched nerve. Well, that doesn't sound too serious, but many people have to undergo an operation for this condition. I was told very bluntly that I "was too old to have one"! I was eighty, almost eighty-one, at this time. In any case, I was advised by many people not to have a back surgery, so I did not. The doctor said, "You will have to live with it."

I am happy to say the good care and prayers of my friends have helped me considerably, and I am all set to go to England. I just have to pack my suitcase! My good friends Ellen and Johnny Grimes are going to take me to the airport tomorrow week. It is indeed good to have friends and I have been blessed with many along life's journey.

One Day's Living in a Retirement Home and in Service for the Lord 1988

I had been taking care of Milton Slade. He was a resident of the Midrise at Westminister Oaks. My duties were to "bathe and dress him, make breakfast and eat this meal with him and tidy up afterwards, and make his bed."

I also went and helped him to get to bed in the evening. This help was needed because he had been involved in an accident while on his vacation in Alaska. It was October 22, 1988, when I went to hear the Tallahassee Symphony Orchestra; it was an enjoyable program. However, I was extremely tired and had things to do before retiring that night. I was up early next morning to help Milton and then went to a seminar for teachers at the church. I wondered why I should be going because it was for different age groups in which I was involved. However, the first person I saw was Celeste Williams, a precious black lady who had come to the seminar for help with teaching. She had left our church and was being used of God in an all-black church elsewhere.

I immediately was able to tell her about Child Evangelism Fellowship, Inc. and our new director. She was happy to know about this organization and she was a contact for the monthly prayer meeting to which she promised to come.

I learned much about how to work with youth while at the seminar. I was almost home and before turning into Meandering Way, I nearly ran over a chicken in the road; so I stopped at the little farmhouse which is near us to let the people there know about the chicken which had got loose. The resident said it wasn't his. I then engaged him in conversation about going to church. He said his wife went to a certain church, so I was able to remind him that he should be going also and the whole family. I invited him to our church and to the special meetings we were to have the next week. Another contact for a C.E.F. Club seemed imminent also, as there were children in this home—another reason I was led to go to the seminar.

I was still very tired so decided after a quick lunch to undress and rest in bed. I also put a notice on my door saying: "Please do not disturb unless visitors from outside."

I was nicely settled in bed when the phone rang. It was from the prayer chain at the church. "Would you pray for three-and-a-half-year-old Elizabeth Murphy?" This sweet child had fallen on her head, resulting in a seizure and was at the Tallahassee Memorial Hospital. I prayed and passed the message on to the next one on the prayer list. It was not long before I heard a big noise next door. I went to see what was wrong. My neighbor had family members there but everything was okay.

Then a short while after that, Mildred Lees was at my door! This dear lady is almost blind and was trying to read my notice on the door, so I went to see who was there. She was sorry to bother me but was in tears and I was able to bring her in. She needed someone to read a letter to her; I was able to console her. She is a lovely Christian lady who was able to share some of her thoughts with me. I found the Lord helping me while I was resting in between times. After that, another lady, Dorothy Harper, locked herself out of her room and came to me to phone for the guard to let her in. So the Lord used me again in some small way.

It was not long again that I had yet another call on the phone. It was my special friend Grace Daffin. She has a severe loss of memory; she had been away for two weeks, and forgot to tell me and no one knew where she was except the main office. She had tried to get me, she said, several times. I was truly glad to hear her voice. The sad thing was she didn't remember she had been away. Another phone call came that afternoon from Ruth Berkhart about showing some work for the fall show; this was settled for her.

This was a day of opportunities of service and I thank God that He can use us in small ways. He gave me the strength that I needed, also. And so it goes, day by day. We must be ready to respond to His call.

New Year Aspirations 1989

This new year may have joys or sorrows. However, each of us must accept whatever comes along. The main thing is to prepare oneself.

As we get older we sometimes find our general health failing, but in my case we do have many facilities to help us, and it is no use doting on some small ailment we may have. I personally have been blessed with generally good health, although I did have a period of ill health this past summer and with good doctor care have recovered.

I desire to be a blessing or help to a few people, as long as the Lord gives me health and strength. Having been a nurse during my working years, I find I am able to help some of my colleagues in simple ways, as well as to give an hour each morning to custodial care to one person which enables him to stay in the Midrise portion of the home in which we live; otherwise he would have to go into the health center.

I am interested in various occupations, and enjoy watercolor painting, so I intend to give a little time to this pastime. I had a little money given me at Christmas, so I have spent it on art supplies. Then, I do hope to get together some notes to bring my life story into focus.

A Surprise in the Mail 1991

My regular letter from Ruthie Ervine came today and contained a surprise. The families are building their retirement homes. I must tell you about my stepfamily. Bill was the only child of my late husband, and his wife has taken it upon herself to do the correspondence for them. Every week I receive a letter from Ruthie telling me what they are doing, with other pertinent news from where they are living.

Bill is a retired electrical engineer, and a fine Christian man who is devoted to his wife and his church; the same can be said about Ruthie. They were both born in northern Ireland and met in the U.S. and fell in love. They are Evangelical Christians, and are committed to serve in the church as teachers of the Word and officers of men's and women's groups. At present, they are members of the Sherwood Congregational Church in Arkansas.

Their three children, now grown-up, have never married and so intend to stay close to one another in retirement years. David is an artist, and his twin brother Jonathan is an all-around handyman, I believe. I haven't gotten to know very much about the boys. Roberta seems to have inherited the "brains" in the family. She is quite a linguist, and can speak several languages. She obtained a Ph.D. in Armenian history and has taught high school for Armenian children for several years in Jerusalem.

The homestead they have now is a large place; it has served its purpose well for a few years, as they have used their home for fellowship meetings and meals. Now they are retired and not so energetic and are bogged down with arthritis. They are desirous of living in smaller quarters.

This letter I received is telling me what their plans are and what they have already accomplished. It appears that they have finished building two homes, and two others are in various stages of completion. They have procured twenty acres of land in the wooded area at Vilonia, Arkansas, and intend to move into these smaller homes soon. It looks like Roberta is building her own place on this same property, and will be joining the family in a country setting. This is a very unusual thing to happen—four or five people in one family to decide to build homes together in one place—but it seems an ideal thing to do. Bill and Ruthie will commute back and forth to church till the Lord leads them to do otherwise. Bill and the boys have worked together on these houses and Ruthie says he ". . . has built this house as solid as he used to build his machines at work."

The boys have seen deer, wild turkeys, road runners, and more while working on the houses. Someone dropped off a puppy on their property, which stayed around and so has become Jonathan's dog. They have named him "Poco," which is Spanish for "little." This surely completes the family. I am trusting the Lord to pour out His blessings upon this new venture.

November 1994. I am happy to say this family sold their house in Sherwood and are happily settled in Vilonia, except Roberta, who is still working.

A Busy Life at Westminister Oaks

At age eighty-six, I still find myself a busy person residing here at Westminister Oaks. Today being Tuesday, there is a Bible study to attend at 11 A.M., and another I will teach at 4 P.M. here in the health center.

It is important to keep oneself bodily fit as we advance in age, so a daily walk through the woods is enjoyed most days and appreciated, especially since a winding cement walk has been provided.

I must say a number of friendships are made at this Presbyterian home of the elderly. A part of my day is spent visiting longtime friends who either live in Oaks, South, or have moved to the Parry Building where specialty care is provided. I am blessed with good friends who are good neighbors on the fifth floor of this building. We surprise one another by taking some delicacy which we have prepared and can enjoy at lunchtime or suppertime. I sometimes make banana nut bread which can be shared. My friend at the end of the corridor, Grace Nash, is good at making soups which I have enjoyed a few times. This lady has gone through adverse circumstances in life, having been interred in a Japanese camp in the Philippines during World War II. She has written a book about her experiences; her musical talent (she is a brilliant violinist) surely helped her in difficult circumstances. Then there is Elizabeth Skinner at the opposite end of this wing of the fifth floor. She is seldom at home as she finds many interests to take up her time. One project she has is sending out a monthly card to all residents, which contains a poem or writing which is selected according to the season and is intended to cheer the recipients.

We have various committees who organize different activities so we can enjoy planned entertainment, educational lectures, and musical artists, who come in from Florida State University, and clergyman from various denominations who come in to serve us once a week, also.

Conclusion of Life's Journey

I would like to see my "life story" published; this is my ambition. You may ask why. Several people with whom I have shared different incidents in my life have urged me to do so. God has been very good to me. I have made mistakes in life like every person, but God has steered me through problems and difficulties. As you have read my story, you may have noticed that through each stage of my life, God has been there to help. He has given me grace, peace, and enlightenment to overcome problems, and to start all over again. I hope it will also help you, my reader, to trust in God at all times, as we are taught to do in God's Word.

I am sure that this could not have been possible without the background training I received as a child. I was raised in a Christian atmosphere, and I thank God for that. He has been very near and dear to me, and each day now as I have reached my senior years, God is closer to me than ever before. Each new day as I awake, I can say, "Thank you, Lord, for another day in which to live." I can take a morning walk through the woods and sing my little ditty:

> Thank you Lord for the world so sweet,
> Thank you God for the food we eat,
> Thank you God for the birds that sing,
> Thank you God, for everything.

So far, I am still able to drive my car in the daytime. I am able also to continue the Bible study for the people in the health center, and join in various activities offered in Westminister Oaks.

My motto in life has been, "Doing does it," and my special Bible verses which have been helpful to me are these:

> Trust in the Lord with all thine heart, and lean not to thine own understanding; in all thy ways acknowledge Him and He shall direct thy paths. (Prov. 3:5–6)

> Thou wilt keep him in perfect peace whose mind is stayed on Thee, because he trusteth in Thee. (Isa. 26:3)

If it pleases the Lord to give me more years in this life, I trust they will be fruitful ones. I pray for peace in this old world and that people in every corner of the earth will come to know Jesus as their Savior, Lord, and coming King.

Do You Believe in Angels?

It was two years since I had visited my sister in England and she had been very ill during that time. In fact, it was only a few weeks after I left in 1992 that she had an emergency operation for adhesions from an operation which she had forty years previously. At the same time, she was needing a hip replacement done; but as she was so ill and almost died, she would not consent to have the second operation done until the pain was unbearable.

Queenie has always kept me ignorant of things pertaining to illnesses, so I found out about her dilemma when I eventually arrived to see her again. We made the best of her disability. She had come through the operation successfully on her hip, this being her second replacement of the same hip. She was now gaining her strength. Some very kind friends in the church borrowed a wheelchair and she was there to meet me at the airport.

She had gone ahead and made reservations for us to have a quiet holiday at Southsea-Portsmouth, which was only thirty miles away from her home. We moved into a very nice guest house where we stayed for two weeks. Our host catered "bed and breakfast" and evening meals for us. We were fairly near the seafront and were able to use the buses, which were plentiful and frequent at this time of the holiday season.

When I first arrived at my sister's bungalow, I was delighted to see everything so neat and pretty, both inside and also out in the small flower garden; nothing had been neglected. She had managed to have the small conservatory rebuilt after storm damage, and a lady gardener had taken care of the plants and flowers.

Queenie had to use crutches while I was with her and she was very persevering. The bus drivers were extremely good in helping her on and off the vehicles.

Up until I arrived, the weather in England had been stormy and wet, but now it was beautiful and remained so all the time we were together, which was four weeks.

We discovered that Portsmouth was a very historical place and were able to visit the places of interest, without overtaxing Queenie's limitations. How good it was to see so many holiday makers parading the seafront. I had often wanted to travel on the hovercraft and now seemed to be an ideal time to do this, so we made reservations to go to the Isle of Wight and were not disappointed with this all-day outing! The island is so beautiful and the bus facilities take one to the many famous places you may have read about. This was one of the highlights of our vacation.

Phil and Brenda Bryan were a godsend to us. They planned the best picnic I have ever experienced. We were fairly near the New Forest and they decided to take us there. They did everything and provided the food. Phil knew some of the best places to go and so it was very enjoyable. As we turned into the picnic area, the tall cedars and other trees were like the columns of a stately cathedral. We basked in ecstatic wonder as we watched others coming to the same spot. On leaving, we discovered other and different beauty spots. Open fields, where the wild horses and donkeys roamed, as well as fields of heather, small lakes, and tiny villages were all part of this time together. Our thanks are due to these dear friends who made this memorable occasion possible.

As my holiday drew to a close, arrangements were made for my return home to Tallahassee. Phil and Brenda were again available and happy to drive us to the airport about sixty miles away. My flight was comfortable and I had not made any plans for someone to meet me on arrival. When it was time to land, I began to wonder about getting home with so much luggage and where to get in touch with a telephone. I had received excellent care so far by Delta Airlines. Somehow, I had not worried about this problem and felt sure things would world work out all right. Here I was being carried off the plane by an attendant, and who should I see looking for me but my good friend Mike Fansler who had brought me to the airport a month previously. This was nothing short of a miracle.

Do you believe in angels? Well, I do! He was God's angel for me at this time. He did not know when I was to return and we had not arranged to meet; however, his wife had suggested I might be on this flight! What a happy ending to this holiday and to my story.

Selected Prayers for Myself

Heavenly Father, I am in thy Hands,
My life is in Thy keeping.
Help me this day and all days,
To make Thy Will my will,
And to walk forward confidently,
Certain that what Thou has planned for me is better
Than anything I can plan for myself.
Speak to me, Lord,
In my lonely, weak hours,
And with Thy grace,
Comfort and strengthen me,
So that I shall live up to the highest I know.
Through Jesus Christ, my Lord.
Amen.

Father in Heaven

I thank Thee for this day,
May I face every moment with courage and cheer.
I pray not for an easy life, but for a useful one.
Give me the wisdom to make right choices,
And give me the confidence to meet the unexpected.
Help me to live in thought and deed in accordance
With Thy Will for my life.
May I always have the consciousness of Thy presence,
Wherever I go and whatever I do.
May the peace which comes alone from Thee,
Be always in my heart.
In Jesus' Name,
Amen.